CANOE TRAILS
OF THE DEEP SOUTH

CANOE TRAILS
OF THE DEEP SOUTH

by
Chuck Estes
Elizabeth F. Carter
Byron Almquist

Menasha Ridge Press
Birmingham, Alabama

Library of Congress Cataloging-in-Publication Data

Estes, Chuck, 1950 -
    Canoe trails of the Deep South / Chuck Estes, Elizabeth F. Carter,
Byron Almquist. --1st ed.
        p.   cm.
    Includes index.
    ISBN 0-89732-066-2
    1. Canoes and canoeing - Southern States - Guide books. 2. Southern
States - Description and travel - 1981 - Guide books.   I. Carter,
Elizabeth F., 1939-   .   II. Almquist, Byron, 1941 - .   III. Title.
GV776.S65E88   1991   91-13632
797.1'22'0975 - dc20   CIP

Menasha Ridge Press
3169 Cahaba Heights Road
Birmingham, Alabama, 35243

Contents

Part Three: ALABAMA

Acknowledgments

Chuck Estes, the author of the section on Mississippi, is deeply appreciative to the following people for their companionship and assistance in this project: Phil McCullough, Milton Everett, and Joe and Robin Johnson, my first canoeing partners and fellow explorers; Jim Trunzler and Ozzie and Eve Wells, my constant paddling companions; Larry Estes of Rivers Expeditions, Incorporated; Sue Noblin, typist, editor, and paddler; the members of the Mississippi Chapter Sierra Club; and especially my bow partner, traveling companion, friend, and wife, Lola.

The author of the section on Alabama would like to express appreciation to the following people for their invaluable assistance: Bob Andrews of Sunshine Canoes in Mobile, Alabama; Butch and Bill Grafton of The Canoe Livery at Newton, Alabama; Donald Stacks of Andalusia, Alabama; his helpful friends, Jack and Francis McGowin and Ernest Cleland; the West Florida Canoe Club in Pensacola, Florida; Grady Hartzog of Eufaula, Alabama; Mrs. Carolyn Emerick of Brewton, Alabama; my good friends and intrepid explorers from the Apalachee Canoe Club in Tallahassee, Don Kelly, Ron Balkoom, John Pearce, Liz and Butch Farmer, Jim and Janet Temkin; and most of all to my advisor, driver, campmaker, best friend and husband, Butch Horn.

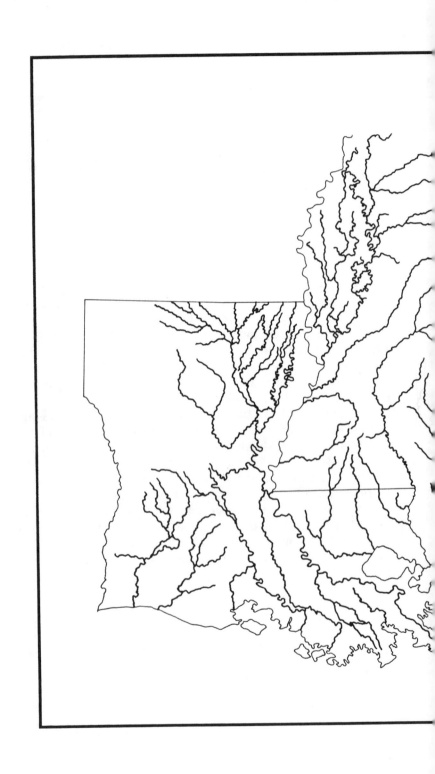

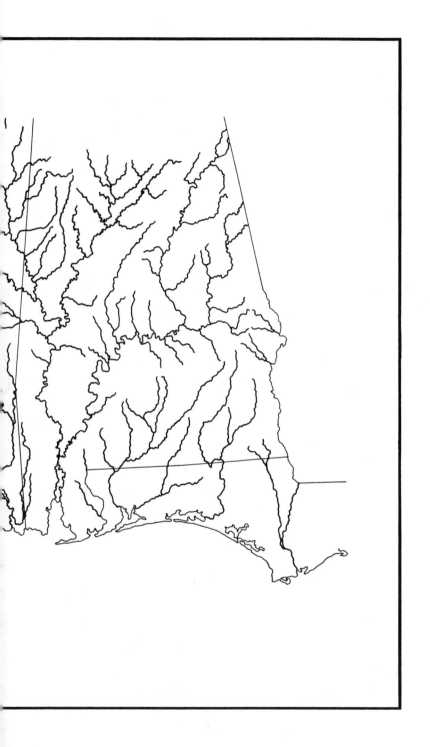

Introduction

The great Southern writer William Faulkner wrote of an earlier time when there was a deep, impenetrable Southern wilderness. Men and machines have long since disposed of any true wilderness in the South. However, along some of the creeks and rivers of the region, vestiges of that long ago wilderness can be sensed. Because of difficult terrain and limited access, most of the land surrounding streams remains forested. These mature forests are home to a diverse wildlife population and are a beautiful backdrop to many scenic streams.

In recent times, it seems the natural streams of the South have been rediscovered, as witnessed by the increasing recreational use. This may be explained partially by the increased stresses of peoples' lives and the need to seek an outdoor release. Several rivers with canoe rentals currently receive heavy recreational pressure. In addition, most of the streams described in this book are within reasonable driving distance from urban areas. One of the purposes of the book is to increase knowledge of the region's rivers and creeks, and in turn take pressure off those already crowded streams. It is also our hope that, after exposure to these streams, people will work to protect an already diminished natural resource.

There are, however, people who very simply love to run rivers for the sheer exuberance and freedom of the experience. It is for these people, river runners, that this book is written. The authors drew upon their knowledge gained from actual experiences on many Southern rivers to select and describe streams with the highest qualities. We have given a description of each stream including maps and information on location, access, difficulty, distance, and scenery. Many of the county or rural roads referred to in the stream descriptions have no identification or road numbers in the field. Therefore, the maps that are provided should be relied upon to find accesses. Large rivers with motorized traffic such as the Apalachicola, Escambia, Alabama, Pascagoula, and Mississippi intentionally have not been included.

Writing a guide book with three authors has been a challenge. Although our styles may be different, we hope that our love for these streams and our descriptions of them bridge over the differences. Elizabeth had the responsibility for the section on Alabama streams, Byron covered Louisiana and southwest Mississippi, and I was responsible for the remainder of the Mississippi streams and the material preceding the stream sections.

Byron, Elizabeth, and I wish you safe and memorable trips. Enjoy. See you on the river.

Chuck Estes

General Information

Geology of the Deep South

The primary physiographic province of the region is the Gulf Coastal Plain, which has low topographic elevations and extensive tracts of marshy land.

The streams of the Deep South are a product of the climate and geology of the region. The geologic history shows the region to be an emerged sea bed. Since the time of the dinosaurs, the Gulf shoreline has been receding. This is partially due to land building by such rivers as the Mississippi with its heavy load of sediment transported from the north. A large section of the Gulf Coastal Plain is part of the Mississippi Embayment, which was previously occupied by sea but gradually filled with sediments ranging in thickness from a few feet to several thousand feet.

With the absence of an ocean covering it, this exposed plain still bears a strong resemblance to the Continental Shelf. Its materials are similar, stratified the same way, and have the same featureless surface on emergence from the sea. Some of the formations beneath the plain are partly consolidated but remain in their original deposited condition as sand, gravel, clay, or marl – –not sandstone, conglomerate, shale, or limestone. Thus, the heavy rainfall of the humid climate in the Deep South meets only slight resistance in eroding the relatively unconsolidated land. This results in differential weathering of the exposed stratus, forming a belted coastal plain. The physiographic regions of the Gulf Coastal Plain created by this weathering are indicated in Figure 1.

Streamflow Characteristics

The annual rainfall in the Gulf Coastal Plain averages from 48 to 68 inches over the region. About 50 percent of the precipitation evaporates or is

3

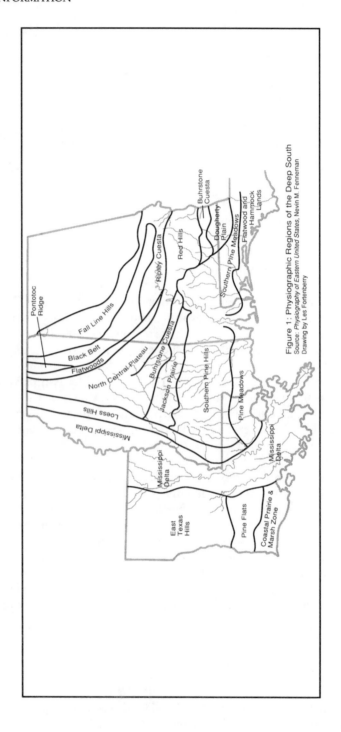

Figure 1: Physiographic Regions of the Deep South
Source: *Physiography of Eastern United States,* Nevin M. Fenneman
Drawing by Les Fontenberry

transpired by vegetation, about 10 percent infiltrates to the water table, and about 40 percent runs off as streamflow.

Streamflow is made up basically of two runoff components. These are direct runoff, or the water that flows over the ground or just under the surface during and immediately after a rainstorm, and groundwater storage that comes out in seeps and springs for days and weeks after the rain. Direct runoff supplies most of the volume of streamflow in flood periods. Groundwater runoff feeds streams in the periods between rains.

The proportion of total streamflow that comes from direct runoff and groundwater runoff varies among streams, depending on such watershed features as elevation of the land and the density and type of vegetation.

Streams that have entered the Gulf Coastal Plain from more rugged physiographic regions carry heavy loads of sediment. Streams originating in the Gulf Coastal Plain generally carry very little sediment except in areas of intensive agricultural activity. The streams of the lower Gulf Coastal Plain flow through sandy soil, so their waters are clear and sparkling, colored a reddish tint by tannic acid derived from decayed vegetation. Streams in this region meander through broad swampy floodplains.

An interesting feature of Deep South streams is the formation of oxbow lakes. It is the nature of moving water to erode the outside of river bends and deposit much of the eroded matter on the inside of the turn, thereby forming a sand- or gravel bar. The result in more mature streams is a meander or the formation of a series of horseshoe-shaped and geometrically predictable loops in the river (see Figure 2). A series of such undulating loops markedly widens the valley floor. Often, as time passes, the current erodes the neck of a loop and creates an island in midstream thereby eliminating a curve in the river. Eventually the entrances of the loop fill in, and an oxbow lake is formed.

Major River Basins of the Deep South

The Apalachicola River basin is comprised of the Flint, Chattahoochee, and Apalachicola rivers. The Apalachicola River is formed by the confluence of the Flint and the Chattahoochee rivers at the Jim Woodruff Dam. It then flows 107 miles southward to Apalachicola Bay in the Gulf of Mexico. The Florida Department of Environmental Regulation has designated the Apalachicola River as "outstanding Florida water" and protects its water quality. Many excellent tributaries of these rivers feed the basin. Because the Flint, Chattahoochee, and Apalachicola rivers are used by power boats in their lower sections, the highest quality canoeing experiences are found on the tributaries.

Rivers in the Choctawhatchee-Escambia basin rise in southeastern Alabama and flow through northwestern Florida to the Gulf. The basin is an

Figure 3: River Basins of the Deep South
Source: *National Water Summary 1985*, United States Geological Survey, Water Supply Paper 2300. Drawing by Les Fortenberry

area of great runoff ranging from 20 to 40 inches per year. Groundwater in the basin discharges to tributary streams that are generally connected with the aquifers. The combination of rainfall runoff and groundwater discharge produces the large runoff in the basin. Principal rivers in this basin include the Choctawhatchee, Yellow, Shoal, Escambia, and Perdido rivers. The basin is mostly rural and largely undeveloped, and the rivers are used mainly for recreation.

The Alabama River basin begins in northwestern Georgia from the headwaters of the Coosa and the Tallapoosa rivers. The headwater rivers originate in the Piedmont, Valley, and Ridge physiographic regions. Large dams and hydroelectric plants are located on these rivers in the steep reaches above the coastal plain. The Coosa and the Alabama river systems have long been used for transportation as a link to Alabama's port at Mobile. Dams were constructed for hydroelectric power generation, flood control, and navigation locks on these rivers beginning in 1914.

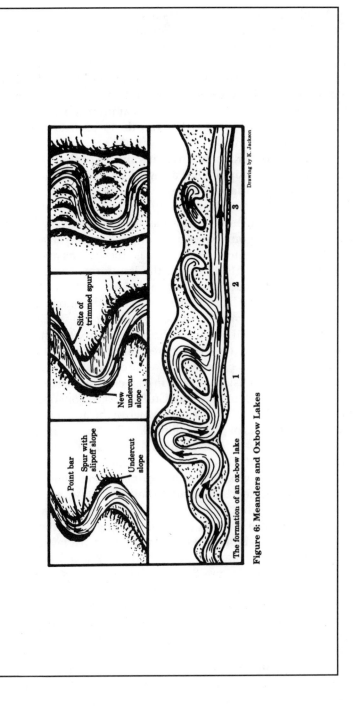

Figure 6: Meanders and Oxbow Lakes

The Mobile-Tombigbee River basin's headwaters are at the origins of the Tombigbee River in the hills of northwestern Mississippi. The Tombigbee River then flows southward 254 miles through Alabama and joins the Alabama River 45 miles north of Mobile to form the Mobile River. The river system is used extensively for transportation of coal, lumber, and timber products to Mobile. A series of locks and dams has been constructed on the Tombigbee and Black Warrior rivers to aid transportation activities. Reservoirs created by the locks and dams are the focus of most fishing and boating activities in the basin.

The Pascagoula River basin drains an area of about 8,900 square miles in southeastern Mississippi. The Pascagoula River is formed by the confluence of the Chickasawhay and the Leaf rivers. The river then flows southward for about 80 miles before emptying into the Gulf. The Escatawpa River, located mostly in Alabama, flows into the Pascagoula River very near the Gulf Coast. Much of the Pascagoula River basin and the coastal area that drains directly into the Gulf is forested. Near the coast these areas are low-lying flatlands and marshlands. Farther inland, the landforms consist primarily of low, rolling hills and broad, flat floodplains.

The Mississippi Coastal basin consists of the Biloxi, Jourdan, Tchoutach-abouffa, and Wolf rivers. The basin is heavily forested and receives a large amount of rainfall. All streams in the basin are free flowing. Fishing and light boating activities are the primary recreational uses within the basin.

The Pearl River basin drains an area of about 8,700 square miles in Mississippi and Louisiana. Rising in east-central Mississippi, the Pearl River flows for almost 490 miles to the Gulf. Other major streams in the basin are the Strong and Bogue Chitto rivers. Much of the upper two-thirds of the Pearl River basin consists of gently rolling to hilly terrain. In the southern part of the basin, the land is much flatter. More than 60 percent of the basin is forested, and about 30 percent of the basin is farmed.

The Amite-Tangipahoa basin is formed in southwestern Mississippi. The principal streams are the Amite, Comite, Tickfaw, and Tangipahoa rivers, which flow through southeastern Louisiana and eventually drain into Lake Pontchartrain. The basin is primarily forested and the terrain consists of gently rolling hills in the upper part, but is almost level near the coast. The streams of the basin are some of the most scenic in the region.

The Lower Mississippi-Big Black basin drains portions of north-central and southwest Mississippi. The Big Black, Bayou Pierre, Homochitto, and Buffalo rivers are the major streams of the basin. The Big Black River drains a 3,500-square-mile area about 160 miles long and 20 to 25 miles wide. There are no major tributaries of the Big Black River. Elevations in the basin range from about 50 feet to a little more than 500 feet above sea level. The basin is sparsely populated and is hilly to gently rolling and largely forested, with much cattle ranching and farming. The Big Black River receives significant amounts of sediment and agricultural chemicals.

The Yazoo River basin drains about 14,000 square miles in northwestern Mississippi. The basin includes a hilly upland in north-central Mississippi where four headwater tributaries originate, and extensive flat lowlands in the Mississippi Alluvial Plain or the Delta. The Delta, part of the Mississippi River floodplain, is some of the world's most fertile and productive farmland. The upland part of the basin is sparsely populated, consisting largely of forests, pastures, and small farms. Because of the heavy farming activities in the basin, streams here receive large amounts of sediment and agricultural chemicals as well.

The Ouachita River basin drains parts of southeastern Arkansas and northeastern Louisiana. The upper part of the Ouachita River flows through hilly terrain that is primarily forested. A major tributary is the Tensas River, which flows parallel to the Mississippi River. The Tensas River basin contains extensive bottomland hardwood tracts. Several locks and dams are located on the Ouachita River to provide commercial transportation for the basin.

The Louisiana Coastal basin drains the southern part of Louisiana. The major streams of the basin are the Atchafalaya, Teche, Vermillion, Calcasieu, and the Mermentau rivers. Of these rivers, possibly the most important is the Atchafalaya River. Its swamps are the most extensive remaining in the South. A diverse and dense wildlife population is found in the basin. Water quality in the basin is threatened by municipal and industrial discharges, agricultural discharges, and saltwater encroachment in the lower reaches.

Climate of the Deep South

The Deep South generally has a humid subtropical climate. Climatic variations are determined by the large landmass to the north and west and by the Gulf of Mexico to the south. These surface areas generate alternate flows of cold air moving southward and warm moist air moving northward. The mean annual temperature of the region averages 66°F. Daytime maximum temperatures exceeding 90° F sometimes occur every day in July or August. During the summertime, exposure to the sun should be carefully monitored. Even hazy overcast days have the potential for sunburn; proper coverage using sunscreen or clothing should be used. During the winter, minimum temperatures ranging from 35° to 43° F are common. The combination of cold water and cold air create ideal conditions for hypothermia in the winter season even in the South.

Rainfall in the Deep South averages about 58 inches a year, with the heaviest rainfall in the southern part of the region near the coast (see figure 4). The period of highest rainfall is December through April, with monthly averages of almost 6 inches. During the dry season in late summer and fall, the average monthly rainfall, derived mostly from thundershowers, ranges from 2 to 4 inches. Frontal actions produce most of the precipitation during the period of heavy rain in winter and early spring. High-intensity storms, generated in Texas or the western Gulf, move east-northeastward where they clash with cold fronts moving southeastward over the region.

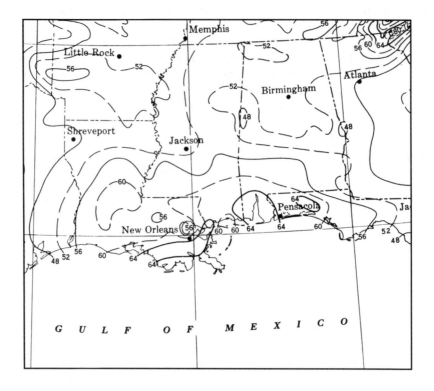

Thunderstorms can occur up to 80 days per year near the Gulf Coast. During the summertime the coastal area experiences about 90 percent of thunderstorms between dawn and dusk. Further inland the storms occur more frequently between noon and midnight. During warm, humid weather, severe thunderstorms may spawn tornadoes. Tornadoes vary considerably in intensity, area covered, and duration. Though they may occur at any hour, their greatest frequency of occurrence is from noon to dusk. The Deep South also lies in the path of hurricanes moving landward from the Gulf. Some of the heaviest rainfalls of record have been those accompanying hurricanes, which occur primarily from June to November.

Biting Creatures

The Deep South is a region of abundant rainfall and vegetation, and there are healthy populations of insects and reptiles. Some of these creatures are annoying at times. However, by using common sense and keeping a watchful eye, most problems associated with these critters can be avoided.

Several types of insects make life unpleasant during the warm months. Mosquitoes, biting midges (no-see-ums), deer flies, and black flies are most prevalent at dusk and can be controlled with insect repellent, oily lotions, and adequate clothing for good skin coverage. Mosquitoes are especially fond of woods and areas of heavy vegetation. By camping in open areas like sandbars, exposure to mosquitoes can be minimized.

The bald-faced hornet builds a beautiful nest that looks like an oversized football. It is very common to see these hornets' nests in trees overhanging southern streams. Do not let your curiosity carry you too close; hornets are not very hospitable! Certain species of paper wasps, such as the yellow jacket, build nests in low bushes near streams. Fire ants, with their very painful bite, are a relatively new invader from Mexico. Fire ants are normally found in high, dry areas, but are occasionally found in creek bottoms. The ants' nest, characterized by a loose mound of soil ranging from several inches to a foot in height, should be avoided.

It is not unusual to see any of the species of snakes found in the South along a river at some time. However, most snakes encountered on southern streams are not poisonous. Several species of aquatic snakes, including the diamondback and yellow-bellied water snake, are the most common. These beneficial snakes primarily eat fish and frogs, and are often killed needlessly. The diamondback water snake unfortunately looks similar to the poisonous cottonmouth water moccasin. The non-poisonous water snakes are usually not aggressive unless they feel threatened. The water moccasin, however, is surprisingly aggressive at times.

Vandalism

Many river accesses are in remote areas. In the past, there have been cases of vehicle break-ins at some of these. Take caution to lock and protect vehicles and property left at all river accesses. If you must leave valuables in your vehicle, store them out of sight. You also might consider making arrangements to park at nearby homes, churches, or businesses. Remember that most local residents are happy to assist you, and are usually very interesting folks to get to know.

A paddler's legal right to run a river is based on the concept of navigability. This is somewhat unfortunate since navigability as a legal concept has proven both obscure and somewhat confused over the years. The common law test of navigability specifies that ony those streams affected by the ebb and flow of the sea tides are navigable. Fortunately, most states expressly repudiate the common law test and favor instead the so-called civil law test —thus a stream is considered navigable if it is capable of being navigated in the ordinary sense of that term, which relates essentially to commerce and transportation. But even if a stream is not navigable from a legal perspective according to the civil law test, it may still be navigable in fact. This means that its navigability does not depend on any legislative act, but is based rather on the objective capability of the stream to support navigation. Thus a creek swollen by high waters may become navigable for a period of time.

If a stream is navigable in the legal sense (civil law test), ownership of the bed of the stream is public. In this case the public possesses all navigation rights as well as incidental rights to fish, swim, and wade. Property rights of those who own land along a navigable stream extend only to the ordinary low water mark. If the water later recedes or islands form in the bed of the stream, the property remains that of the state.

On the other hand, if a stream is only navigable sometimes (as in the case of a seasonal stream) the title of the land under the water belongs to the property owners over whose land the stream passes. However, the ownership is subject to a public easement for such navigation as the condition of the stream will permit.

Regardless of the question of navigability, the right of landowners to prohibit trespassing on their land along streams (if they so desire) is guaranteed. Therefore, access to rivers must be secured at highway rights-of-way or on publicly owned lands if permission to cross privately owned land cannot be secured. Landowners, in granting access to a river, are extending a privilege that should be appreciated and respected. Do not betray a landowner's trust if extended the privilege of camping, putting in, or taking out. Do not litter, drive on grass or planted fields, or forget to close gates. In some cases property owners may resent people driving for hundreds of miles to float through what the landowner may consider private domain. Indeed, it is not unusual for landowners to firmly believe that they "own" the river that passes through their land.

On the other hand, good manners, appreciation, and consideration go a long way in approaching a landowner for permission to camp or launch. The property owner may be interested in paddling and flattered that the paddler is interested in the countryside, and so may be quite friendly and approachable. Cultivate and value this friendship and avoid giving cause to deny paddlers access to the river at some time in the future.

Legally, paddlers are trespassing when they portage, camp, or even stop for a lunch break if they disembark from their boats onto the land. If approached by a landowner while trespassing, by all means be cordial and explain your reason for being on the property (portage, lunch break, etc.). Never knowingly camp on private land without permission. If you do encounter a perturbed landowner, be respectful.

Ecological Considerations

Many of the streams listed in this guide flow through national forests, state-owned forests, wildlife management areas, and privately owned lands that in some cases are superior in quality and aesthetics to lands under public ownership. It is the paddling community's responsibility to uphold the integrity of these lands and their rivers by exercising ecologically sound guidelines. Litter, fire scars, pollution from human excrement, and the cutting of live trees is unsightly and affects the land in a way that threatens to ruin the outdoor experience for everyone.

Paddlers should pack out everything they packed in: all paper litter and such nonbiodegradable items as cartons, foil, plastic jugs, and cans. Help keep our waterways clean for those who follow. If you are canoe camping, leave your campsite in better shape than you found it. If you must build a fire, build it at an established site, and when you leave, dismantle rock fireplaces, thoroughly drown all flames and hot coals, and scatter the ashes. Never cut live trees for firewood (in addition to destroying a part of the environment, they don't burn well). Dump all dishwater in the woods away from water courses, and bury all excrement.

Hazards and Safety

Hazardous situations likely to be encountered on the river must be identified and understood for safe paddling. The lure of high adventure has in part explained why there are so many more paddlers these days. Unfortunately, an alarming number are not prepared for what they encounter.

American Whitewater Affiliation Safety Code

The American Whitewater Affiliation's safety code is perhaps the most useful overall safety guideline available.

I. **Personal Preparedness and Responsibility**
   A. **Be a competent swimmer** with ability to handle yourself underwater.
   B. **Wear a life jacket.**
   C. **Keep your craft under control.** Control must be good enough at all times to stop or reach shore before you reach any danger. Do not enter a rapid unless you are reasonably sure you can safely navigate it or swim the entire rapid in the event of capsize.
   D. **Be aware of river hazards and avoid them.**
      Following are the most frequent killers:
      1. **High Water.** The river's power and danger, and the difficulty of rescue, increase tremendously as the flow rate increases. It is often misleading to judge river level at the put-in. Look at a narrow, critical passage. Could a sudden rise in the water level from sun on a snow pack, rain, or a dam release occur on your trip?
      2. **Cold.** Cold quickly robs your strength, along with your will and ability to save yourself. Dress to protect yourself from cold water and weather extremes. When the water temperature is less than 50°F,

a diver's wet suit is essential for safety in event of an upset. Next best is wool clothing under a windproof outer garment such as a splashproof nylon shell; in this case one should also carry matches and a complete change of clothes in a waterproof package. If, after prolonged exposure, a person experiences uncontrollable shaking or has difficulty talking and moving, he or she must be warmed immediately by whatever means available.

   3. **Strainers**—brush, fallen trees, bridge pilings, or anything else that allows river current to sweep through but pins boat and boater against the obstacle. The water pressure on anything trapped this way is overwhelming, and there may be little or no whitewater to warn of danger.

   4. **Weirs, reversals, and souse holes.** Water drops over an obstacle, then curls back on itself in a stationary wave, as is often seen at weirs and dams. The surface water is actually going *upstream*, and this action will trap any floating object between the drop and the wave. Once trapped, a swimmer's only hope is to dive below the surface where current is flowing downstream or to try to swim out the end of the wave.

E. **Boating alone is not recommended.** The standard preferred minimum is three craft.

F. **Have a frank knowledge of your boating ability.** Don't attempt waters beyond this ability. Learn paddling skills and teamwork, if in a multiperson craft, to match the river you plan to boat.

G. **Be in good physical condition** consistent with the difficulties that may be expected.

H. **Be practiced in escape** from an overturned craft, in self-rescue, and in artificial respiration. Know first aid.

I. **The Eskimo roll should be mastered** by kayakers and canoeists planning to run large rivers or rivers with continuous rapids where a swimmer would have trouble reaching shore.

J. **Wear a crash helmet** where an upset is likely. This is essential in a kayak or covered canoe.

K. **Be suitably equipped.** Wear shoes that will protect your feet during a bad swim or a walk for help, yet will not interfere with swimming (tennis shoes recommended). Carry a knife and waterproof matches. If you need eyeglasses, tie them on and carry a spare pair. Do not wear bulky clothing that will interfere with your swimming when waterlogged.

II. Boat and Equipment Preparedness

A. **Test new and unfamiliar equipment** before relying on it for difficult runs.

B. **Be sure the craft is in good repair** before starting a trip. Eliminate sharp projections that could cause injury during a swim.

C. **Inflatable craft should have multiple air chambers** and should be test inflated before starting a trip.

D. **Have strong, adequately sized paddles or oars** for controlling the craft, and carry sufficient spares for the length of the trip.

E. **Install flotation devices in noninflatable craft.** These devices should be securely fixed and designed to displace as much water from the craft as possible.

F. **Be certain there is absolutely nothing to cause entanglement** when coming free from an upset craft; e.g., a spray skirt that won't release or that tangles around the legs; life jacket buckles or clothing that might snag; canoe seats that lock on shoe heels; foot braces that fail or allow feet to jam under them; flexible decks that collapse on boaters' legs when trapped by water pressure; baggage that dangles in an upset; loose rope in the craft or badly secured bow and stern lines.

G. **Provide ropes to allow you to hold on to your craft** in case of upset, and so that it may be rescued. Following are the recommended methods:

1. **Kayaks and covered canoes** should have 6 inch-diameter grab loops of one-fourth-inch rope attached to bow and stern. A stern painter 7 or 8 feet long is optional and may be used if properly secured to prevent entanglement.

2. **Open canoes** should have bow and stern lines (painters) securely attached consisting of 8 to 10 feet of one-fourth- or three-eights-inch rope. These lines must be secured in such a way that they will not come loose accidentally and entangle the boaters during a swim, yet they must be ready for immediate use during an emergency. Attached balls, floats, and knots are not recommended.

3. **Rafts** should have taut perimeter grab lines threaded through the loops usually provided on the craft.

H. **Respect rules for craft capacity** and know how these capacities should be reduced for whitewater use. (Life raft ratings must generally be halved.)

I. **Carry appropriate repair materials:** tape (heating-duct tape) for short trips, complete repair kit for wilderness trips.

J. **Cartop racks must be strong and positively attached** to the vehicle, and each boat must be tied to each rack. In addition, each end of each boat should be tied to the car bumpers. Suction cup racks are poor. The entire arrangement should be able to withstand all but the most violent accident.

III. Leader's Preparedness and Responsibility

A. **River conditions.** Have a reasonable knowledge of the difficult parts of the run, or, if an exploratory trip, examine maps to estimate the feasibility of the run. Be aware of possible rapid changes in river level and how these changes can affect the difficulty of the run. If important,

17

determine approximate flow rate or level of the river. If the trip involves important tidal currents, secure tide information.

B. **Participants.** Inform participants of expected river conditions and determine whether the prospective boaters are qualified for the trip. All decisions should be based on group safety and comfort. Difficult decisions on the participation of marginal boaters must be based on group strength.

C. **Equipment.** Plan so that all necessary group equipment is present on the trip: 50- to 100-foot throwing rope, first aid kit with fresh and adequate supplies, extra paddles, repair materials, and survival equipment, if appropriate. Check equipment as necessary at the put-in, especially: life jackets, boat flotation, and any items that could prevent complete escape from the boat in case of an upset.

D. **Organization.** Remind each member of individual responsibility in keeping the group compact and intact between the leader and the sweep (a capable rear boater). If the group is too large, divide into smaller groups, each of appropriate boating strength, and designate group leaders and sweeps.

E. **Float plan.** If the trip is into a wilderness area, or for an extended period, your plans should be filed with appropriate authorities or left with someone who will contact them after a certain time. Establishing of checkpoints along the way from which civilization could be contacted if necessary should be considered. Knowing the location of possible help could speed rescue in any case.

IV. In Case of Upset

A. **Evacuate your boat immediately** if there is imminent danger of being trapped against logs, brush, or any other form of strainer.

B. **Recover with an Eskimo roll** if possible.

C. **If you swim, hold on to your craft.** It has much flotation and is easy for rescuers to spot. Get to the upstream side of the craft so it cannot crush you against obstacles.

D. **Release your craft if this improves your safety.** If rescue is not imminent and water is numbingly cold, or if worse rapids follow, then strike out for the nearest shore.

E. **When swimming rocky rapids,** use backstroke with legs downstream and feet near the surface. If your foot wedges on the bottom, fast water will push you under and hold you there. Get to slow or very shallow water before trying to stand or walk. Look ahead. Avoid possible entrapment situations: rock wedges, fissures, strainers, brush, logs, weirs, reversals, and souse holes. Watch for eddies and slackwater so that you can be ready to use these when you approach. Use every opportunity to work your way to shore.

F. **If others spill, go after the boaters. Rescue boats and equipment only if this can be done safely.**

V. International Scale of River Difficulty

If rapids on a river generally fit into one of the following classifications, but the water temperature is below 50°F, or if the trip is an extended one in a wilderness area, the river should be considered one class more difficult than normal.

Class I   Moving water with a few riffles and small waves; few or no obstructions.

Class II   Easy rapids with waves up to 3 feet, and wide, clear channels that are obvious without scouting; some maneuvering is required.

Class III   Rapids with high, irregular waves often capable of swamping an open canoe; narrow passages that often require complex maneuvering; may require scouting from shore.

Class IV   Long, difficult rapids with constricted passages that often require precise maneuvering in very turbulent waters. Scouting from shore is often necessary, and conditions make rescue difficult. Generally not possible for open canoes; boaters in covered canoes and kayaks should be able to Eskimo roll.

Class V   Extremely difficult, long, and very violent rapids with highly congested routes that nearly always must be scouted from shore. Rescue conditions are difficult, and there is significant hazard to life in event of a mishap. Ability to Eskimo roll is essential for kayaks and canoes.

Class VI   Difficulties of Class V carried to the extreme of navigability. Nearly impossible and very dangerous. For teams of experts only, after close study and with all precautions taken.

Injuries and Evacuations

Even allowing for careful preparation and attention to the rules of river safety, it remains a fact of life that people and boats are somewhat more fragile than rivers and rocks. Expressed differently, accidents do occur on paddling trips, and *all* boaters should understand that it can happen to them. Although virtually any disaster is possible on the river, there seems to be a small number of specific traumas and illnesses that occur more frequently than others. These include:

1. Hypothermia
2. Dislocated shoulder (especially common in decked boating)
3. Sprained or broken ankles (usually sustained while scouting or getting into or out of the boat)
4. Head injuries (sustained in falls on shore or during capsize)
5. Hypersensitivity to insect bite (anaphylactic shock)
6. Heat trauma (sunburn, heat stroke, heat prostration, dehydration, etc.)
7. Food poisoning (often resulting from sun spoilage of lunch foods on a hot day)

8. Badly strained muscles (particularly of the lower back, upper arm, and the trapezius)
9. Hand and wrist injuries
10. Lacerations

What happens when one of the above injuries occurs on the river? Many paddlers are well prepared to handle the first aid requirements, but are unfortunately ill prepared to handle the residual problems of continued care and evacuation. The following is an excerpt from *Wilderness Emergencies and Evacuations* by Ed Benjamin: "When a paddler is injured during a river trip he can usually be floated out in a canoe. Unfortunately, however, circumstances do sometimes arise when the victim is non-ambulatory, or when lack of open canoes or the nature of the river preclude floating the injured party out. In such a situation, the trip leader would have to choose between sending for help or performing an overland evacuation."

When sending for help, send at least two people. Dispatch with them a marked map or drawing showing your location as exactly as possible. (Yes, that means pencil and paper should be part of every first aid kit.) Also send a note giving directions for finding you, plus information on the nature of your emergency and the type of assistance you require. Have your messengers call the proper agencies, such as local police, a rescue squad, the U.S. Forest Service, the state police, plus any unofficial parties such as professional river outfitters who could lend special expertise to the rescue. This having been done, the messengers should be instructed to report the situation simply and factually to the families of the persons involved.

Many paddlers, unfortunately, do not know where they are except in relation to the river, and all too few carry topographical maps. Rescuers need to know exactly where you are in terms of the land, roads, etc. A helicopter pilot will not make much sense of the information that your victim is on the left bank below Lunchstop Rapid.

Establish shelter for youselves and the victim; any rescue is going to take a long time. In the time it takes your messengers to walk out, organize help, and return to you, many hours or perhaps days will pass. Psychologically prepare yourself for a long wait. To expedite the rescue attempt, build a smoky fire to help your rescuers locate you.

Many people believe that if they are ever hurt in the wilderness, a helicopter will come fly them out. This is not necessarily so. Only if you are near a military air base or a civilian air rescue service do you have a good chance of getting a helicopter. Even if one is available, there are several serious limitations. A rescue helicopter will not fly in bad weather, over a certain altitude, or at night. A helicopter needs a clear, reasonably level area, about 150 feet in diameter, in order to land. Moreover, the pilot will probably need some sort of wind indicator on the ground such as a wind sock or a smoky fire. All helicopters are not the same; most do not have cable on which to raise a victim, and all have limitations on where they may hover. If a helicopter is successful in landing near you, do not approach the craft until the crew signals you to do so, and then only as the crew directs. In most situations the availability or usefulness of a helicopter is doubtful. More likely you will be rescued by a group of volunteers who will drive to the nearest roadhead, reach you on foot, and carry the victim out. Volunteer rescue teams are usually slow and sometimes lack adequate training (particularly for a river rescue).

If help cannot be obtained, or if you have a large, well-equipped group, it may be possible to carry the victim out yourself. A litter can be improvised from trees, paddles, packs, etc. It should be strong enough to protect the victim from further injury. If you do attempt to evacuate the victim yourself, be advised that overland evacuations (even with the best equipment) are extremely difficult and exhausting and are best not attempted unless there are eight or more people to assist. When carrying a litter, a complement of six bearers is ideal. Not only does this spread the load, but, if one bearer loses footing, it is unlikely that the litter will be dropped. Bearers should be distributed so that there are two by the victim's head, two by the feet, and one on each side in the middle. Those carrying at the head of the victim must pay careful attention to the victim. An unconscious victim requires constant checking of vital signs. A conscious victim will be uncomfortable and frightened and will need reassurance. Bear in mind that a day warm enough to make a litter carrier perspire may be cool enough to induce hypothermia in an unmoving victim. Always have one bearer set the pace and choose the safest and easiest route. Go slow and easy and be careful. Always use a rope to belay the littr from above when ascending or descending a slope—a dropped litter can slide a long way. Paddlers should insist that their partners learn first aid. First aid gear (including pencil and paper), extra topographical maps, and rope should be carried in the sweep boat.

Hypothermia

Hypothermia, the lowering of the body's core temperature, and death from drowning or cardiac arrest after sudden immersion in cold water, are two serious hazards to the winter, early spring, and late-fall paddler. Cold water robs the victim of the ability and desire to save him or herself. When the body's temperature drops appreciably below the normal 98.6°F, a person becomes sluggish, breathing is difficult, coordination is lost, pupils dilate, speech becomes slurred, and thinking irrational. Finally unconsciousness sets in, and then, death. Hypothermia can occur in a matter of minutes in water just a few degrees above freezing, but even 50° water is unbearably cold.

To make things worse, a paddler may panic when faced with a long swim through rapids. Heat loss occurs quickly. A drop in body temperature makes swimming almost impossible, and tragically, the harder you struggle, the more heat your body loses. Body temperatures below 90°F lead to unconsciousness, and a further drop to about 77°F usually results in death. (But this

21

same lowering of the body temperature slows metabolism and delays brain death in cases of drowning, therefore heroic rescue efforts have a higher chance of success.)

Paddlers subjected to spray and wetting from waves splashing into an open boat are in almost as much danger of hypothermia as a paddler completely immersed after a spill. The combination of cold air and water drains the body of precious heat at an alarming rate, although it is the wetness that causes the major losses since water conducts heat away from the body 20 times faster than air. Clothes lose their insulating properties quickly when immersed in water, and skin temperatures will rapidly drop to within a few degrees of the water temperature. The body, hard pressed to conserve heat, will then reduce blood circulation to the extremities. This reduction in blood flowing to arms and legs make movement and heavy work next to impossible. Muscular activity increases heat loss because blood forced to the extremities is quickly cooled by the cold water. It's a vicious, deadly cycle.

The best safeguards against cold weather hazards are: recognizing the symptoms of hypothermia, preventing exposure to cold by wearing proper clothing (wool and waterproof outerwear or wet suits), understanding and respecting cold weather, knowing how the body gains, loses, and conserves body heat, and knowing how to treat hypothermia when it is detected. Actually, cold weather deaths may be attributed to a number of factors: physical exhaustion, inadequate food intake, dehydration of the body, and psychological elements such as fear, panic, and despair. Factors such as body fat, the metabolic rate of an individual, and skin thickness are variables in a particular person's reaction and endurance when immersed in cold water. Since the rate of metabolism is actually the rate at which the body produces heat from burning fats, carbohydrates, and proteins, one person may have a higher tolerance for cold weather than another. Stored fatty tissues also help the body resist a lowering of its core temperature. Shivering is "involuntary exercise"—the body is calling on its energy resources to produce heat. Proper food intake and sufficient water to prevent dehydration are important in any cold weather strenuous exercise, especially paddling.

The key to successfully bringing someone out of hypothermia is understanding that their body must receive heat from an external source. In a field situation, strip off all wet clothes and get the victim into a sleeping bag with another person. Skin-to-skin transfer of body heat is by far the best method of getting the body's temperature up. Don't let the victim go to sleep, and feed him or her warm liquids. Build a campfire if possible. Mouth-to-mouth resuscitation or external cardiac massage may be necessary in extreme cases when breathing has stopped, but remember that a person in the grips of hypothermia has a significantly reduced metabolic rate, so the timing of artificial respiration should correspond to the victim's slowed breathing.

How to Use This Guide

For each stream in this guide you will find a general description and at least one stream data list and map. (A stream is flowing water and may be a river, a creek, or a branch or fork of a river.)

Stream Descriptions

These are intended to give you a feel for the stream and its surroundings, and they are presented in general, nontechnical terms.

Stream Data

Each stream data list provides the necessary technical and quantitative information for each of the streams listed, as well as some additional descriptive data. Occasionally certain facts are covered in both the general description and in the data list for added emphasis. Listed below are fuller explanations of many of the categories found in the data lists.

Each list begins with the specific stream **section** to which the data apply and the **counties** in which the stream is located.

Suitable for∇While most streams described in this book are best for day cruising, some provide the opportunity for canoe camping.

Appropriate for—This item was included strictly for convenience. For definitional purposes, *families* connotes adults of various skill levels who want to take nonswimming adults or children in the canoe with them. We always assume that personal flotation devices (PDF's), e.g., life jackets, will be worn by all parties on moving water.

Beginners are paddlers with a knowledge of strokes and self-rescue who can maneuver a boat more or less intuitively on still water (lakes and ponds). True *intermediates* meet all beginner qualifications, have a working knowledge of river dynamics, have some ability in rescuing others, and (for our purposes) are competent and at home on Class II whitewater. Needless to say, these definitions could be refined or elaborated ad infinitum. They are not intended to be all-inclusive, but rather to give you a reasonable idea of how to classify yourself and how experienced practitioners of the sport may tend to class you.

Months Runnable—The months given are based on the average rainfall for a year. Different sections of rivers may be runnable at different times. Some rivers are not necessarily runnable at a given time of year but are only runnable after a heavy rainfall.

Interest Highlights—This category includes special *scenery, wildlife, whitewater, local culture* and *industry, historical locations,* and unusual *geology.*

Scenery—Taste is relative, and in the absolute sense ours is no better or worse than anyone else's. Our preference is that you form your own conclusions about the comparative beauty of the streams listed in this guide. Knowing, however, that it would take a long time to run most of these streams, we were presumptuous enough to include a comparative scenery rating based strictly on our own perceptions. The ratings run from *unattractive* to *uninspiring,* through gradations of *pretty* and *beautiful,* to *spectacular.*

Difficult—The level of difficulty of a stream is given according to the International Scale of River Difficulty inthe table found on page 00. Such ratings are relative and pertain to the stream described under more or less ideal water levels and weather conditions. For streams with two International Scale ratings, the first represents the average level of difficulty of the entire run and the second (expressed parenthetically) represents the level of difficulty of the most difficult section or rapids on the run. Paddlers are cautioned that changes in water levels or weather conditions can alter the stated average difficulty rating appreciably.

Average Width—Rivers tend to start small and widen as they go toward their confluence with another river. Pools form in some places, and in other places the channel may constrict, accelerating the current. All of these factors affect the width and make the average width an approximate measure.

Velocity—This represents the speed of the current, on the average, in nonflood conditions. It can vary a great deal from section to section on a given stream depending on the stream's width, volume, and gradient at any point along its length. Velocity is a partial indicator of how much reaction time you need on a certain river. Paddlers sometimes describe a high velocity stream as "coming at them pretty fast," meaning that the speed of the current does not allow them much time for decisions and reactions.

Rivers are described here as *slack, slow, moderate,* and *fast.* Slack rivers have current velocities of less than a half mile per hour; slow rivers have velocities of over a half mile per hour but less than two miles per hour. Moderate velocities range between two and four miles per hour, and fast rivers are those that exceed four miles per hour.

Hazards—Hazards are dangers to navigation. Because of the continuous action of the water, many of these hazards may change, and new ones might appear. *Low-hanging trees,* which can be a nuisance, may become *deadfalls, blowdowns,* and *strainers.* Human intervention creates hazards such as *dams, low bridges, powerboat traffic,* and *fences* (an especially dangerous "strainer").

Rescue Index—Many of the streams in this book run through wild areas. A sudden serious illness or injury could be an urgent problem if you can't get medical attention quickly. To give you an idea of how far you may be from help, a brief description is given of what might be expected. *Accessible* means that you might need up to an hour to secure assistance, but evacuation is not difficult. *Accessible but difficult* means that it might take up to three hours to get help and evacuation may be difficult. *Remote* indicates it might take three to six hours to get help; and *extremely remote* means that you could expect to be at least six hours from help and would need expert assistance to get a disabled person out.

Source of Additional Information—Various sources of additional information on water conditions are listed. Professional outfitters can provide both technical and descriptive information and relate the two to paddling. Other sources listed (forest rangers, fish and wildlife officers, etc.) will normally provide only descriptive information, e.g., "the creek's up pretty good today," or, "the river doesn't have enough water in it for boating."

Maps

The maps in this guide are not intended to replace topographic quadrangles for terrain features. Rather, they are intended to illustrate the general configuration of the stream, its access points, and surrounding shuttle networks.

Some of the maps are congested to the point that access letters may not be exactly where they should, but are only in the general vicinity. You may have to scout the area before launching. Approximate river miles and car shuttle miles from one access point to the next are provided with the maps. Additionally, the names of the topographic quadrangles on which the streams appear are provided with the maps. To order these maps, see the address list in "Where to Buy Maps" in the appendix, item B.

Table 1. Rating the River*

Points	Secondary Factors — Factors Related Primarily to Success in Negotiating			Primary Factors — Factors Affecting Both Success and Safety				Secondary Factors — Factors Related Primarily to Safe Rescue			
	Obstacles, rocks and trees	Waves	Turbulence	Bends	Length (feet)	Gradient (ft/mile)	Resting or rescue spots	Water Velocity (mph)	Width and depth	Temp	Accessibility °(F)
0	None	Few inches high, avoidable	None	Few, very gradual	<100	<5, regular slope	Almost anywhere	<3	Narrow (<75 feet) and shallow (<3 feet)	>65	Road along river
1	Few, passage almost straight through	Low (up to 1 ft) regular, avoidable	Minor eddies	Many, gradual	100<EN>-700	5-15, regular slope		3-6	Wide (>75 feet) and shallow (<3 feet)	55-65	<1 hour travel by foot or water
2	Courses easily recognizable	Low to med. (up to 3 ft), regular, avoidable	Medium eddies	Few, sharp, blind; scouting necessary	700-5,000	15-40, ledges or steep drops		6-10	Narrow (<75 feet) and deep (>3 feet)	45-55	1 hour to 1 day travel by foot or water
3	Maneuvering course not easily recognizable	Med. to large (up to 5 ft), mostly reg., avoidable	Strong eddies and cross currents		>5000	>40, steep drops, small falls	A good one below every danger spot	>10 or flood	Wide (>75 feet) and deep (>3 feet)	<45	>1 day travel by foot or water
4	Intricate maneuvering; course hard to recognize	Large, irregular, avoidable; or medium to large, unavoidable	Very strong eddies, strong cross currents								
5	Course tortuous, frequent scouting	Large, irregular unavoidable	Large scale eddies and crosscurrents, some up and down								
6	Very tortuous; always scout from shore	Very large (>5 ft), irregular, unavoidable, special equip. required						Almost none			

Source: Prepared by Guidebook Committee—AWA (from "American White Water," Winter 1957).

Table 2. Ratings Comparisons

International Rating	Approximate Difficulty	Total Points (from Table 1)	Approximate Skill Required
I	Easy	0–7	Practiced Beginner
II	Requires Care	8–14	Intermediate
III	Difficult	15–21	Experienced
IV	Very Difficult	22–28	Highly Skilled (Several years with organized group)
V	Exceedingly Difficult	29–35	Team of Experts
VI	Utmost Difficulty– Near Limit of Navigability		

1. Much of the information in this section was derived from *National Water Summary 1985*, United States Geological Survey, Water-Supply paper 2300.

Part One

LOUISIANA

Atchafalaya Basin

Located in southern Louisiana, the Atchafalaya Basin is a huge floodplain of the Atchafalaya River. The cities of Baton Rouge and Lafayette are located outside of its midpoints and it is bisected by I-10. The Atchafalaya Basin is America's largest bottomland hardwood forest swamp.

The Atchafalaya has been impacted by man. Portions of the northern half, above I-10, have been cleared for farming. In the lower half are canals dug in past decades to allow for oil exploration and drilling. Despite these intrusions, the basin is a vast wilderness area of hardwood forests. In the forest is a complex network of major rivers, with smaller creeks, bayous, and seasonal sloughs that feed off the larger streams. The greatest appeals of the Atchafalaya are the lakes that tend to be long and slender, dotted with cypress, and often tied together by narrow channels.

The paddling opportunities in the Atchafalaya are limitless. Not only are there numerous public launches, there are roads that parallel the levees that hold the Atchafalaya in check. An adventuresome paddler can launch from the levee at almost any point and paddle off to explore lakes or sloughs. Because the water level fluctuates as much as 20 feet over a year's time, another dimension is added for the paddler.

There are references in the following route descriptions to specific water levels of the Atchafalaya Basin. To find the current water levels, look in the New Orleans daily newspaper, *The Times-Picayune*. Each day the water levels of the Atchafalaya River are published on the "weather" page.

The gauge at Krotz Springs, Louisiana, is the one that is the most relevant for the routes described here. This gauge, however, is 40 miles upstream and on the west side of the Atchafalaya Basin; it gives paddlers an approximation of what water levels will be found in the Bayou Pigeon and Bayou Sorrell areas.

The following two descriptions of specific routes give the paddler some insights into the adventures offered by this Louisiana wilderness forest swamp.

Upper Flat Lake

In the Atchafalaya Basin there are numerous lakes of varying sizes and descriptions. One that is readily accessible to the paddler is Upper Flat Lake, located approximately 10 miles northwest of the town of Bayou Sorrell. A paddler could reach Upper Flat in about 30 minutes from a public launch.

The lake itself is approximately three to four miles long, depending on the water level. Its width is 1,000 feet at the widest point and the banks sporadically feature majestic, mature bald cypress. The lower half of the lake is open water that tapers down to an outflow channel leading to Upper Grand River.

The upper half of the lake is where paddlers find the most adventure. Because the open water extends into the forest, there is a labyrinth of channels and islands. Depending on the water level, the paddler may be able to explore this maze of open water and forested land.

Often there is considerable bird life, so bring binoculars. At times of low water, mudflats become exposed. Upon these, lush grass that attracts insects grows quickly, which in turn attracts birds. Flocks of ibis, egrets, and herons are seen in the fall when feeding conditions are optimum.

The way to access Upper Flat depends upon the water level. At high water, paddle up Upper Grand River into Bayou Marigoin, then through an unnamed lake east of Upper Flat into Upper Flat at its midpoint. At low water the only choice is to paddle up Upper Grand River to the outflow channel of Upper Flat itself.

The best water level for visiting Upper Flat is below eight feet on the Krotz Springs, Louisiana, gauge. Readings of 4 feet at Krotz Springs mean numerous islands are exposed, often with flocks of feeding birds.

To reach the public launch, drive north along the levee 8 miles from Bayou Sorrell. Cross over the levee to a large public launch where electrical lines also cross over the levee.

Section: Upper Flat Lake

Counties: Iberville Parish (LA)

USGS Quads: Grand River, Grosse Tete, SW (LA)

Suitable for: Beginners or anyone with binoculars

Appropriate for: Cruising, camping at low water

Months Runnable: All

Interest Highlights: Scenery, wildlife—especially bird life

Scenery: Beautiful—classic lake scene with cypress and moss

Difficulty: Class I

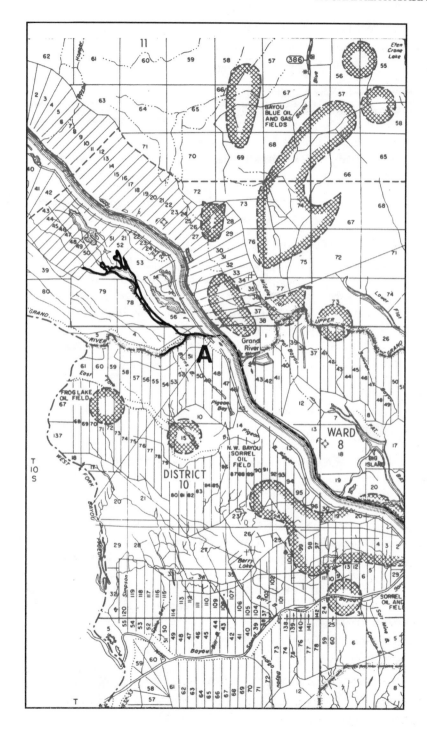

Average Width: Entrances 30 ft., lake 1,000 ft.

Velocity: Entrance at flood requires strenuous upstream paddling

Hazards: Fish hooks, strong currents

Rescue Index: Very accessible

Source of Additional Information: Canoe & Trail Adventures, 129 North Hennessy Street, New Orleans, LA 70119; (504) 486-2355.

Access Points	Access Code	River Miles	Shuttle Miles
A-A	1357	6*	0

To far end of the lake and return by most direct route. Following shorelines would lengthen the distance.

Access Key:

1	Paved road	7	Clear trail
2	Unpaved road	8	Brush and trees
3	Short carry	9	Launching fee charged
4	Long carry	10	Private property, need permission
5	Easy grade	11	No access, reference only
6	Steep incline		

Bayou Pigeon

The bayou Pigeon route gives the paddler two choices. One is to explore a series of interconnected lakes; another is to explore a variety of sloughs that provide a most intimate view of the swamp.

The city of Bayou Pigeon is located on the east side of the Atchafalaya at the end of LA 75. The launch is located 1.5 miles up the levee road from the bridge that provides access to Bayou Pigeon. The actual put-in spot can be the public launch, which means paddling eight-tenths of a mile north to the pipeline canal. Or, the alternative is to drive up the levee road eight-tenths of a mile, then portage the canoe over to a site directly opposite the pipeline canal. The choice should be based on the strength of the current flowing south in the intracoastal canal.

If the more northern put-in is chosen, carefully cross the intracoastal canal to an unnamed canal 30 feet wide that is directly across from the put-in. The current moves into the swamp with a velocity that depends on the water level. Proceed down this canal 2.2 miles to where a northeast-south-west canal intersects the east-west canal. At the intersection of these canals is the tip of a three-mile-long, unnamed Atchafalaya lake that makes this point a six-way crossing of waterways. This lake leads into a complex of other similar lakes.

A paddler with curiosity and a topo map can spend unlimited time exploring this complex of "skinny" lakes. Some lakes come complete with their own cypress-covered islands. Others connect with smaller lakes that wander off in various directions, some to dead ends, and others to intersections with still other lakes. All the lakes have shorelines dotted with very old cypress that have escaped the lumberman's saw.

Exploring the lakes can provide a full day of paddling, birding, eating lunch, and possibly hiking. If one is not camping, then while time and energy allow, a prudent paddler should return to the original put-in spot via the same pipeline canal.

Optimum levels for exploring the lakes are approximately from 8 to 12 feet on the Krotz Springs gauge. At this water level, the base of the cypress are exposed, there are no strong currents, and there is dry ground for stops. Higher water levels mean that a paddler can cut through the woods, but the forest swamp is not as attractive as at lower levels.

Another alternative to exploring the lakes is exploring the sloughs off the east-west pipeline canal. One possible trip is to paddle the 2.2 miles to the six-way intersection referred to above. Then turn right to the northeast to follow a much narrower and much older canal. Proceed one-half mile northeast and then turn with the canal due east. The man-made waterway seems natural in appearance. At eight-tenths of a mile from the turn, there is a crucial departure out of the canal into a very narrow, natural slough. This slough eventually meanders back to the original east-west pipeline canal. En route, one has the feeling of truly paddling through the forest. The contrast is extreme between this intimate slough, and the miles of open, long lakes described earlier.

Upon arrival at the east-west pipeline canal, if there is still time, energy, and curiosity, paddle across the canal into what the topo map calls Bayou Teche. Again, reenter a slough with a canopy overhead and tree trunks at paddle length. After approximately 1 mile, you will come out in Bayou Pigeon, a large waterway. By turning left, the public launch is eight-tenths of a mile upstream.

Another slough is found approximately three-tenths of a mile downstream or to the right of the exit from Bayou Teche. This unnamed slough is some 2 miles long with cross sloughs at its midpoint. Depending on current, time, etc., explore as much of this slough as desired, then return to Bayou Pigeon and the public launch. Optimum water levels for paddling sloughs would be around ten feet on the gauge at Krotz Springs.

It is essential that a paddler have the topo map, Pigeon LA, to make sense of the area. The Atchafalaya offers wildlife, vastness, and wilderness to those who explore its inner reaches.

Section: Bayou Pigeon

Counties: Iberville Parish (LA)

USGS Quads: Bayou Sorrell, Pigeon (LA)

Suitable for: Beginners

Appropriate for: Cruising, camping at low water

Months Runnable: All

Interest Highlights: Scenery, wildlife, especially bird life

Scenery: Pretty to beautiful

Difficulty: Class I

Average Width: Canal and sloughs 60–300 ft., lakes 500–1,000 ft.

Velocity: Slack

Hazards: Crossing the Intracoastal Waterway

Rescue Index: Very accessible

Source of Additional Information: Canoe & Trail Adventures, 129 North Hennessy Street, New Orleans, LA 70119; (504) 486-2355.

Access Points	Access Code	River Miles	Shuttle Miles
A–B	1357	9*	0 or .8 mile
B	1357	6**	

* To far end of the lake and return by most direct route.

** To combine canals and sloughs and Bayou Pigeon.

Access Key:

1	Paved road	7	Clear trail
2	Unpaved road	8	Brush and trees
3	Short carry	9	Launching fee charged
4	Long carry	10	Private property, need permission
5	Easy grade	11	No access, reference only
6	Steep incline		

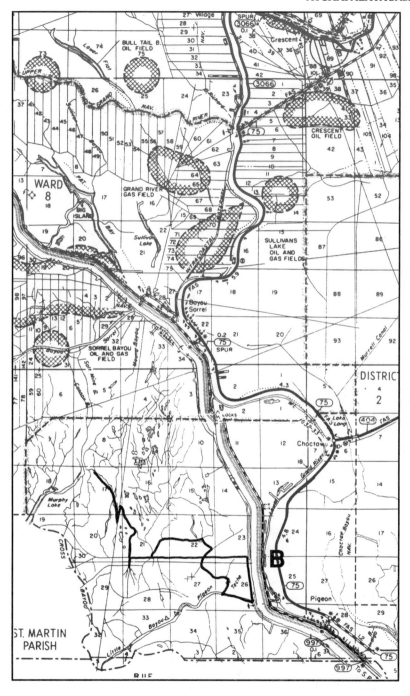

Bayou La Branche and Bayou Trepagnier

West of New Orleans, in the swamps and marshes that surround Lake Pontchartrain, are numerous bayous. These bayous are waterways that are really extensions of the lake itself. The water level is directly related to the lake level, which can be influenced by very modest tides or by strong winds that "tilt" the lake's water toward one shore or the other. The current in a bayou can flow in either direction, but it usually moves toward the lake. Bayous often have abundant bird and reptile life. They can be bordered by marshes or by a forest swamp.

An example of these bayous is Bayou La Branche, which is located west of New Orleans next to the Bonnet Carre Spillway. The spillway is a two-mile-wide emergency runoff path used when the Mississippi River reaches flood stage.

There is no guarantee that you will spot wildlife, but in Bayou La Branche and Trepagnier, there are often wading birds—egrets, ibis, and herons. The chances of surprising, or being surprised by, an alligator are good, especially near marshland. Often there are nutria, fur-bearing rodents, walking along or swimming in the bayou, usually indifferent to observers. There may be a scattering of snakes, turtles, and other assorted wildlife. To sum up, you are very likely to observe wildlife in this type of habitat.

To reach the put-in site, drive down the east levee of the spillway 3.1 miles to a semi-official launch. Paddle one half mile east in a canal to reach Bayou La Branche. By turning right (south), you will find 3.5 miles of bayou to explore. (At the end of 3.5 miles, the bayou becomes a canal, Cross Bayou Canal, and is of less interest to a paddler.) The bayou itself is bordered by a row of bushes and trees. Behind that strip are picturesque stands of cypress. Depending on the water levels, there are narrow, shallow waterways that can be used to gain access to the cypress stands. These stands are of the classic image, with flaring trunks, egrets about, and Spanish moss swaying in the breeze.

An alternative to paddling the length of La Branche is exploring Bayou

Trepagnier. The entrance to Bayou Trepagnier is found one half mile south of the intersection of Bayou La Branche and the entrance canal.

This second bayou is much, much narrower, more shaded, and meanders more than its parent bayou. As with the larger bayou, when the water is up there are opportunities to leave it and explore small open ponds and still more cypress stands. Bayou Trepagnier may continue for a full 3 miles from its mouth at Bayou La Branche to an abrupt end at a refinery.

Still another alternative for the paddler, after reaching La Branche, is to turn left (north) and paddle one-half mile out to Lake Pontchartrain. Once there, follow the shoreline of the lake. The shore to the east offers shell beaches, marshes, modest dunes, and cypress trees.

You may continue to paddle along the shore. Note the transition from lake to marsh. Occasionally there are opportunities to paddle out into large ponds that form the hollow centers of marshlands. Flocks of wading birds can sometimes be observed, as they prefer the open spaces that the marsh offers.

If a paddler chooses to explore this wetland of bayous, marshes, swamps, shallow ponds, and shorelines, the reward will be uncommon scenery, bountiful bird life, and an appreciation of one portion of the Gulf Coast environment.

Section: Bayou La Branche and Bayou Trepagnier

Counties: St. Charles Parish (LA)

USGS Quads: La Branche, Laplace (LA)

Suitable for: Cruising

Appropriate for: Beginners

Months Runnable: All

Interest Highlights: Scenery, wildlife

Scenery: Pretty to beautiful

Difficulty: Class I

Average Width: 30–60 ft.

Velocity: Slow

Hazards: Fishing hooks, powerboats, high winds

Rescue Index: Accessible by boat

Source of Additional Information: Canoe & Trail Adventures, 129 North Hennessy Street, New Orleans, LA 70119; (504) 486-2355.

Access Point	Access Code	River Miles	Shuttle Miles
A–A	2357	7.8 round-trip (if Bayou La Branche) 8.0 round-trip (if Bayou Trepagnier)	

Access Key:

1	Paved road	7	Clear trail
2	Unpaved road	8	Brush and trees
3	Short carry	9	Launching fee charged
4	Long carry	10	Private property, need permission
5	Easy grade	11	No access, reference only
6	Steep incline		

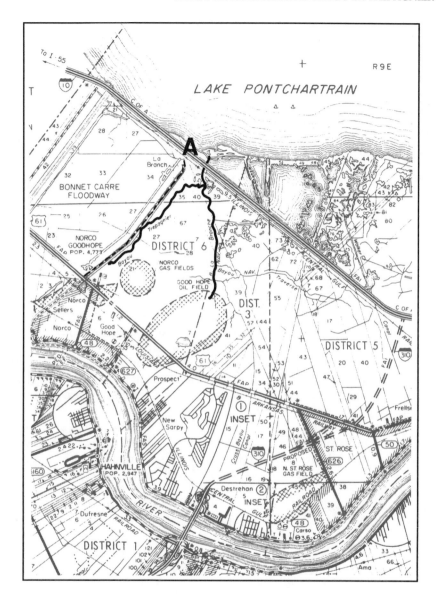

Jean Lafitte National Historical Park Barataria Unit

Jean Lafitte National Historical Park, headquartered in New Orleans, is composed of several segments. The two best known are the French Quarter in New Orleans proper, and the Chalmette Battlefield, located downstream from the city. A third segment is the Barataria Unit, which offers the paddler canals, bayous, and marsh ponds to explore. Located south of New Orleans off of LA 45, the Barataria Unit consists of 8,600 acres, plus another 8,000 acres in a protection zone.

The Barataria Unit is a mixture of various kinds of wetlands. There are forests of hardwoods—maples, oaks, and sweetgum—which can be paddled through or walked through on boardwalks. There are pockets of cypress-tupelo stands, which can be paddled into. And there are marshes, which offer considerable bird life, laced by canals.

Water levels fluctuate only a few feet at most, but since the bayous and canals are very, very shallow, a two-foot difference can make a waterway accessible or inaccessible to a paddler.

Perhaps the best months to paddle in the Barataria Unit are in the spring, March and April, when the trees and other vegetation are turning green, and in the fall months. The winter months are cooler, but do not offer much color. In the summer, in the open, it can be very warm and insects are a problem.

The Barataria Unit has a visitor's center, (504) 689-2002, which is open from 9 A.M. to 6 P.M. daily. The park itself is open from 7 A.M. to 7 P.M. Rangers on duty advise on the daily fluctuations of the water level in the various canoe trails. Maps of the park, which have enough detail for locating access points and routes to paddle, are available. The rangers offer canoe trips during which flora and fauna information is provided. At the time of this writing, there is a possibility of more canoe trails being designated. Even more

42

ambitious is the thought of providing camping platforms so that paddlers could spend the night amid the sounds of a Louisiana swamp.

The following are specific canoe routes that provide access into Louisiana wetlands, and thus opportunities for observations of wildlife and natural vegetation.

Bayou Coquille access (A) is from a parking lot on LA 45, seven-tenths of a mile north of the visitor's center. Coquille meanders through forests of hardwoods. On the lands adjacent to the bayou are maples, oaks, sweetgums, plus an understory of palmetto and bushes. In the bayou itself are tupelo trees and scattered cypress. There are even open spaces free of all vegetation. Near its western end, there is a stand of several acres of young cypress complete with Spanish moss. Bayou Coquille is the most appealing of the canoe trails now available in the Barataria Unit. It is very shallow, so sufficient water level is necessary to paddle through. This canoe trail is a very good example of a Louisiana bottomland hardwood swamp.

Kenta Canal is a century-old canal that extends out of a forested area to a transition zone from forest to marsh. Access (B) is from LA 301, 2 miles from the visitor center. One end of Kenta terminates in two-tenths of a mile in the Intracoastal Waterway. The other ends in a pipeline canal that runs through the marsh. The length is 3 miles overall. Because the canal is so old, the banks are covered with vegetation that gives it a natural appearance. Nutria are frequently seen along the banks. There are alligators and otters in the canal itself. Flocks of wading birds are common, like ibis, egrets, and herons. At the marsh end, there is a viewing platform built by the National Park Service. From there a paddler can look over the marsh and the pipeline canal. Options are turning into Bayou Coquille or paddling south-southeast in the pipeline canal for one-tenth of a mile. Turn left into very shallow ponds to get a close-up of a Louisiana marsh. An easier option is to paddle into the trenasses—mini-canals—dug by trappers to give them access to the marsh and its fur-bearing inhabitants. Kenta Canal combined with Bayou Coquille give a paddler a view of the habitat found in the Barataria Unit.

Bayou des Familles runs parallel to, but away from, LA 45. The bayou is buffered from the highway by trees and bushes so that there is a feeling of wilderness. Access to this canoe trail is from the same parking lot used for Bayou Coquille.

Bayou des Familles extends for 3.5 miles. It is still another choice for exploring this national park. Bayou Coquille intersects Bayou des Familles on its east end, and Kenta Canal on its west end. Using these other trails, a paddler can reach every designated trail from the parking lot described above.

Section: Jean Lafitte National Historical Park, Barataria Unit
Counties: Jefferson Parish (LA)
USGS Quads: Bertrandville, Lake Cataouatche East
Suitable for: Daytime exploring
Appropriate for: Beginners
Months Runnable: Year-round
Interest Highlights: Scenery, wildlife
Scenery: Pretty
Difficulty: Class I
Average Width: 30-75 ft.
Velocity: None to slow
Rescue Index: Accessible by boat
Source of Additional Information: National Park Service, 423 Canal, New Orleans, LA 70130-2341; (504) 589-2330.

Access Points	Access Code	River Miles	Shuttle Miles
AA (Bayou Coquille)	1357	4.0*	0
BB (Kenta Canal)	1357	5.6	0

Estimated

Access Key:
1 Paved road
2 Unpaved road
3 Short carry
4 Long carry
5 Easy grade
6 Steep incline
7 Clear trail
8 Brush and Trees
9 Launching fee charged
10 Private Property, need permission
11 No access, reference only

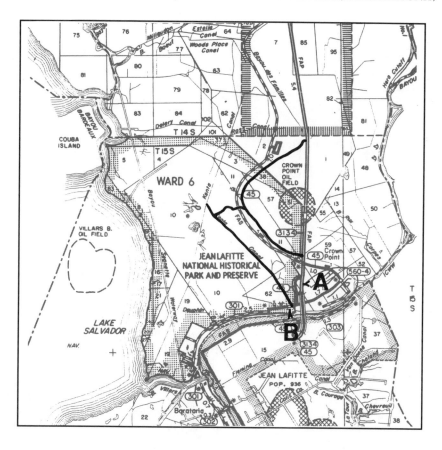

Pearl River Basin
Honey Island Swamp

Located along the Louisiana-Mississippi border is the Pearl River Basin, known locally as the Honey Island Swamp. The basin is the floodplain for the Pearl River. It extends southward for 50 miles from near Bogalusa, Louisiana, to the Mississippi Sound. Its total area is approximately 300 square miles (192,000 acres), the vast majority being heavily wooded. The forest is bottomland hardwood trees of oaks, maples, sweetgums, etc., with ponds of tupelo and scattered cypress. The forest is laced with a network of waterways composed of rivers, creeks, bayous, lakes, ponds, and sloughs. This network provides the adventurous paddler a tremendous opportunity to explore a wilderness area. The Pearl River annually fluctuates as much as 10 to15 feet, yet remains at different levels for weeks at a time, providing considerable variety to the Pearl River Basin experience.

This wilderness area has been little impacted by man. Except for two interstates, one highway, and scattered lumbering, the length and width of the Pearl River Basin is largely as it has always been. Three large segments of the basin are now public property: one is the Bogue Chitto National Wildlife Refuge, a second is Mississippi's Old River Wildlife Management Area, and the third is the state of Louisiana's Pearl River Game Management Area. In the future, hopefully more of the basin acres can be acquired and protected from any further alterations.

There are references in the following route descriptions to specific water levels of the Pearl River. To find the current water levels look in the New Orleans daily newspaper, *The Times-Picayune*. Each day the water levels of the Pearl River are published on the "weather" page.

The following three descriptions of specific routes give the paddler insights into one of America's least impacted forest swamps.

Socias Lake

Socias Lake is a modest-sized body of water in the forests of the upper Pearl River Basin. Part of its attraction is in the challenge of finding it. At low water, it is accessible only by canoe. It can be reached from the Mississippi side, but only via an intricate route that includes waterways not on the topo map. The topo map accurately shows the sequence of the Pearl River, Gum Bayou, and Socias Lake. It is simple to paddle to this Mississippi lake from the Louisiana side. The sense of triumph is considerable when the lake is reached—hence the appeal of Socias Lake!

From the launch, paddle across the canal to a set of tracks on the opposite bank. Portage the canoe along the tracks for 100 yards, then launch into the Pearl River. (The portage avoids a sill that at low water is extremely dangerous for canoes.)

Paddle down the Pearl River for a mile and a half to the third right-hand turn. Pass through the left-hand bank, the Mississippi side, with the current into a 20-foot wide cut. (Ignore an earlier cut on the second right-hand turn at approximately one mile.)

The slough, Gum Bayou, is a rarity in that it is one of only a handful that flows into the basin at even the lowest of water levels. It is classic in appearance with high, steep banks and overhanging hardwood trees. The stream may be interrupted by trees that are partially or completely blocking the path. If a way through is not handy, the paddler must finesse or power his way through. There are no decision-causing major forks. After 1.5 miles in a generally southeastern direction, a persistent paddler will be pleasantly surprised to enter a modest-sized lake. This is Socias Lake—approximately three or four football fields long and one football field wide. It is very appealing with its shore of individual cypress trees. About a third of the way down the right-hand side is a concentrated stand of out-of-the-water cypress that make for a superb lunch spot.

To return to the launch, reverse the route. Since the current will then be against you, consider the return an opportunity for some aerobic exercise. Despite the oncoming current, the return is not difficult, especially in the Pearl River where the current on the inside of the turns is almost nil.

The woods paralleling the slough are open and inviting. Take advantage of exploring them if they are accessible, which occurs only in the dry autumn.

Section: Socias Lake
Counties: Pearl River County (MS)
USGS Quads: Henleyfield, MS

Suitable for: Intermediate paddlers

Appropriate for: Day trips, camping (when the Pearl is low)

Months Runnable: All, although best at low water

Interest Highlights: Scenery, wildlife, exploring

Scenery: At low water, beautiful

Difficulty: Class I

Average Width: Gum Bayou, 25 ft.; Socias Lake, 100 yds.

Velocity: In Gum Bayou slow to moderate

Hazards: Trees down in Gum Bayou, getting lost, fatigue

Rescue Index: Accessible by boat

Source of Additional Information: Canoe & Trail Adventures, 129 North Hennessy Street, New Orleans, LA 70119; (504) 486-2355.

Access Point	Access Code	River Miles	Shuttle Miles
A	1357	6	0

Access Key:

1	Paved road	7	Clear trail
2	Unpaved road	8	Brush and trees
3	Short carry	9	Launching fee charged
4	Long carry	10	Private property, need permission
5	Easy grade	11	No access, reference only
6	Steep incline		

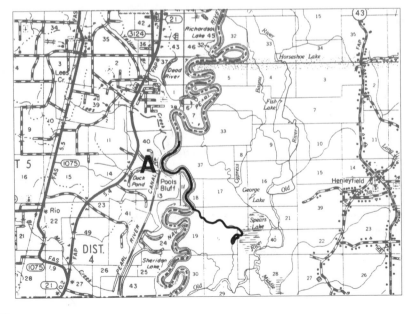

Sheridan Lakes

Many facets make up the whole of bottomland hardwood swamp. This route gives a paddler an unusual opportunity to explore a variety of waterways, each representative of one aspect of the forest swamp. In one day's time, you may go from the Pearl River into narrow, cool sloughs, and emerge into modest-sized lakes. After a portage over a levee, return to the launching site via a man-made canal.

The public launching point is called Pool's Bluff. This is a Corps of Engineers landing on the Pearl River south of Bogalusa, Louisiana. To locate, drive south from Bogalusa on LA 41 for 5 miles, or north from Sun, Louisiana, on LA 41 for 5 miles, to a Corps of Engineers sign, "Pool's Bluff." Follow the all-weather road east a half mile to the public launch.

Launch directly into the canal and paddle straight across to a set of tracks on the opposite bank. Portage your canoe along these tracks for 100 yards, then launch into the Pearl River. (The portage is to avoid a sill which, at certain water levels, is extremely hazardous to small boats.)

Paddle on the Pearl River only until you can leave it and adventure into the forest itself via a slough. If the water level is above 14 feet on the Bogalusa gauge, the first slough will have enough water to float a canoe. It is located just 300 yards downstream on the right side. Turn into it and enter a world where the slough is so narrow that both banks can often be touched by an extended paddle. Overhead is a canopy of branches furnished by a mixture of oaks, maples, sweetgums, and tupelo. Approximately 300 yards from the Pearl, the slough forks; take the left fork which, in 1.5 miles, enters the upper Sheridan Lake. En route the slough is joined by two other sloughs coming in from the Pearl. There are also stretches of open water with high, pine-covered banks on the right and low ground on the left. Continue to follow the main current that passes through some very pretty tupelo-lined sloughs until you reach the Sheridan Lake.

In the event that the Pearl River is too low at the first slough, continue around the bend, and at approximately 1.1 miles from the sill there is another obvious slough on your right. Within 500 yards, this alternative slough enters the main slough coming down from the right (north). If this slough is not accessible, continue another 1.2 miles on the Pearl to the third slough. Use this one to paddle into the interior of the floodplain.

Upon reaching upper Sheridan Lake, either turn left and explore its length or continue straight ahead until you reach the lower and larger Sheridan Lake. The northern edge of this lake is lined with cypress that are beautiful at low water levels. There are beaver at the far end of the lake, so be alert for them.

In the southeastern corner of lower Sheridan is high ground. It makes an excellent place to stop for a snack or to stretch your legs. This high ground is an island of pines when the Pearl is above flood stage.

To return to the launch, paddle to the southwestern corner of the lake through lilypads to an obvious groove in the levee. Portage over the levee and turn right. The landing is 1.4 miles up the canal.

This is an excellent one-day float that has an unusual amount of variety to it. There are opportunities for observing wildlife, especially birds and reptiles, which only enhance the memories of this route.

Section: Sheridan Lakes (Pearl River Basin)

Counties: Washington Parish (LA)

USGS Quads: Henleyfield (MS)

Suitable for: Exploring, camping

Appropriate for: Beginners

Months Runnable: Year-round, but prettiest when the Pearl is below flood

Interest Highlights: Scenery, wildlife

Scenery: Beautiful

Difficulty: Class I

Average Width: 25-600 ft.

Velocity: Gentle, except at highest water levels

Hazards: Fish hooks, getting lost

Rescue Index: Very accessible

Source of Additional Information: Canoe & Trail Adventures, 129 North Hennessy Street, New Orleans, LA 70119; (504) 486-2355.

Access Points	Access Code	River Miles	Shuttle Miles
A	1357	6*	0

Assuming that the longest route is taken, which is the third slough, and that the length of both lakes are paddled.

Access Key:	1	Paved road	7	Clear trail
	2	Unpaved road	8	Brush and trees
	3	Short carry	9	Launching fee charged
	4	Long carry	10	Private property, need permission
	5	Easy grade	11	No access, reference only
	6	Steep incline		

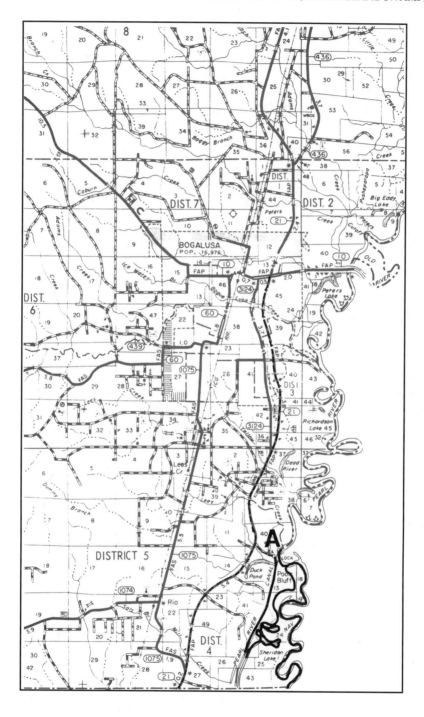

Peach Lake

Peach Lake is a long, narrow lake of about 4 miles that extends north and south into the very heart of Honey Island Swamp. Peach Lake is always accessible, evenat the lowest levels of the Pearl River. An access to the entrance to the lake is via a public launch, Davis Landing.

From New Orleans, proceed on I-10 to the Slidell exit (Hwy. 190) and exit to the right. Proceed 1.8 miles to LA 1090. Turn left onto LA 1090 (shopping center on the left), and proceed 2 miles. (En route go over I-10.) Turn right onto Davis Landing Road immediately in front of a Time Saver store. Proceed seven-tenths of a mile to a stop sign. Turn left and proceed 1.1 miles to Davis Landing. (The road makes 90° and 45° turns during that 1.1 mile distance.)

The lake itself is free of trees or islands, but is bordered by the familiar tupelo and cypress. Adjacent lands have a forest of maples, oaks, sweetgum, and other varieties of trees. The wildlife includes birds such as egrets and ibis. There are alligators in the lake, but they are shy and seldom seen.

The south end of the lake has the deepest water, the largest, oldest cypress, and the greater width. Paddling toward the north end, the lake gradually narrows, the route becomes more twisted, and the banks rise. Eventually, the open lake just disintegrates into sloughs that spread out in different directions. At low-water levels, there are considerable hiking opportunities on the dry lands that border the lake.

The entrance to the lake contrasts with the openness of the lake itself. The entrance extends for about 1.5 miles from the Middle River to the lake. When coming through the entrance, dodge snags and fallen trees as you admire the overhead canopy of hardwood trees. There are turns to negotiate on the approach to the lake, but most of the paddling is through the tunnel-like slough that provides access to the lake.

To reach Peach Lake, launch from Davis Landing public launch, paddle out of the canal, and turn right onto the wide West Pearl. Descend for about 1.5 miles to where the Middle River splits off to the left. Turn into it, descend a third of a mile and then turn left again into the entrance to Peach Lake.

After exploring the lake, exit through the entrance, turn right, and go up the Middle River. Upon reaching the West Pearl, turn left and paddle downstream 1.25 miles to Crawford Landing, another public launch.

The gauge at Pearl River is the best indicator of water levels and river currents in Peach Lake. Water levels can vary from 4 to plus 20 feet. The best time to explore Peach Lake is when the level is 8 feet and below. Since you exit out of the lake against the current, the effort to leave at higher levels becomes considerable.

The route from Davis into Peach Lake and then out to Crawford is especially recommended for moonlight paddling. In the swamp at night, there is an orchestra of sounds to absorb. To paddle into Peach Lake before sunset, have a campfire meal at sunset, and then exit by moonlight is a special event for anyone.

Section: Peach Lake (Honey Island Swamp)

Counties: St. Tammany Parish (LA)

USGS Quads: Haaswood

Suitable for: Exploring (no overnight camping allowed)

Appropriate for: Beginners

Months Runnable: Whenever the Pearl River is below 8 ft. on the Pearl River gauge

Interest Highlights: Scenery, wildlife

Scenery: Pretty

Difficulty: Class I (when the Pearl River gauge is below 8 ft.)

Average Width: 20–600 ft.

Velocity: Gentle, except when the Pearl is at flood stage

Hazards: Wasp nests, fish hooks, getting lost

Rescue Index: Very accessible

Source of Additional Information: Louisiana Wildlife and Fisheries, 2001 Quail Drive, Baton Rouge, LA 70898; (504) 342-5874.

Access Points	Access Code	River Miles	Shuttle Miles
A–B	1357	7.0*	4.2
B	1357		

Assuming the paddler goes to a distinctive "split" in the lake. To the right the channels dead-end; to the left the channel continues.

Access Key:

1	Paved road	7	Clear trail
2	Unpaved road	8	Brush and trees
3	Short carry	9	Launching fee charged
4	Long carry	10	Private property, need permission
5	Easy grade	11	No access, reference only
6	Steep incline		

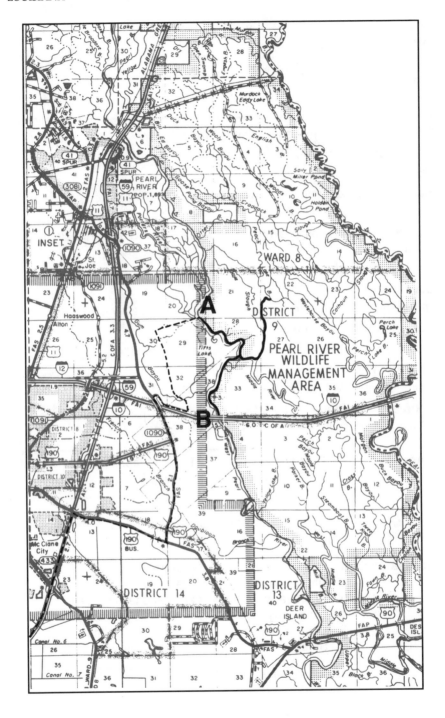

Maple Slough

Maple Slough in the Pearl River Basin is one of the finest among the most beautiful and interesting wetland habitats in the transition zone where a southern hardwood swamp gives way to freshwater marsh. Local adventurers enjoy it by putting in on the West Pearl at the U.S. Highway 90 public launch. Paddle 1 mile upstream to the open oxbow on the west bank of the river, then up the oxbow until it makes a sharp turn to the right. The entrance to Maple Slough is on the left bank.

A canopy of giant cypress covers the narrow channel. No longer than a half mile, Maple Slough should be explored slowly. Its course, sometimes no broader than the width of two canoes, meanders through huge, ancient cypress, then abruptly ends in open marsh.

Instead of grounding out in the grass, Maple Slough offers a "turning basin" the size of a tennis court that is an excellent observation deck for the rich wetland environment.

The marsh reaches to the horizon on the south and north, while a tree-top forest crowds the skyline a quarter-mile to the west. Birds use the open marsh as a flyway, giving visitors a chance to spot egrets, herons, marsh hawks, and occasionally anhingas. During the winter months, a pair of bald eagles are often seen flying food patrols from their nest, hidden from sight to the south-southeast.

Sunset is a special time to experience Maple Slough. The light softens, and a chorus of insects joins with bullfrogs to serenade the evening procession of roosting flights by numerous bird species. Maple Slough has been preserved by the Louisiana Nature Conservancy. One trip should convince anyone the effort was worthwhile.

Section: Maple Slough

Counties: St. Tammany Parish (LA)

USGS Quads: Rigolets (LA)

Suitable for: Beginners at low water, strong paddlers only at high water

Appropriate for: Day, twilight, and moonlight

Months Runnable: Year-round

Interest Highlights: Scenery, wildlife

Scenery: Pretty

Difficulty: Class I at low water

Average Width: 6–8 ft. wide

Velocity: In the West Pearl, at high water a moderate current; in Maple Slough no current

Hazards: Upstream paddling

Rescue Index: Accessible

Source of Additional Information: Canoe & Trail Adventures, 129 North Hennessy Street, New Orleans, LA 70119; (504) 486-2355.

Access Point	Access Code	River Miles	Shuttle Miles
A	1357	3	0

Access Key:

1	Paved road	7	Clear trail
2	Unpaved road	8	Brush and trees
3	Short carry	9	Launching fee charged
4	Long carry	10	Private property, need permission
5	Easy grade	11	No access, reference only
6	Steep incline		

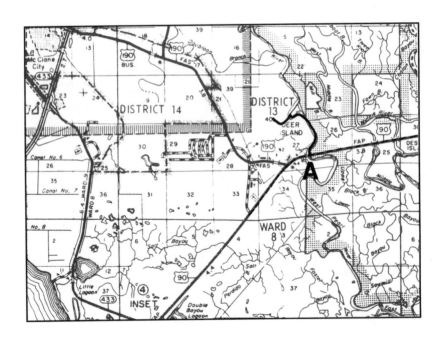

Amite River

The Amite River is the boundary between two Louisiana parishes, St. Helena and East Feliciana. It is a stream that offers gentle turns, numerous sandbars, and sloping banks. The river is formed by the confluence of the east and west forks of the Amite. The meeting of the two forks occurs just 1 mile south of the Mississippi-Louisiana state line. At that point, the stream changes character from the creeklike appearances of the forks to a river. A suggested overnight canoe trip is one day on the shaded East Fork, and one day on the Amite itself, out in the open, using the gravel bars for stopping places.

The upper Amite River has been proposed as the location of a dam as a flood-control project for the lower Amite. The lake behind the dam would extend back up toward the state line.

East Fork of the Amite River

Located in Mississippi due south of Liberty, the East Fork of the Amite River is a creeklike stream. The East Fork has high banks, overhanging branches, and, depending on water level, a fair amount of logs and trees in the streambed. There are several small islands that split the already narrow stream. Opposite these islands, the congestion of downed trees is likely. You may even choose to stop at the head of the island and scout both channels to determine which is the less obstructed choice.

The 10.5-mile section from Amite River East Fork rural bridge (MS) to LA 432, west of Chipola (LA), (access A–access B) offers not only two states but also two contrasting streams. First comes the creek, narrow and shady, with tight turns and modest islands that appear and disappear as the stream changes. Depending on water level, logs and trees may obstruct the paddler's way. (These can be hazardous at medium or higher water levels.) There is no sign or mark at the Mississippi-Louisiana border. At about the 5-mile mark, the East Fork of the Amite is joined by the West Fork and the two become the Amite River. The stream then makes a transition to a river with much broader, gentler turns and sandbars. Within a mile of the two forks, there is a cluster of at least ten lunching/camping beaches. This is significant because, with one exception, these are all the beaches found along this section. It is a good one-day float in the summer or a very leisurely wintertime overnight canoe trip.

To reach access A, the rural bridge in Mississippi north of Chipola, Louisiana, from the I-55 interchange near Kentwood, Louisiana, proceed 17 miles west on LA 38 to Chipola, Louisiana. Turn right in Chipola onto LA 1044 and proceed 6.8 miles to a rural intersection (at 5.8 miles crossing into Mississippi), turn left and proceed 1.2 miles to a rural bridge over the East Fork of the Amite River.

The Amite River continues for another 6 miles from LA 432 to LA 10 (access B–access C) much the same pace with the same scenery. The river does have numerous sandbars, which are evenly distributed along the way. In the first 2 miles on the west bank, there are at least two dozen camps. In the second half of this section, the current is quicker than in the first half, giving the paddler a little faster ride. The combination of these two sections would make a fine overnight float during the summer.

To reach the LA 432 bridge west of Chipola, Louisiana, access B, in Chipola turn onto LA 432 and proceed west 3.9 miles to the bridge over the Amite River.

LA 10 to LA 37

The section from LA 10 (Coleman) to LA 37 (Grangeville) (access C–access D) measures 16.5 miles between public bridges—an unusually long stretch for the Gulf Coast region. The result is a remote, little used, gentle stream that appeals to those who want "to get away from it all." The distance discourages a day paddler, so the best use of this section of the Amite is a leisurely overnight camping trip.

There are numerous spacious gravel bars that can be used for camping or resting. There are no towns and only a few camps to intrude on the remote feeling. The banks and adjacent lands are forested, consisting of the usual mix of hardwoods. The current is not hurried but neither is it terribly sluggish, as it still has many miles to go before emptying into Lake Maurepas.

One feature of this section that a paddler should be aware of is that, within 2 miles of the start, the Amite River divides. The resulting channels are approximately 1.6 miles (west) and 1.2 miles (east) long. Stop and do some scouting along the banks before choosing a channel. When a stream splits, the current in channels is almost always faster than in the main stream, and often there are trees that span the channel. Yet, despite these words of caution, the split of the Amite is an opportunity to briefly return to creek paddling with its higher banks, overlapping branches, and tight turns. If the objective of the canoe trip is to be by yourself at a deliberate pace, then paddle this long stretch of the Amite River.

To reach access C, from Darlington, Louisiana, proceed west on LA 10 4.3 miles to the bridge over the Amite. (Darlington is 15 miles west of I-55 on LA 10.)

To access D, LA 37 bridge southwest of Grangeville, Louisiana, from Grangeville, Louisiana, proceed 0.5 mile southwest on LA 37. (Grangeville, Louisiana, is 23 miles west of Amite, Louisiana, on LA 16 and LA 63.)

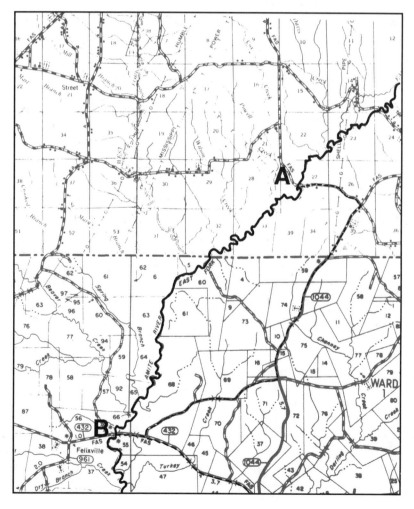

Section: Amite River, East Fork to LA 37 (to Grangeville)

Counties: Amite (MS), East Feliciana, St. Helena parishes (LA)

USGS Quads: Liberty (MS); Chipola, Hatcherville (LA)

Suitable for: Cruising, camping

Appropriate for: Families, beginners

Months Runnable: All

Interest Highlights: Scenery, wildlife

Scenery: Pretty, especially the East Fork

Difficulty: Class I

Average Width: 30–80 ft.

Velocity: Slow to moderate

Hazards: Deadfalls and low-hanging trees

Rescue Index: Accessible to accessible-but-difficult

Source of Additional Information: Canoe & Trail Adventures, 129 North Hennessy Street, New Orleans, LA 70119; (504) 486-2355.

Access Points	Access Code	River Miles	Shuttle Miles
A–B	2357	10.5	9.5
B–C	1357	6.0	5.2
C–D	1357	16.5	12.9
D	1467		

Access Key:

1	Paved road	7	Clear trail
2	Unpaved road	8	Brush and trees
3	Short carry	9	Launching fee charged
4	Long carry	10	Private property, need permission
5	Easy grade	11	No access, reference only
6	Steep incline		

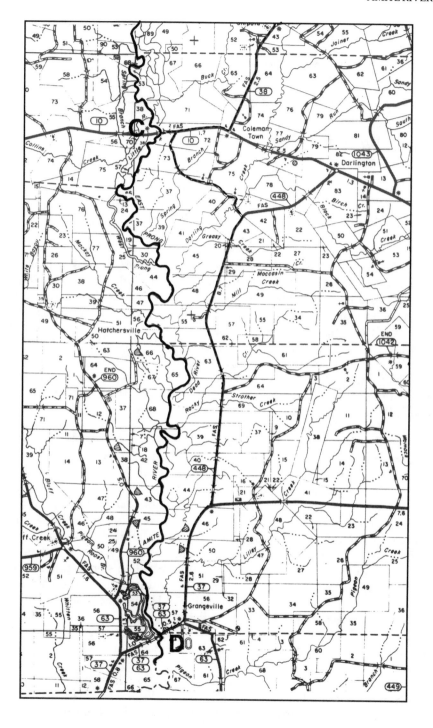

Tangipahoa River

The Tangipahoa River begins southwest of McComb, Mississippi, as the outlet for Percy Quin State Park. It flows south and southwest through farms and forests without ever passing through a city. Eventually it enters Lake Pontchartrain on its northeast shoulder, contributing its fresh water to this brackish lake. The stream is recognized by the state legislatures of both Mississippi and Louisiana as a state scenic river.

As most Gulf Coast streams do, it begins as a creek, makes the transition to a river, and then finishes as a bayou. The 36 miles described here are the most attractive sections—the lower creek and upper river—that the Tangipahoa River offers paddlers.

Tangipahoa River driving directions are as follows: To reach access A at Osyka, Mississippi, from the intersection of U.S. 51 and MS 584, in Osyka, Mississippi, proceed on MS 584 1.1 miles east and north to a rural bridge. To access B at Greenlaw, Louisiana, from the intersection of U.S. 51 and LA 1054, in Greenlaw, Louisiana, proceed east on LA 1054 1.6 miles to a rural bridge. To reach access C at Kentwood, Louisiana, from the intersection of I-55 and LA 38 west of Kentwood, Louisiana, proceed 2.2 miles east on LA 38 to a rural bridge. To reach access D at Tangipahoa, Louisiana, from the intersection of I-55 and LA 440 west of Tangipahoa, Louisiana, proceed 2.3 miles east on LA 440 to a rural bridge. To reach access E at Arcola, Louisiana, from Arcola, Louisiana, proceed 0.6 mile east on LA 10 to a rural bridge. To reach access F at Amite, Louisiana, from the intersection of U.S. 51 and LA 16 in Amite, Louisiana, proceed east on LA 16 1.5 miles to a rural bridge. And finally, to reach access G at Independence, Louisiana, from the intersection of U.S. 51 and LA 40 in Independence, Louisiana, proceed east on LA 40 1.3 miles to a rural bridge.

The section from MS 584 (Osyka) to LA 1054 (Greenlaw) (access A–access B) is 3.6 miles. For paddlers who like creeks and the challenge of the somewhat unknown, starting at Osyka, Mississippi, offers both. It is possible to paddle even farther upstream than Osyka on the Tangipahoa River, but this starting point is a very reasonable choice given the uncertainty of low water and logs and trees upstream.

The Tangipahoa River is at this point a creek with distinct close banks, broad-leaf trees extending out over the stream, and almost endless tight turns.

There certainly may be logs, even entire trees, across the entire width of the streambed. These change with every flood, so much so that a paddler can know that they exist, but not how many.

There are also islands that come and go, although this happens over a period of years, not seasons, as with the trees. Some are tiny; others require you to make deliberate decisions about what ways to go around them, and hope that the chosen routes are clear of obstructions. There are no sizable beaches. Any camping is confined to the woods above the stream.

The section from LA 1054 to LA 38 (Kentwood) (access B–access C) is 5.2 miles. This segment of the Tangipahoa River continues as a creek. One additional feature is that a few hundred yards to the east and parallel to the stream is a 70-foot ridge. Occasionally, the stream brushes up against it, giving the Gulf Coast paddler the rare circumstance of having to really look up to find the top of the sloping bank.

The foliage along the stream alternates between open woods and heavy undergrowth. At times there is a delightful canopy completely covering the streambed. There are also modest tributaries that sometimes join the river; these can be worth exploring.

It is 6.5 miles from LA 38 to LA 440 (Tangipahoa, access C–access D). This segment has several features of interest for a paddler. For most of the distance, the stream continues as a creek. The ridge mentioned above has moved off to the east. There are scattered tributaries, but mostly you'll enjoy the forest above and around. At approximately 4.5 miles, the stream splits around a hefty-sized island. (In a straight line the island is seven-tenths of a mile long, but the channels that parallel it are approximately twice as long —1.5 miles.)

Take time to check out which is the preferred channel around the island. The major item to note is how many trees or logs there are across each channel. Due to the narrowness of the stream, the channels are often blocked. The novelty of lifting over a chest-high log or pushing through a fully branched tree is soon lost, so take the clearer route.

After the joining of the two island channels, the Tangipahoa makes an abrupt transition from a creek to a river. Now the paddler has sand-and-gravel bars, wider streambeds, and gentle turns. Almost simultaneously, the stream flows past Camp Moore, which is now a Confederate cemetery, a Louisiana commemorative area. During the Civil War, Camp Moore was a training site for Louisiana volunteers. Finally, you arrive at Kentwood, the source of the famous spring water that is sold commercially in several states.

The preceding three segments of the Tangipahoa, 15.3 river miles, make an excellent overnight camping-canoeing weekend. The water needs to be of sufficient level to clear most of the obstacles, but not high or strong enough to sweep unwary or inexperienced paddlers into them.

The section from LA 440 to LA 10 (Arcola, access D–access E) is 8.4 miles. There are numerous sand-gravel bars, which are excellent for rest breaks, picnics, or overnight campouts. The stream is wide enough so that no tree spans its entire width. There still may be a considerable number of embedded logs and branches that need to be dodged, but in general, the paddling is easier than it is upstream. The rate of flow is gentle and consistent with the upstream segments. The trees are the same hardwoods, but are behind the sand-gravel bars; no longer are they overhead. Scattered along the west banks are both active and abandoned commercial gravel-dredging operations. They are not readily seen, however, and are not intrusive to a paddler.

For the next 5.2 miles, from LA 10 to LA 16 (Amite, access E–access F), the Tangipahoa River continues upstream with a gentle current, spacious and frequent sand-gravel bars, and wide, sweeping turns. In this segment, the river flows over a 100-foot contour. (There will be a slight bump for the discerning paddler.) At 3.8 miles, By Creek enters on the left (east). It is the largest tributary encountered so far on this stream. There are scattered commercial gravel-separation operations, but again, they are not too visible to the paddler.

The next section runs for 8.3 miles, from LA 16 to LA 40 (Independence, access F–access G). The Tangipahoa River flows farther south toward its rendezvous with Lake Pontchartrain. After having been quite consistent in its rate of flow, the current for the first half is a little faster than it is farther upstream. The 50-foot-high ridge line which had been parallel to the river is closer, and even becomes the bank at 3.5 miles. Below this point, the current slows substantially, the banks are more forested, and there are few sand-gravel bars.

Section: MS 584 (Osyka, MS) to LA 90 (Independence, LA)

Counties: Pike (MS), Tangipahoa Parish (LA)

USGS Quads: Osyka (MS); Spring Creek, Kentwood, Chesbrough, Roseland, Loranger (LA)

Suitable for: Cruising, camping

Appropriate for: Families, beginners

Months Runnable: All

Interest Highlights: Scenery, wildlife

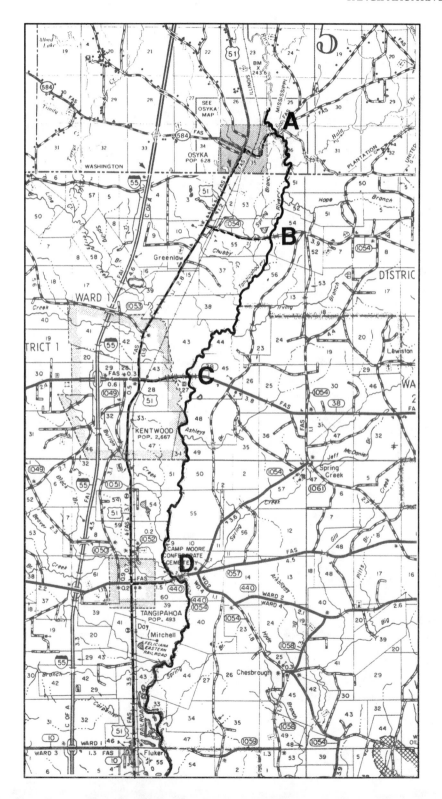

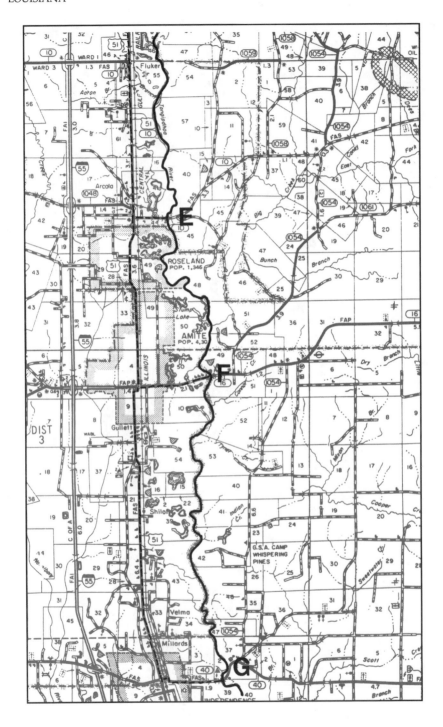

Scenery: Pretty to beautiful
Difficulty: Class I
Average Width: 20–80 ft.
Velocity: Slow to moderate
Hazards: Downed trees
Rescue Index: Accessible
Source of Additional Information: None known

Access Points	Access Code	River Miles	Shuttle Miles
A–B	1357	3.6	4.2
B–C	1357	5.2	6.0
C–D	1357	6.5	7.0
D–E	1357	8.4	8.3
E–F	1357	5.2	5.6
F–G	1357	8.3	9.2

Access Key:
1 Paved road
2 Unpaved road
3 Short carry
4 Long carry
5 Easy grade
6 Steep incline
7 Clear trail
8 Brush and trees
9 Launching fee charged
10 Private property, need permission
11 No access, reference only

Part Two

MISSISSIPPI

Bogue Chitto River

From the MS 570 bridge to the MS 44 bridge (access A–access B) is a 3.9-mile run of moderate difficulty through excellent scenery, as in most sections of the Bogue Chitto. To reach Access A (Highway 570 northeast of McComb, Mississippi), from the split of MS 44 and MS 570 in eastern McComb, Mississippi, proceed 7.3 miles east and north on MS 570 to a rural bridge.

This section of the Bogue Chitto River is like a creek. As always for this type of stream, the paddler comes across a narrow channel, occasional islands, high, wooded banks, and a decent current to help him along. There are no significant hills, bluffs, or tributaries on this section. There may be logs and snags, depending on the water level. There are only a few small beaches found in this section. In the late summer and fall, this section may be too low to run. If so, move down the Bogue Chitto until there is enough water to float a canoe.

From the MS 44 bridge (locally called the Quinn Bridge) to the Holmesville bridge (access B–access C) is another moderately difficult run of 6.9 miles. Access B, MS 44 east of McComb, Mississippi, is known as Quinn Bridge. From the split of MS 44 and MS 570 in eastern McComb, Mississippi, proceed 5.4 miles east on MS 44 to a rural bridge.

In this section, the Bogue Chitto is still more like a creek than a river. The banks are consistently in close; there are several small beaches, and the current's movement averages out to be the quickest on the river. The woods on both banks appear to be little disturbed by man and give a sense of paddling along a forest. In the third mile, there is a small island to negotiate. Early in the fourth mile, on the right, a hill ultimately tops out 90 feet above the river. The remainder of this section sustains a respectable current. In the last 2 miles, the stream meanders, leaving you to wonder what is next. There are only scattered houses with very little else to intrude on the river. This section is best for day paddling because there are few beaches available for camping.

The section from Holmesville, Mississippi, to the U.S. 98 bridge (access C–access D) continues at a moderate level of difficulty for 4.2 miles. From Tylertown, Mississippi, take U.S. 98 West 12 miles to a county road, turn right, and travel 1.7 miles to the bridge just east of Holmesville, Mississippi.

This section is a busy, eventful stretch of the Bogue Chitto River. The course is constantly meandering—more so than anywhere else on the river. Within the first mile on the right is a hill 80 feet above the water's edge, then at 1.5 miles the Topisaw Creek enters from the left. The Topisaw adds substantially to the volume of the Bogue Chitto. It is by far the largest tributary of the layer stream. Just before the 3-mile distance, the paddler comes to an island that splits the river. Go left around the far side of the one-third mile-long island. On the left, after the island, there will be a small stream, Leatherwood Creek. The section finishes with some faster and more shallow stretches that are similar to some stretches further upstream. There are a few camping beaches, but not enough to make this section a good one to count on for the evening.

The next section, from the U.S. 98 bridge to the Bogue Chitto Water Park (access D–access E), is an easy 2.3-mile paddle, through excellent Bogue Chitto scenery. Access D is from Highway 98, located between McComb, Mississippi, and Tylertown, Mississippi. From the intersection of U.S. 98 and MS 27 west of Tylertown, Mississippi, proceed west on U.S. 98 for 9.6 miles to a modern concrete bridge.

This short section is attractive and wandering with a few beaches and a moderately fast current. There are very few signs of people along this section.

Bogue Chitto Water Park to Walker Memorial Water Park (access E–access F) is an easy 4.5-mile paddle through good scenery, flowing from Pike into Walthall County. From Tylertown, Mississippi, travel west on U.S. 98 for 10.6 miles. (At 9.8 miles cross over the Bogue Chitto.) Turn left (south) at sign "Bogue Chitto Water Park." Continue southeast approximately 2 miles to the entrance to the park. This public facility has camping—tent and RV—and a public launch where a canoe can be launched for a fee.

This section is the gentlest portion of the upper Bogue Chitto River. The stream consists of mostly pools with few tributaries and few serious meanders. There is very little sign of human presence, only glimpses of farms behind the row of trees. Camping on this section is not easy since there are few beaches of any size.

The next 6.5 miles, from Walker Memorial Water Park (MS 48) to a county bridge (Lexie) (access F–access G), return the paddler to excellent scenery and a moderate level of difficulty. From Tylertown, Mississippi, travel west on highways U.S. 98 and MS 48 to the edge of Tylertown where the two highways split. Take MS 48 west 5.9 miles to the Bogue Chitto River. Just past the bridge, turn left (south) and proceed a half mile to Walker Memorial Water Park on the left. The park has a public launch, toilets, pump water, picnic benches, and a parking lot.

The Bogue Chitto continues at a fairly gentle pace for the first two-thirds of this section. There are at least two camping beaches per mile, often three. The trees are set back behind low banks. There are just a couple of houses or camps to remind you of human presence. The only tributary of note is Silver Creek which comes in from the right at about the 2-mile mark. At about the 4.5-mile mark, the Bogue Chitto picks up its pace as it flows through a newly created channel. Over 1 mile of meandering river is reduced to a third of a mile by this self-constituted channel. The result is the fastest 500 yards of the entire Bogue Chitto River. If you are prepared, the new channel is fun to bounce through. For the unwary or inept, the new slot can be an upsetting experience. The river continues at a quickened pace to the Lexie bridge. Local residents call this Stallins Bridge, although that name does not appear on any topo or county map.

The section from the Lexie county bridge (Stallins) to the Dillon county bridge (access G–access H) is 3.6 miles and continues to be moderately difficult. To reach this access, take an unnumbered highway west of Lexie. From the intersection with MS 27 and an unnumbered highway in Lexie, Mississippi, proceed 3.8 miles west on the unnumbered highway.

The first 2 miles of this section complete the fastest 4 miles on the Bogue Chitto River. These miles are to be savored by paddlers who want to use the faster current to practice their skills. Maneuvers such as ferryglides and eddy turns can be accomplished by taking advantage of the current. There are numerous spacious sand-gravel bars that can be used for rest breaks, lunches, or campsites.

Approximately two-thirds of the way through this section, the paddler comes to the Bogue Chitto "falls." It is an irregular sandstone ledge that the river flows over. Rather than merely read about the billowing clouds of mist, thunderous roars, and the beauty of plunging water, it is best that each paddler discover and experience the falls for him or herself. After the falls, the Bogue Chitto resumes a more normal pace. Seven-tenths of a mile below the falls, Magees Creek enters from the left. This stream has 11 miles of creek paddling which is described in the next chapter. The take-out for this section can either be beneath the public bridge on the right, or at a canoe rental business that is 200 yards further downstream on the left.

The section from the Dillon bridge (unnumbered county road) to LA 438 (Warnerton) is 3.7 miles (access H–access I). It offers the paddler several features of interest. Access is from Dillon bridge on an unnumbered highway off of MS 27. From the Louisiana-Mississippi state line, proceed north on MS 27 for 2.0 miles, turn left (west) onto an unnumbered highway, and proceed 1.5 miles to a rural bridge. The stream, in terms of velocity and width, is a continuation of the segment immediately above it. A unique feature is that for the first 3 miles there is almost a continuous sand-gravel bar that alternates from one side to the other. There is also a clay shoal riffle found nowhere else on the Bogue Chitto.

Also of interest to paddlers is the passing from one state to another— Mississippi to Louisiana. Since there is no sign, paddlers with the two appropriate topo maps, Tylertown, Mississippi, and Clifton, Louisiana, can decide for themselves where the state line ought to be.

The section from LA 438 to LA 38 (Clifton) is 6.3 miles. This section (access I–access J) continues as before in terms of width, although the velocity is a little less than upstream. Travel from Warnerton, Louisiana, on Hwy. 438. From the intersection of LA 25 and LA 438 in Warnerton, Louisiana, proceed west on LA 438 to a rural bridge. The main thing to remember about this section is that there has been extensive sand-gravel dredging and processing along the banks. The topo map of Clifton, Louisiana, shows nine symbols where Bogue Chitto has been disturbed. This stretch is tolerable if you are passing through on a longer trip. However, it has been the most adversely impacted section on the Bogue Chitto, making it the least attractive to a paddler seeking natural outdoor scenery.

With a little over 10 miles between bridges, the segment from LA 38 to LA 25 (Franklinton) (access J–access K) can be a good one-day float. To reach Access J at Clifton, Louisiana, from the intersection of LA 25 and LA 38 in Clifton, Louisiana, proceed west of LA 38 to a rural bridge.

The river continues to offer a respectable current and a variety of sandbars, obstacles, and bends to keep a paddler occupied. There are four named tributaries that enter the river. Springs Creek is 3 miles downstream and is the largest and most interesting.

There are sand and gravel bars along the banks and some dredging/processing operations. These, however, are much less apparent than the operations found upstream. Despite the fact that the stream flows west of Franklinton, Louisiana, the only town along its entire route, there is little evidence of its proximity.

To Access K (Highway 25 west of Franklinton, Louisiana), from the intersection of LA 16 and LA 25 in Franklinton, Louisiana, proceed west on LA 25 for six-tenths of a mile to a rural bridge.

Section: MS 570 (McComb, MS) to LA 25 (Franklinton, LA)

Counties: Pike and Walthall (MS); Washington and St. Tammany parishes (LA)

USGS Quads: McComb North, Pricedale, Holmesville, Progress, Tylertown (MS); Franklinton, Enon, Sun, Industrial (LA)

Suitable for: Cruising, camping

Appropriate for: Families, beginners, intermediates

Months Runnable: All

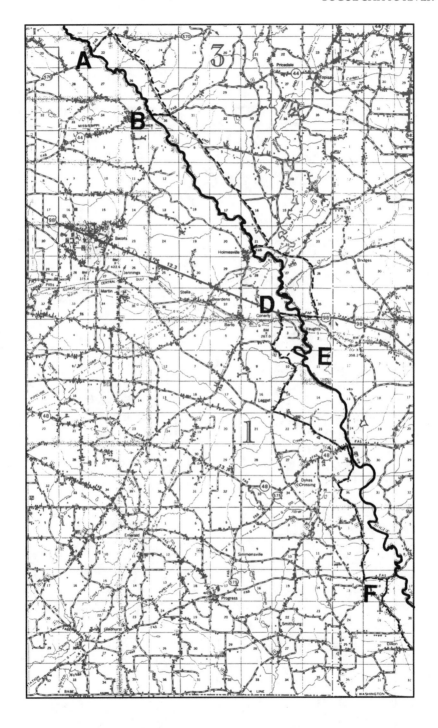

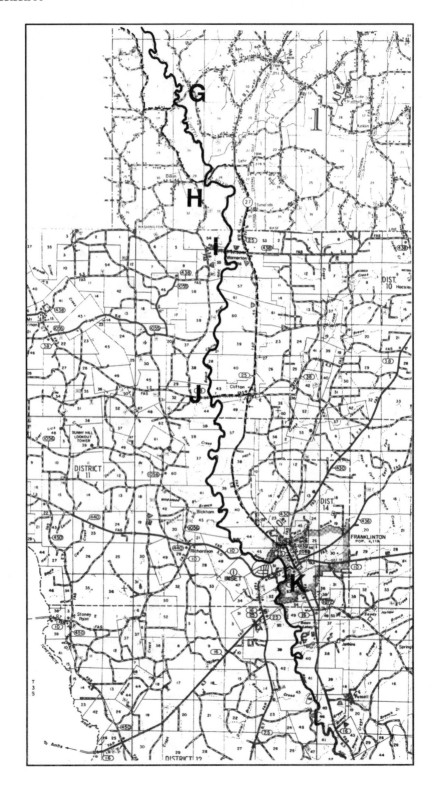

Interest Highlights: Scenery, wildlife

Scenery: Pretty

Difficulty: Class I

Average Width: 40–80 ft.

Velocity: Slow to moderate

Hazards: Fallen trees, logs in streams

Rescue Index: Accessible

Source of Additional Information: Canoe & Trail Adventures, 129 North
Hennessy Street, New Orleans, LA 70119; (504) 486-2355.

Access Points	Access Code	River Miles	Shuttle Miles
A–B	All access	3.9	3.4
B–C	points are	6.9	6.6
C–D	1357s with	4.2	3.6
D–E	the length	2.3	2.0
E–F	of carry	4.5	7.8
F–G	and grade	6.5	6.0
	varying but		
G–H	in no case	3.6	3.4
H–I	an extremely	3.7	3.6
I–J	difficult	6.3	6.7
J–K	put-in.	9.8	8.0

Access Key:

1	Paved road	7	Clear trail
2	Unpaved road	8	Brush and trees
3	Short carry	9	Launching fee charged
4	Long carry	10	Private property, need permission
5	Easy grade	11	No access, reference only
6	Steep incline		

Magees Creek

Magees Creek is a true creek that flows past Tylertown, Mississippi for 11 miles to empty into the Bogue Chitto River. The creek has high banks, tiny islands, overhangingVeven overlappingVbranches, a couple of mild shoals, one very high (50- to 70-foot) bluff, and a twisting, quick, cornering course through Walthall County.

The creek is best for a one-day float. Put in at the public water park on the east side of Tylertown, and then take out at the Dillon bridge or at a private launch 200 yards further downstream from Dillon. This float includes almost a mile of the Bogue Chitto River, making the total length approximately 11 river miles.

During these 11 miles, Magees drops some 50 feet from 240 to 190 feet, which is an average of 4.5 feet per mile. For streams in southern Mississippi and southern Louisiana, this is more of a drop than is common. The stream has long pools with little movement and then sections where the current moves along more swiftly. The minor shoals are fun to paddle through and even better if you park the canoe and refloat the shoals in a life vest.

As for water levels, it is difficult to know the exact level. There are no gauges on the bridges and no resident rangers at the water park in Tylertown. Commercial canoe rental businesses are the best sources for current conditions.

In a typical year, the water level is too low in the late summer and early fall for really enjoyable floating down the stream. Also, when Magees Creek has a rise on it of a couple of feet, it would be wise to stay off it. Paddle instead on the nearby Bogue Chitto. With high banks, quick turns, logs in the streambed, plus a pushing current, Magees becomes hazardous. Very few paddlers have the ability to quickly stop their onrushing momentum when logs are encountered and backferry their canoes to a bank.

Magees Creek is a remote, largely secluded, adventurous stream. There are only a couple of very small sandbars, so overnight camping is not easily done. Magees is best for a one-day float that includes lunch and time to enjoy the parade of superb scenery that this stream offers.

The 5.3 miles from the Tylertown bridge (U.S. 98) to the Lexie bridge (access A–access B) are moderately difficult. In Tylertown, travel seven-tenths of a mile east from the intersection of MS 27 (north and south) and U.S. 98 (east and west) to Holmes Water Park where there is a public launch.

This section of Magees is a classic creek. The stream is often narrow, the banks are often high (20 feet above the water), and the course is at times extremely meandering. The trees above consist of oaks, maples, sweetgum, and magnolias with the branches occasionally forming a shady canopy of leaves. The current is at a six-foot drop per mile quicker than on most streams found in southern Mississippi and Louisiana. There are a few clay shoals and a few dark pools, but no substantial beaches. Depending upon rainfall levels and time of year, springs may drip from the clay banks. One half mile from the Lexie bridge on the left-hand side is a dirt bluff that is some 50 to 70 feet above the water's edge—an uncommon feature for the area.

It's four miles from the Lexie bridge to the Highway 27 bridge (access B–access C). Lexie is 3 miles southwest of Tylertown, on MS 27. From Lexie, travel southeast eight-tenths of a mile to a bridge on an unnumbered county road.

This next section of Magees Creek is a continuation of the upstream section. Although the current is slower, the stream is a little bit wider and there are a few modest gravel beaches. The stream is still very attractive. On a hot summer day, Magees is cool and shady with both shallow depths and deeper pools. About halfway through the section on the left is a 6-foot-wide, 6-inch-deep gravel bottomland stream, Kirklin Creek, that is a typical tributary to larger streams such as Magees Creek. The combination of these two sections—9.3 miles—makes an excellent float. However, most paddlers opt to continue on for 2 miles and finish up at a take-out on the Bogue Chitto.

The 2 miles from the Highway 27 bridge to the Dillon bridge (access C–access D) continue through beautiful scenery at a similar level of difficulty as in previous sections. From Lexie, travel south 3 miles to a bridge on   MS 27.

Magees retains creek-like characteristics for its last 1.4 miles before entering the Bogue Chitto River. From this confluence, continue on six-tenths of a mile to a county bridge or to a canoe rental service 200 yards on the left beyond the bridge.

Section: U.S. 98 (Tylertown) to Dillon bridge
Counties: Walthall (MS)
USGS Quads: Tylertown

Suitable for: At low levels, beginners on up

Appropriate for: Cruising

Months Runnable: All except autumn

Interest Highlights: Scenery, wildlife

Scenery: Beautiful

Difficulty: Class I

Average Width: 30–45 ft.

Velocity: Slow to moderate

Hazards: Downed trees, obstacles in the streambed

Rescue Index: Accessible

Source of Additional Information: Canoe & Trail Adventures, 129 North Hennessy Street, New Orleans, LA 70119; (504) 486-2355.

Access Points	Access Codes	River Miles	Shuttle Miles
A–B	1357	5.3	4.5
B–C	1467	4.0	3.6
C–D	1357	2.0	2.0
D	1357		

Access Key:

1	Paved road	7	Clear trail
2	Unpaved road	8	Brush and trees
3	Short carry	9	Launching fee charged
4	Long carry	10	Private property, need permission
5	Easy grade	11	No access, reference only
6	Steep incline		

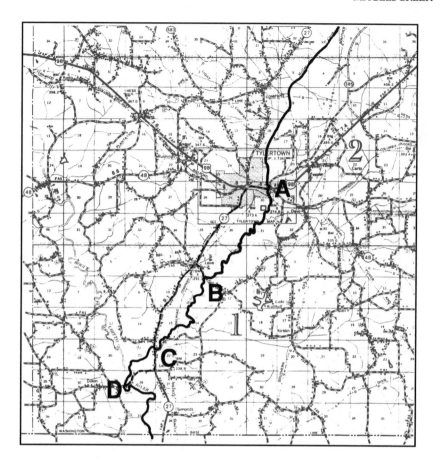

Wolf River

The Wolf River is a stream that offers considerable variety as it makes the transition from a creek to a small river. Beginning in south-central Mississippi, the Wolf flows south and becomes a tidal bayou before entering the estuary bay next to the city of Bay St. Louis. Because the Wolf is never near any city, the recommended paddling sections are usually free (for a Gulf Coast stream) of signs of human encroachment.

Because the Wolf River flows through rural Mississippi, the access points to the Wolf are unusually challenging to find. The Wolf River is bracketed by two interstates, I-59 to the north and I-10 to the south. The best canoeing is found centered between the two. From Silver Run Bridge to Sellers Bridge (U.S. 53), the distance (access A–access B) is 13.1 miles.

If the paddling is going to end at Sellers (B), then the better access is from I-59. To reach Silver Run (A), exit at Millard Exit #6 and proceed 2.2 miles east on an unnumbered county road. At an intersection there, turn right onto another county road and proceed 3.2 miles to U.S. 53. Cross over U.S. 53 and proceed 8.0 miles to the Silver Run bridge. If going to Sellers (B), at the intersection with U.S. 53 turn right onto U.S. 53, and proceed 13.5 miles to Sellers.

If the canoe trip is to begin at Sellers (B), then the better access is from I-10. Take the Bay St. Louis Exit #13 and proceed north on MS 43 for 6.4 miles (through Kiln). Turn right onto MS 603 and proceed 13.6 miles to U.S. 53. Turn right and proceed 5 miles to the Sellers (B) bridge.

If your destination is the river access at the cemetery (C), proceed across Sellers bridge 3.2 miles to an intersection with an unnumbered county road. Turn right (south) and proceed 1.8 miles. Turn right again on an unnumbered county road and proceed 4.4 miles to a cemetery. Turn right and proceed two-tenths of a mile to the bank of the Wolf River.

To reach Cable bridge (D) from the south, take Exit #24 off of I-10 and proceed 3.0 miles southeast to a crossroads, De Lisle. Turn sharply left (north), and proceed 6.4 miles on an unnumbered county road. Turn right (east), and proceed 2.0 miles to what is known locally as the Cable bridge.

The 13.1 miles from Silver Run bridge to Sellers bridge (U.S. 53) of the Wolf River is like a creek with high banks, nearby trees, and a very meandering course. Between these two bridges, the stream drops some 70 feet over a 10-mile section, which means there is a respectable current. There are at least 30 sandbars suitable for group camping. This section also has at least seven sets of clay shoals and one clay chute. (These chutes seem to be unique to the Wolf River.) The chutes are just that—channels cut out of clay by the current that will accommodate a canoe. Most are a few canoe lengths long and average 1 to 2 feet deep. (The only negative point about this section is that it gets too low to paddle during dry periods.)

The section from Sellers bridge to the cemetery (a sandy lane off an unnumbered county road) (access B–access C) is 8 miles. This second section is very different from its upstream segment. Here, the Wolf becomes a small river with gentle turns and large sand-and-gravel beaches with trees set back to the edge of them. There are at least 20 beaches that can be used for group camping, and at least two more clay shoals. Because the gradient has flattened out, this section is almost always runnable in the late summer and early fall.

The third section of the Wolf, from the cemetery to Cable Bridge Road (access C–access D), is very similar to the section immediately above it. One highlight is Sandy Creek, which is a tributary of the Wolf that appears a half mile before the take-out at Cable bridge. Sandy Creek is an attractive side stream with its own spring-fed waters and beaches. And finally, within sight of the take-out bridge, there is a nice set of clay shoals to complete your adventure on the Wolf River. A paddler could continue downstream to a take-out below I-10. However, the better paddling is upstream of the Cable bridge access.

Section: Silver Run bridge to Cable Bridge Road

Counties: Pearl River, Hancock, and Harrison (MS)

USGS Quads: Silver Run, Sellers, Vidalia

Suitable for: Beginners

Appropriate for: Cruising and camping

Months Runnable: All

Interest Highlights: Scenery

Scenery: Pretty

Difficulty: Class I

Average Width: 30–50 ft.

Velocity: Gentle

Hazards: Downed trees and obstacles in the streambed

Rescue Index: Accessible

Source of Additional Information: Adventure Canoe, 10072 Lobuoy Road, Pass Christian, MS 39571; (601) 255-9783.

Access Points	Access Codes	River Miles	Shuttle Miles
A–B	1357	13.1	12.7
B–C	1357	8.0	9.5
C–D	2357	3.5	4.7
D	1357		

Access Key:

1	Paved road	7	Clear trail
2	Unpaved road	8	Brush and trees
3	Short carry	9	Launching fee charged
4	Long carry	10	Private property, need permission
5	Easy grade	11	No access, reference only
6	Steep incline		

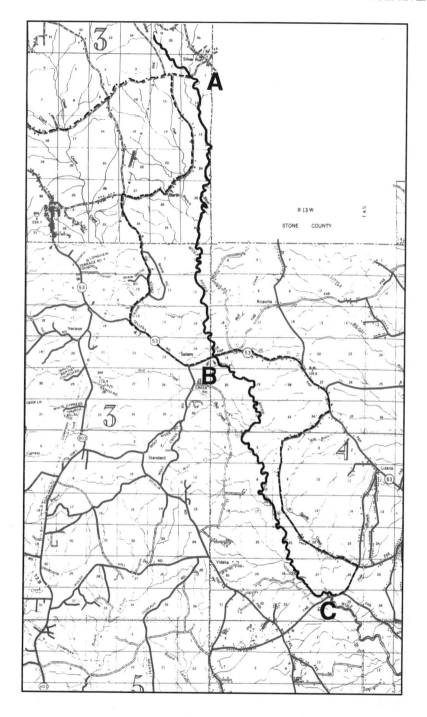

Strong River

The Strong River is a tributary of the Pearl River, with its headwaters in central Mississippi. The stream receives a moderate amount of canoeing traffic on weekends since it is the closest river with lively shoals within driving distance of the urban area in and around Jackson, Mississippi. In its upper stretches (access A–access D), the river is a small, fairly shallow stream with dense vegetation surrounding it. River birches, maples, and willows form a canopy over the stream in most places. The Strong River flows through a rural area so that, recessed in the fairly steep banks, the paddler experiences a sense of remoteness. The only intrusion you may encounter is the sometimes strong odor from commercial chicken houses near Pinola.

The stream is generally runnable all year, although summer and fall levels are unpredictable and depend on local rains. No gauge is available, but the operators of the water park should be able to give advice on water level conditions. Although the river may be runnable at high water levels, paddlers must be cautious and use good judgement when the water gets out of the banks into the trees.

The first reliable access to the river is at the D'Lo Water Park (access A) northwest of Mendenhall. From the U.S. 49 bridge over the Strong River, travel one half mile northwest to a paved road on the left (west) with a sign directing to the D'Lo Water Park. Continue traveling a half mile to the southwest to a road on the left that leads to the water park. Check the shoal at the water park before putting in. If there is sufficient water to allow a boat to find a path through the shoal, there will be ample water to make the shoals further downriver boatable and fun.

The river segments from access points A–D are typically utilized for day trips. During low water conditions, the 5-mile section (access A–access B) from the D'Lo Water Park to Merit bridge may be too scrappy to paddle. If so, put in at the Merit bridge, an old iron bridge located on a county road 1 mile northwest of MS 43 at the community of Merit. The 7.5-mile section from access points B–D contains most of the good shoals on the river, making the section a perfect summertime day trip. If you are not pressed for time, a delightful diversion is to wade up the cool, clear waters of Riles Creek which enters the Strong River on river left just below the Merit bridge.

The main characteristic of the upper sections of the Strong River is the intermittent clay outcroppings that form shoals from D'Lo to just below MS 28 near Pinola. These are great fun to maneuver and make a cool lounging spot for reclining during the summer heat. One particularly long shoal with fun waves is located at the county bridge (access C) 2 miles north of Pinola. The takeout at MS 28 (access D) is a very difficult, steep haul up the clay bank upstream and river left of the bridge.

The 12.5-mile section (access D–access F) from MS 28 to the confluence with the Pearl River begins with the most difficult shoals on the river. Careful maneuvering is required at the shoal that stretches for a couple of hundred yards. Below the shoal, the river changes its character to a slower-moving stream with more frequent sandbars. Because of these, this section is the most suited for canoe camping. This stretch of the river is more isolated from civilization except for fishermen searching for the catfish and bluegill of these slower waters. The most prominent landmark of the river, Strong River Bluff, is found on this lower section. The striking yellow clay wall rises 90 feet above the river on river left, approximately 5 miles below MS 28 (access D). The scenic quality of the bluff is such that it was chosen as a wedding site by an outdoor-loving couple.

The Union bridge (access E) on a county road 3 miles south of MS 28 and the community of Union is the last take-out before the Strong River reaches the Pearl River. You may continue the additional 3.5 river miles to the confluence with the Pearl River where the Georgetown Water Park (access F) may be reached by ferrying across the Pearl River to the water park boat ramps.

Section: D'Lo Water Park to Georgetown Water Park on Pearl River
Counties: Simpson, Copian (MS)
USGS Quads: Mendenhall West, Harrisville, Schley, Georgetown
Suitable for: Cruising, camping
Appropriate for: Families, beginners, intermediates
Months Runnable: All
Interest Highlights: Scenery, wildlife
Scenery: Pretty in spots to beautiful in spots
Difficulty: Class I (II)

Average Width: 40–90 ft.

Velocity: Slow to moderate

Hazards: Deadfalls

Rescue Index: Accessible to accessible but difficult

Source of Additional Information: D'Lo Water Park, D'Lo, MS; (601) 847-4310.

Access Points	Access Code	River Miles	Shuttle Miles
A–B	1357	5.1	6.2
B–C	2367	4.6	7.3
C–D	1367	3.1	4.0
D–E	1467	9.2	8.3
E–F[1]	1357	3.4	8.1
F[1]	1357		

[1] On the Pearl River

Access Key:

1	Paved road	7	Clear trail
2	Unpaved road	8	Brush and trees
3	Short carry	9	Launching fee charged
4	Long carry	10	Private property, need permission
5	Easy grade	11	No access, reference only
6	Steep incline		

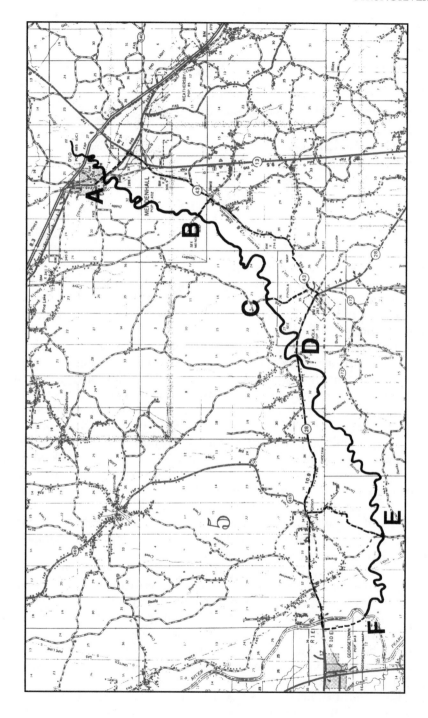

Okatoma Creek

Flowing through south-central Mississippi, Okatoma Creek contains some of the liveliest water in the state. It is the combination of exciting shoals and rapids and the superb scenery along the stream that has made Okatoma Creek the standard by which all other Mississippi streams are measured. Born by springs in the upper watershed, the Okatoma eventually combines with Bowie Creek north of Hattiesburg to form the Bowie River. In the mid 1980s, the Soil Conservation Service attempted to conduct a stream channelization project on Okatoma Creek. This extremely destructive project was halted by the efforts of concerned locals, landowners and conservationists. Although the project was terminated, everyone who cares about the creek should remain alert to ensure that this irreplaceable resource is not lost.

Several rapids and small drops are found at claystone outcroppings on Okatoma Creek. River birches and magnolias stretch over the creek, filtering the sun. The fishing for bass and bluegill is excellent. Below Seminary, fishing is more successful on weekdays due to less canoeing traffic than on weekends. Be aware that alcoholic beverages are illegal in Covington County. The sheriff's officers and game wardens routinely check boaters for proper safety equipment (such as life jackets) and illegal beverages at the Seminary access (B), and at unannounced points downstream.

The Okatoma Creek is usually runnable all year below Seminary. An old gauge painted on a bridge pier at the Seminary access (B) can be used to judge the water level. With a gauge reading of minus 1.0 feet there is sufficient flow to get through most shoals. If the creek's drainage area has received normal rainfall, the gauge level should be just above zero. Advanced paddlers like to catch the stream gauge at 2.5 to 3.0 feet. At that level big waves are formed that can be surfed (riding on the upstream side of a wave). Only experienced paddlers should be on the creek above 3.0 feet, since the increased current makes rescue of an overturned boat very difficult. A gauge reading of over 5 feet indicates that the stream is getting out of its banks and into the trees,

90

approaching flooding conditions, and should be paddled only by expert boaters.

The first good access to the creek is south of Collins on a county bridge (access A) 1 mile east of U.S. 49 near the small community of Kola. The stream width varies from 20 to 50 feet in this section with several pullovers at lower water levels. Although you encounter some pastures, the stream flows primarily through a dense forest. With the exception of a rapid formed by a ledge near the end, this 7-mile section lacks the exciting shoals and rapids of the lower sections. However, this is offset by the tranquility of beautiful scenery and few people.

The most popular access to the creek is at the town of Seminary, one half mile east of U.S. 49, where MS 590 (access B) crosses the stream. A local church owns the property adjacent to the access on river left so paddlers should respect their property. Because of the excellent scenery and multitude of shoals and rapids, the 9-mile section (access B–access D) is considered by many to be the best canoeing day trip in the state. This is verified by the large number of recreational users during summer weekends. If solitude is what you want, this section should be paddled on weekends in late fall, winter, or early spring.

At Seminary, the creek starts out as a quiet, 50-foot wide, canopied stream. At the end of the first quarter of a mile, the action picks up when a shoal is encountered that should be run on the far left. A large pool below offers excellent swimming. Paddlers practice ferrying and peeling out in the fast current here. The most demanding rapid on the creek is found approximately 2.5 miles downstream of Seminary in a right-hand bend. A horizon line alerts the paddler to The Chute. Here, a claystone shelf forms a barrier to the stream. Erosion by the creek at low water has formed a channel on river left. The channel snakes through the claystone outcropping to give the paddler an exciting ride. Begin the run by lining up on the right side of the river left channel. Angle the bow slightly to the right when entering the drop, then turn the boat sharply to the right to make the 90-degree turn. At normal water levels, the bottom of the rapid is very aerated with some tricky crosscurrents to negotiate. The clay shelf on river left makes a nice spot for a rest break, lunch or just for viewing other paddlers running the rapid.

Continuing downstream you can relax and enjoy the botanical variety along the creek. The dense green of the white titi shrubs creates a buffer for the paddler; and in the spring, wild azalea and mountain laurel add color to the scenery.

Two miles below The Chute is a 3-foot drop known as Okatoma Falls. The shoal that precedes the drop starts in a sharp right-hand bend. Maneuver through the shoal to approach the drop on the left center of the stream. The pool below the drop is a favorite swimming hole of locals and paddlers alike. The claystone outcrop that forms the drop creates a perfect lounging area in the shoal. There is nothing like soaking in cool, clean water to break the summer heat.

Fairchild's Landing (access C), located off a private dirt road 1 mile northeast of U.S. 49, is some 200 yards below Okatoma Falls on river right. This is privately owned land and not a public access. If you want to take out here, you can arrange for a shuttle (for a fee) with the Okatoma Outpost in Sanford. Another take-out, one quarter of a mile downstream on the left, can be used by arranging for a shuttle with Lonnie's Canoe Rental in Seminary. The creek slows down below Fairchild's Landing where there are fewer shoals. However, this 4.5-mile section is very scenic and remote. In several places the creek is cutting new channels, allowing the paddler to observe this interesting natural process. Be cautious of downed trees and debris in these spots. The next access is at the MS 598 bridge (access D) 3 miles east of U.S. 49 or the Okatoma Outpost launching area on river right downstream of the bridge.

Below MS 598, the creek meanders 6 miles to the community of Lux. There are several fun shoals in this section and one small drop in the first 2 miles. Small sandbars appear more frequently, so camping spots are more available in this section. To get to the Lux bridge (access E), travel south on U.S. 49 approximately 4.5 miles from its intersection with MS 598 to a point where a county road enters from the left (east). Then proceed east 1.5 miles on the county road to the Lux bridge, where access is on river left. The creek continues another 1.5 miles to the confluence with Bowie Creek.

Section: County bridge south of Collins to Peps Point Road on Bowie River

Counties: Covington, Forrest (MS)

USGS Quads: Collins, Williamsburg, Seminary, Sanford, Eastabuchie

Suitable for: Cruising, camping

Appropriate for: Families, beginners, intermediates

Months Runnable: All

Interest Highlights: Scenery, wildlife

Scenery: Pretty in spots to beautiful in spots

Difficulty: Class I (II)

Average Width: 40–80 ft.

Velocity: Slow to moderate

Hazards: Deadfalls

Rescue Index: Accessible to accessible but difficult

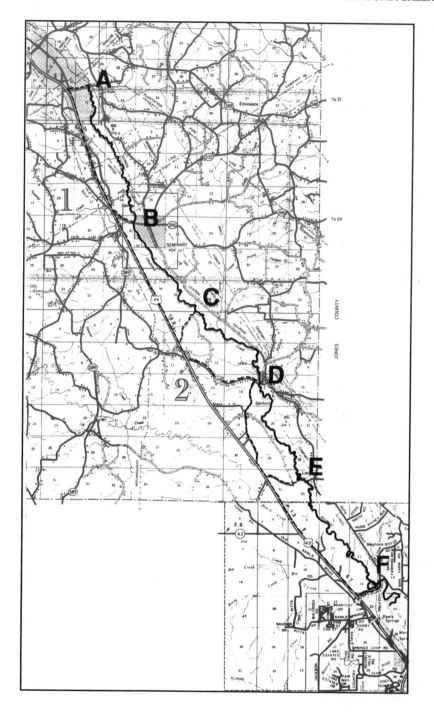

Source of Additional Information: Okatoma Outdoor Post, Sanford, MS; (601) 722-4297. Lonnie's Canoe Rentals, Seminary, MS; (601) 722-4301. River Expeditions, Jackson, MS; (601) 362-6049. Out 'N' Under, Meridian, MS; (601) 693-5827.

Access Points	Access Code	River Miles	Shuttle Miles
A–B	1357	7.2	6.3
B–C	1357	4.6	6.3
C–D	23579, 10	4.6	4.5
D–E	1357	6.1	6.5
E–D[1]	2357	5.6	7.3
D[1]	1367		

[1]On the Bowie River

Access Key:

1	Paved road	7	Clear trail
2	Unpaved road	8	Brush and trees
3	Short carry	9	Launching fee charged
4	Long carry	10	Private property, need permission
5	Easy grade	11	No access, reference only
6	Steep incline		

Bowie Creek and Bowie River

Flowing out of Covington and Jefferson Davis counties in south-central Mississippi, Bowie Creek joins with Okatoma Creek to form the Bowie River just north of Hattiesburg. Bowie Creek shares a lot of similar forest and vegetation features with its sister stream the Okatoma, but that is where the similarities end. Except for a few occasions, Bowie Creek does not have the many clay outcroppings which create the shoals and rapids so typical of Okatoma Creek. However, Bowie Creek does have one distinct advantage over its sister stream—you will probably not see anyone else on the creek. The primary attraction is the pristine setting and feeling of remoteness found on the creek. Unfortunately, after becoming the Bowie River and flowing around Hattiesburg, these qualities are attacked by gravel dredges and a chemical plant.

During the spring and after periods of local rain, floating on the creek can begin below a county bridge (access A) 4.4 miles southwest of Seminary. Here the creek is fairly narrow with a width of 20 to 40 feet. Local fishermen generally keep the creek open from downed trees; nevertheless, caution should be taken. The creek meanders often in this upper section, requiring constant maneuvering with several log pullovers at low water levels. This section is not suitable for canoe camping due to pullovers and a lack of sandbars. Float fishing is fair in this section of the stream.

After floating approximately 6 miles, you reach the MS 589 bridge (access B). It is approximately 7 miles south of Seminary and the access is upstream and river left of the bridge. Here several tributaries increase the flow of the creek, making boating downstream at this point possible most of the year. There are no gauges on the Bowie, so floating conditions are a judgment call. Human intrusion is minimal along the creek. Even though the banks are not very steep, the dense vegetation of titi and myrtle bushes helps to create a green barrier along the creek, increasing the sense of isolation. Some shoals are found in this section, but the scenery and solitude are the primary attractions. After paddling 10.5 miles, you reach a steep access on river left at the U.S. 49 bridge (access C).

Below U.S. 49, Bowie Creek slowly flows the three-quarters of a mile to its junction with Okatoma Creek. In the 5.5-mile section after the junction, the stream (now the Bowie River) travels through wooded lands with increasing signs of civilization. The banks are fairly steep in this section, and some good sized bluffs are encountered. The fishing improves as the river deepens in this section. A nice shoal with a drop of 2 feet provides some excitement just above the Peps Point bridge (access D). This bridge is 1 mile east of U.S. 49, but access is very bad there. It is recommended that the access at the I-59 bridge (access E) 4.5 miles farther downstream be used.

After leaving the I-59 bridge, the Bowie River flows 3 miles through a more developed area to the community of Glendale. The river has been mined for gravel above and below Glendale, so that small lakes have been created by hydraulic dredging. Just below the Glendale bridge (access F), a local chemical company has restricted the river for a water supply. The restriction is made of broken concrete. A river-right channel provides an exciting run. There are several standing waves here that are inviting to play on. Be aware, however, that steel reinforcing rods and other construction materials in the restriction are hazardous. There have been several drownings reported here, so exercise caution. The Glendale bridge, a half mile north of MS 42, is the last good access before the Bowie River reaches the Leaf River near the town of Petal.

Section: County bridge southwest of Seminary to Glendale bridge

Counties: Covington, Forrest (MS)

USGS Quads: Sumrall, Sanford, Eastabuchie, Hattiesburg

Suitable for: Cruising, camping

Appropriate for: Families, beginners

Months Runnable: All except during dry spells

Interest Highlights: Scenery, wildlife

Scenery: Pretty in spots to beautiful in spots

Difficulty: Class I

Average Width: 40–80 ft.

Velocity: Slow to moderate

Hazards: Deadfalls, concrete/steel reinforcing rods near Glendale

Rescue Index: Accessible to accessible but difficult

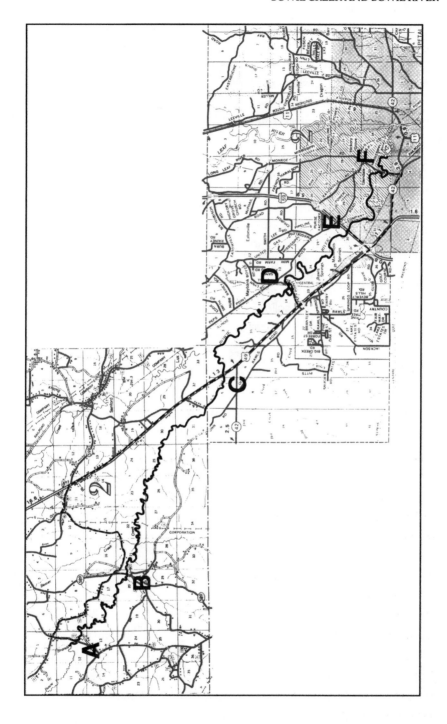

Source of Additional Information: Okatoma Outdoor Post, Sanford, MS; (601) 722-4297.

Access Points	Access Code	River Miles	Shuttle Miles
A–B	1357	6.2	5.2
B–C	1357	10.6	11.1
C–D	1367	5.7	4.1
D–E	1468	4.5	5.6
E–F	1467	2.0	4.3
F	1467		

Access Key:

1	Paved road	7	Clear trail
2	Unpaved road	8	Brush and trees
3	Short carry	9	Launching fee charged
4	Long carry	10	Private property, need permission
5	Easy grade	11	No access, reference only
6	Steep incline		

Tallahala Creek

Tallahala Creek originates in Jasper County and flows south through Jones, Lamar, and Perry counties before emptying into the Leaf River west of New Augusta. The Tallahala is a delightful, seldom used, float stream. Although it does not have claystone outcroppings to provide exciting rapids like some of its neighbors, there are occasional gravel shoals, and snags in the creek to maneuver through and around. This is primarily a stream for relaxing and enjoying the pleasant scenery and excellent fishing. There are no gauges on the creek to determine water levels. However, below MS 29 the creek is generally runnable all year, except during low water levels in summer.

The best uppermost access for the creek is at a put-in on river left at the MS 29 bridge (access A), 1.5 miles east of Ellisville. Above this point, the Tallahala flows through the urban areas of Laurel and Ellisville, and its water quality and scenery are both diminished. In this 4-mile section (access A–access B), the creek has low sandy banks with dense shrubs providing shade. The current is very slow since the stream takes many 90-degree turns. Stands of bald cypress and water tupelo are occasionally found. This section is suitable only for day trips because there are few camping spots.

A county road 2 miles south of Ellisville is the next access (B) on river left. This 9-mile section down to the Moselle to Ovett road (access C) is another good day trip. Give yourself plenty of time since there are several pullover spots. The creek is still very small, in a forest of mixed hardwoods and pines. Bream fishing is good in this section. The take-out (access C) on river right at the Moselle to Ovett road is steep.

The 4.5-mile section (access C–access D) from the Moselle to Ovett road to the Morriston road makes for a leisurely day trip. This is a remote section with little signs of civilization except for a couple of pipeline crossings. Be prepared to walk your boat through a few gravel shoals if the water level is low. The access at the Morriston road (access D) is an easy take-out on river right.

In the next stream segment, access D–access F, the streambed gradually widens to nearly 80 feet as the creek travels the 5.5 miles to the MS 42 bridge. There are more numerous sandbars and wading birds such as the great blue heron. After paddling approximately 4 miles, you reach a county bridge (access E) a quarter of a mile west of the community of Tallahala. This access should not be used because the road has been closed. There is a better access on river left at MS 42 (access F) west of Runnelstown. To get to the MS 42 access, drive to the ball field in Runnelstown and go west to the creek on the dirt road that parallels MS 42.

Below Runnelstown, the creek slows and meanders through a densely forested floodplain. In the next 3.5 miles you pass several oxbow lakes, giving evidence that the stream is dynamic and ever-changing. This section usually has adequate water for floating except during dry spells in the summer and fall.

An easy access at a county bridge (access G) south of Runnelstown starts the best canoe camping section of the Tallahala. Drive 3 miles south of Runnelstown on MS 29 and turn right onto a county road that crosses the creek in a half mile. The best access is on river left. There are sufficient sandbars for camping along the stream. This section also has several oxbow lakes formed by the creek; these may be hard to spot through the dense vegetation. Because the fishing is good, the stream is usually kept clear of pullovers by local fishermen. After paddling 10.5 miles, you come to the last access (H) on Tallahala Creek at a county road crossing approximately 3 miles northwest of New Augusta. This is an easy take-out on river left with room for vehicle parking under the bridge. Tallahala Creek joins the Leaf River a half mile below this bridge. The next access is at a boat ramp on the Leaf River at New Augusta.

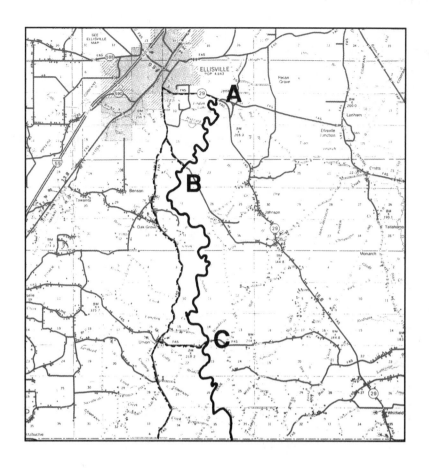

Section: MS 29 at Ellisville to MS 29 at New Augusta
Counties: Jones, Perry, Forrest (MS)
USGS Quads: Ellisville, Barrontown, Carterville, Ovett SE, New Augusta
Suitable for: Cruising, camping
Appropriate for: Families, beginners
Months Runnable: All except during dry spells
Interest Highlights: Scenery, wildlife
Scenery: Pretty in spots to pretty
Difficulty: Class I
Average Width: 40–100 ft.
Velocity: Slow to moderate

Hazards: Pullovers, deadfalls

Rescue Index: Accessible to accessible but difficult

Source of Additional Information: Mississippi Department of Wildlife Conservation, Fisheries Division, Hattiesburg Office, Hattiesburg, MS; (601) 269-8616.

Access Points	Access Code	River Miles	Shuttle Miles
A–B	1357	4.0	4.1
B–C	1357	8.9	9.5
C–D	1367	4.6	7.3
D–E	1357	4.1	5.6
E–F	11	1.5	2.5
F–G	1357	3.5	3.6
G–H	1357	10.5	8.3
H–P[1]	1357	4.4	2.1
P[1]	1357		

[1] On the Leaf River

Access Key:

1	Paved road	7	Clear trail
2	Unpaved road	8	Brush and trees
3	Short carry	9	Launching fee charged
4	Long carry	10	Private property, need permission
5	Easy grade	11	No access, reference only
6	Steep incline		

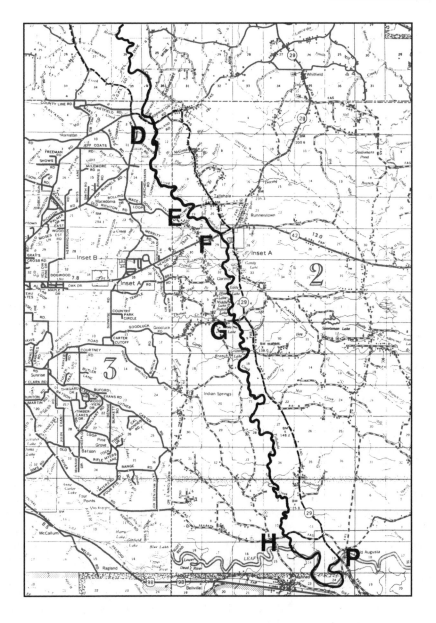

Bogue Homo Creek

Bogue Homo Creek is a tributary of the Leaf River that flows southerly, draining portions of Jasper, Jones, and Perry counties. This is a small stream throughout its length. The creek does not flow past any highly populated areas, so it's possible to feel solitude nearing a wilderness experience. The current flows at a moderate pace, and the water quality is usually excellent because of the undisturbed land surrounding the creek. There are no gauges on the creek, but there is generally enough water for floating all year below MS 42.

The most reasonable uppermost access is at a county bridge (access A) one half mile west of the town of Ovett. Put in on river right. This 9-mile section is wild and very scenic. Many pullovers from fallen trees and logjams are encountered. Because of the pullovers, the section is suitable for day trips only. Give yourself plenty of time to enjoy the heavily forested surroundings and negotiate obstacles.

The next access is at a new county bridge (access B), 7 miles northwest of Richton, which replaced one that collapsed. An exciting claystone shoal is just downstream of the bridge. If there is enough water to pass easily over the rapid, the remainder of the trip should be enjoyable. Take the time to enjoy the many interesting pools and banks formed by the clay outcroppings in this section. An unusual shoal is found approximately a mile upstream of the MS 42 bridge. Here the rushing water has sliced through a clay outcrop, forming several narrow channels. Small towers of clay are left as monuments to the water's erosive powers. After paddling this 3.5-mile section, a boat ramp on river right provides a good take-out at MS 42 (access C).

The 9-mile section below MS 42 (access C–access D) makes an excellent overnight canoe camping trip when there have been enough local rains. Otherwise, be prepared to walk boats through some of the gravel shoals and occasional pullovers. Several large sand and gravel bars are found in this section. Numerous small sandbars can provide camping spots for small groups. Be alert for sightings of osprey (a fish hawk) which have been spotted on past trips. The last access on Bogue Homo Creek is at a county bridge (access D) 4.5 miles northeast of New Augusta. The access is on river left and is steep and poorly developed due to very little traffic. The Bogue Homo continues on for another 3 miles before entering the Leaf River. Access is available at the Wingate bridge on the Leaf River just east of New Augusta.

Section: County bridge at Ovett to Wingate bridge on Leaf River

Counties: Jones, Perry (MS)

USGS Quads: Ovett, Ovett SE, Richton, Beaumont, New Augusta

Suitable for: Cruising, camping

Appropriate for: Families, beginners

Months Runnable: All except during dry spells

Interest Highlights: Scenery, wildlife

Scenery: Pretty in spots to beautiful in spots

Difficulty: Class I (II)

Average Width: 30-80 ft.

Velocity: Moderate

Hazards: Low hanging trees, deadfalls

Rescue Index: Accessible to accessible but difficult

Source of Additional Information: Mississippi Department of Wildlife Conservation, Fisheries Division, Hattiesburg Office, Hattiesburg, MS; (601) 264-8616.

Access Points	Access Code	River Miles	Shuttle Miles
A-B	1357	8.8	7.5
B-C	2357	3.6	4.1
C-D	1357	8.6	10.2
D-Q	1467	3.9	4.5
Q1	1357		

1On the Leaf River

Access Key:
1	Paved road	7	Clear trail
2	Unpaved road	8	Brush and trees
3	Short carry	9	Launching fee charged
4	Long carry	10	Private property, need permission
5	Easy grade	11	No access, reference only
6	Steep incline		

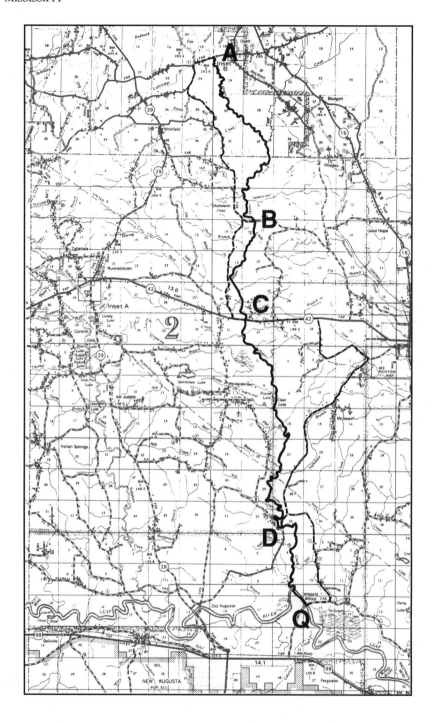

Big Creek

Big Creek springs to life in northern Greene County and flows southerly through the county to meet the Chickasawhay River. The creek is a true canoeing gem in that it passes through scenic rural environs, and has excellent water quality with its headwaters in the DeSoto National Forest. This is an undiscovered stream. Very few people have paddled the upper sections. There are clay outcroppings that form shoals and white sand beaches for lounging. The creek banks are densely populated with titi bushes, and the surrounding forest is primarily pine.

After periods of local rains, Big Creek is runnable below the junction of Kittrell and Indian Camp creeks, at a county road (access A) 4 miles east of the community of Avera. Here the creek is not more than a boat length wide. A crude gauge is painted on a downstream creosote timber pier at the bridge. A gauge reading of near 0 is needed for a good trip. At this level, the creek is lively with a swift current and moderate gradient. Because of the fast current and the clay streambed, the creek stays surprisingly free of pullovers. At a moderate water level, the shoals create a wave train that is so much fun you'll check your map to be sure you are not up north in a whitewater state. With the addition of Hellhole Creek approximately 1 mile below the put-in, Big Creek doubles in size. Several sandy clay bluffs of 30 to 40 feet in height are in this section. Just before reaching the community of Jonathan, having flowed almost 8.5 miles, the creek drops over a fun, river-wide, clay ledge of 1 foot. The take-out at Jonathan (access B) is on river right under the bridge.

Below the Jonathan bridge (access B), the creek begins to slow with less outcroppings of clay. A mile below Jonathan, Big Creek nearly doubles in size again, as Mason Creek enters on river left. With the addition of Mason Creek, the stream takes on a slower pace. After paddling 1.5 miles from Jonathan, you reach the MS 63 bridge (access C). This is an easy take-out on river left under the bridge.

The 12.5-mile section (access C–access F) makes a wonderful canoe camping trip. The creek flows through a remote area forested with river birches, maples, and sycamores near the stream, and pines in the surrounding land. Boating is generally possible year-round below the MS 63 bridge. There are many small sandbars on which to camp. You may get a glimpse of some wildlife, especially deer, supported by the surrounding woods. The last access on Big Creek is at a county bridge (access F) 8 miles southeast of Leakesville. This is an easy access on river left just downstream of the bridge.

Big Creek flows another mile before entering the Chickasawhay River. The first available take-out on the Chickasawhay River is at the U.S. 98 bridge 9 miles northwest of Lucedale. The take-out here is on river right, upstream of the bridge. This is a fairly steep access through a brushy wooded area.

Section: County bridge east of Avera to U.S. 98 bridge at Chickasawhay River

Counties: Greene (MS)

USGS Quads: Avera, Jonathan, Leakesville

Suitable for: Cruising, camping

Appropriate for: Beginners, intermediates

Months Runnable: All except during dry spells

Interest Highlights: Scenery, wildlife

Scenery: Pretty in spots to beautiful in spots

Difficulty: Class I (II)

Average Width: 30–90 ft.

Velocity: Moderate to slow

Hazards: Logjams, deadfalls

Rescue Index: Accessible to accessible but difficult

Source of Additional Information: None known

Access Points	Access Code	River Miles	Shuttle Miles
A–B	2368	8.4	13.4
B–C	1367	1.5	2.1
C–D	1357	3.8	5.8
D–E	1357	3.7	5.3
E–F	1357	5.1	6.4
F–P[1]	1357	8.7	8.1
P[1]	1368		

[1]On the Chickasawhay River

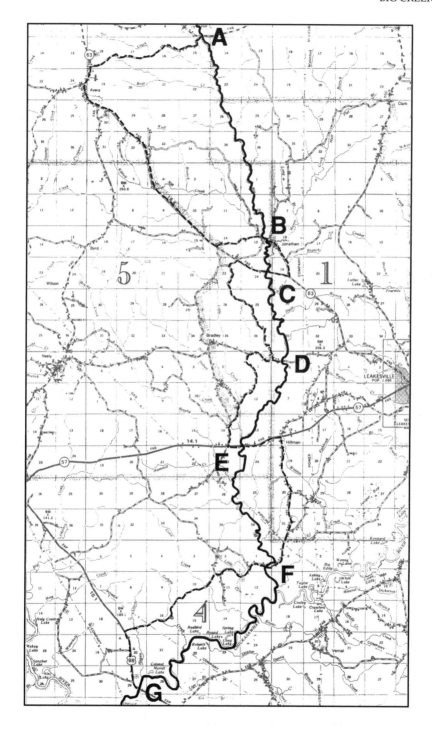

Access Key:

1	Paved road	7	Clear trail
2	Unpaved road	8	Brush and trees
3	Short carry	9	Launching fee charged
4	Long carry	10	Private property, need permission
5	Easy grade	11	No access, reference only
6	Steep incline		

Big Black River

The Big Black River is one of the largest rivers flowing entirely within Mississippi. With its headwaters in Webster County, the Big Black River winds its way through north-central Mississippi, flowing past portions of ten counties. The upper stretches of the river flow through a wide bottomland hardwood forest. The floodplain extends in width from 1 to 2 miles in places. Here the river passes old oxbow lakes and dense woods of oak with cypress, sycamore, maple, birch, and catawpa trees that predominate along the river. The forest of the Big Black River contains a plentiful, diverse wildlife population. Deer, turkey, and beaver are very common. Look closely along the river. You may spot some of these critters; otherwise, you are certain to see tracks and other signs of their activities along the banks. Fishing is excellent in most sections; catfish are the primary game fish. Some locals fish the river by hand-grabbing. You may notice their hollowed logs placed in the river to attract catfish.

Although the Big Black River flows for some 200 miles before emptying into the Mississippi River, this description covers only the uppermost canoeable sections. Agricultural pressures that create erosion and runoff laden with silt, pesticides, and herbicides eventually degrade the river through the middle and lower sections so that canoeing is no longer pleasurable.

The first canoeable section begins one half mile southeast of the town of Kilmichael at the MS 413 bridge (access A). The put-in on river left is actually on a man-made channel. A couple of hundred yards downstream, the natural streambed begins. Twisting routinely in 180-degree turns, the river requires continuous maneuvering by the paddler. Numerous deadfalls and logjams can cause problems in this upper section. In some of the extreme bends, debris jams can be very serious. Because of those potential obstructions, the section above MS 407 should be used primarily as a day trip by more experienced paddlers. It is not a good trip to attempt in the drier seasons of summer and fall unless periods of rain have provided a sufficient water level.

After paddling for almost 6.5 miles from MS 413, you reach the bridge at MS 407 (access B) with a take-out on the right. The bridge is approximately 7.5 miles southeast of Winona.

The next four sections, access B–access F, are all similar in length and characteristics. There are no access points in-between the major highway crossings listed. Therefore, if a day trip is planned, allow for the slow current and meandering nature of the river. The surrounding forest is of hardwoods, but cypress and water tupelo are common in the many swampy areas. The denseness of the woods and width of the floodplain make these sections extremely remote. The banks are steep and muddy, making getting in and out of boats a challenge. Sandbars are not common, so if an overnight trip is planned, be watchful for the few good camping spots in the thick woods. Please be considerate of private landowners, and make sure that any campfires are completely dead.

Section: MS 413 to MS 14

Counties: Montgomery, Carroll, Holmes, Attala (MS)

USGS Quads: Kilmichael, Winona, Vaiden, Hesterville, West, Durant, Owens Wells, Goodman

Suitable for: Cruising, camping

Appropriate for: Beginners, intermediates—in the upper section

Months Runnable: Winter, spring, and rainy periods

Interest Highlights: Scenery, wildlife

Scenery: Pretty in spots to beautiful in spots

Difficulty: Class I

Average Width: 30–120 ft.

Velocity: Slow to moderate

Hazards: Deadfalls, debris jams

Rescue Index: Difficult to remote

Source of Additional Information: None known

Access Points	Access Code	River Miles	Shuttle Miles
A–B	1367	6.4	7.4
B–C	1357	13.8	13.8
C–D	1357	14.3	13.4
D–E	1357	17.4	11.3
E–F	1357	10.3	11.7
F	1357		

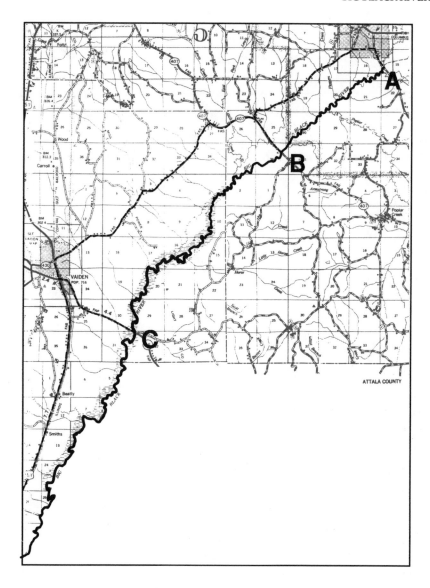

Access Key:

1	Paved road	7	Clear trail
2	Unpaved road	8	Brush and trees
3	Short carry	9	Launching fee charged
4	Long carry	10	Private property, need permission
5	Easy grade	11	No access, reference only
6	Steep incline		

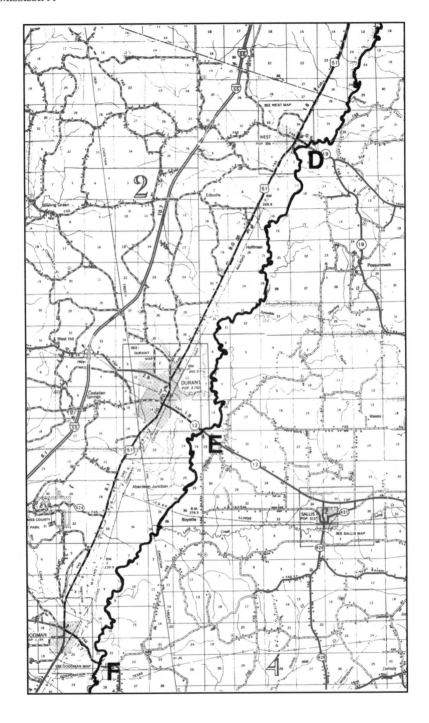

Brushy Creek

Brushy Creek is a small stream with its headwaters in George County. Although it flows for a length of only 6 miles before pouring into the Escatawpa River in Alabama, it represents a microcosm of Mississippi coastal streams. In Brushy Creek's upper reaches, its red tannin waters flow over clay outcrops creating exciting shoals and small rapids. However, as the creek reaches the floodplain of the Escatawpa River, it slows down and takes on the meandering, swampy appearance of blackwater streams.

Brushy Creek is first boatable approximately 7 miles east of Leakesville at a county road crossing (access A). The stream is 20 to 30 feet wide here. There is no gauge, but there is sufficient water level if the stream is easily floatable from bank to bank immediately downstream of the bridge. Also, if the water is slightly over the base of the bushes lining the bank, there will be ample water for the many shoals downstream. The put-in is on river right.

The many twists and shoals require precise maneuvering. Isolated by dense titi bushes along the banks, there are few signs of human activity. Magnolia and birch trees provide shade and help create a sense of intimacy for the narrow streambed.

Camping areas along the creek are limited since there are few sandbars and open areas. Once the Escatawpa is reached, however, many good sandbars are available. After the creek reaches the Escatawpa floodplain, it slowly twists another mile before reaching the Escatawpa River. You reach the take-out for Brushy Creek after traveling a little more than 2 miles on the Escatawpa River to the U.S. 98 bridge (access B). To reach the U.S. 98 bridge, travel 9.5 miles southeast of Lucedale. Access is on the Alabama side on river left.

Section: County bridge east of Leakesville to U.S. 98

Counties: George (MS), Mobile (AL)

USGS Quads: Earlville, Howell

Suitable for: Cruising

Appropriate for: Beginners, intermediates

Months Runnable: All except during dry spells

Interest Highlights: Scenery, wildlife

Scenery: Pretty in spots to beautiful in spots

Difficulty: Class I (II)

Average Width: 30–60 ft.

Velocity: Moderate

Hazards: Low-hanging trees, deadfalls

Rescue Index: Accessible to accessible but difficult

Source of Additional Information: None known

Access Points	Access Code	River Miles	Shuttle Miles
A–B[1]	1357	9.1	7
B[1]	1357		

[1]On the Escatawpa River

Access Key:

1	Paved road	7	Clear trail
2	Unpaved road	8	Brush and trees
3	Short carry	9	Launching fee charged
4	Long carry	10	Private property, need permission
5	Easy grade	11	No access, reference only
6	Steep incline		

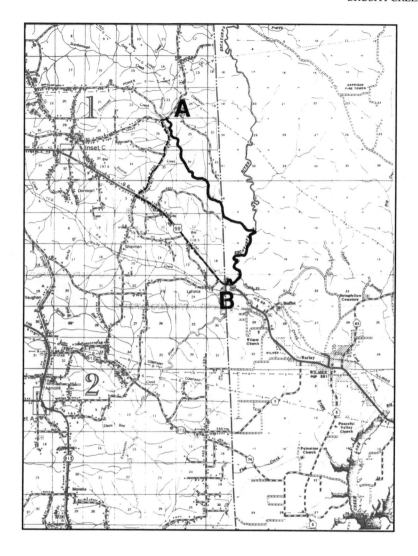

Leaf River

Flowing out of Bienville National Forest in the center of Mississippi, the Leaf River is one of the most scenic streams in the state. The Leaf justifies its name as it travels through heavily forested areas on its journey. Eventually, it joins with the Chickasawhay in the extreme southeastern part of the state to form the Pascagoula River. Beginning as a small 30- to 40-foot-wide stream at the MS 18 bridge, the Leaf becomes a large, slow-moving river, several hundred feet wide in its lower reaches.

In its upper sections, the Leaf is first runnable at the MS 18 bridge (access A) 4 miles east of Raleigh. This meandering 4-mile section has a good number of logjams and deadfalls. It is recommended as a day trip (with a light load) because of the many pullovers. It is best to canoe this segment during moderate water levels in the spring; there is no water level gauge. The take-out is at a county road (access B) 3 miles southwest of Sylvarena where the bridge crossing the Leaf has collapsed.

Access B is generally the best uppermost put-in for canoe camping. There are few pullovers and more sandbars in this 6.5-mile section. West Tallahala Creek joins the Leaf about halfway into this section. Below the junction, the Leaf's volume and size increases which makes paddling easier. The take-out (access C) is at a county bridge 7 miles north of Taylorsville.

The next section, access C–access D, is an 8-mile paddle down to MS 28. There are a number of gravel shoals. Small sand and gravel bars provide camping spots or rest breaks, and there are very few signs of human encroachment along the stream. This is a quiet, easy float that can either be done as a day trip or combined with the section above it (access B–access D) to make an excellent overnight camping trip. The take-out is at a boat ramp at the MS 28 bridge (access D) in Taylorsville.

From MS 28, the river widens as it joins with several good-sized creeks. Numerous pipelines, a transmission line, and a railroad bridge crisscross this segment of the river. It may not be a wilderness float, but it is still a nice trip.

Oakohay Creek supplies more water as it comes into the river approximately 6.5 miles below MS 28. The take-out, a boat ramp at U.S. 84 (access E), is reached after floating 10.5 miles. To get to the U.S. 84 bridge, travel 9.5 miles northeast of Collins.

The 12.5-mile section from U.S. 84 to MS 588, (access E–access F), makes a good overnight float trip. The Leaf meanders slowly in this section. There are several old oxbow lakes which may be hard to spot through the dense vegetation. To find the access at the MS 588 bridge, drive 6 miles east of Ellisville.

Below MS 588, the Leaf becomes a much more interesting canoeing river because there are numerous clay outcroppings and, with them, fun shoals and drops. One drop of nearly 2 feet is particularly exciting and the pool below is a good place to cool off. This 6-mile section, access F–access G, is an excellent day trip. There are a number of gravel bars and clay shelves to relax on, or wade and swim from. The take-out at MS 590 (access G) is 6 miles southeast of Ellisville.

The next section (access G–access I) is a 6-mile run from MS 590 to a county bridge near Moselle, another great day trip. The clay outcroppings in this segment create numerous fun shoals. There are many seeps in the clay formations that allow moss and ferns to thrive. After paddling just over 2.5 miles, you reach a county bridge (access H). It could be an emergency access if necessary. After another 2.5-mile paddle, the I-59 bridge is reached. There is no access at the interstate bridge. Paddle another half mile to a steep take-out near a county road (access I) just west of the town of Moselle.

From Moselle to Eastabuchie, the Leaf River continues to cut through clay formations, creating modest bluffs. The claystone shoals also make an interesting 6-mile paddle. This is a good summertime float because there generally is enough water to provide a steady current. The take-out (access J) is at a boat ramp at a county bridge a half mile west of Eastabuchie.

Below Eastabuchie, the Leaf slows down and its streambed is primarily sand. Absent now are the exciting clay shoals. With the addition of the Bowie River in Hattiesburg, the Leaf becomes a major river. The lower sections of the Leaf are characterized by a wide streambed and many large sandbars that make good camping sites. These sections are heavily fished and generally have good boat ramps at most access points. The Leaf slips slowly by oxbow lakes and swamps until it joins the Chickasawhay River. The two form the Pascagoula River near the town of Merrill.

Section: MS 18 to MS 28

Counties: Smith (MS)

USGS Quads: Louin SW, Center Ridge, Taylorsville

Suitable for: Cruising, camping

Appropriate for: Families, beginners, intermediates

Months Runnable: All except during dry spells

Interest Highlights: Scenery, wildlife

Scenery: Pretty in spots to beautiful in spots

Difficulty: Class I

Average Width: 40–70 ft.

Velocity: Slow to moderate

Hazards: Deadfalls

Rescue Index: Accessible to accessible but difficult

Source of Additional Information: River Expeditions, Jackson, MS; (601) 362-6049.

Access Points	Access Code	River Miles	Shuttle Miles
A–B	1357	4.2	7.3
B–C	2357	6.4	5.3
C–D	2357	7.9	9.4
D	1357		

Access Key:

1	Paved road	7	Clear trail
2	Unpaved road	8	Brush and trees
3	Short carry	9	Launching fee charged
4	Long carry	10	Private property, need permission
5	Easy grade	11	No access, reference only
6	Steep incline		

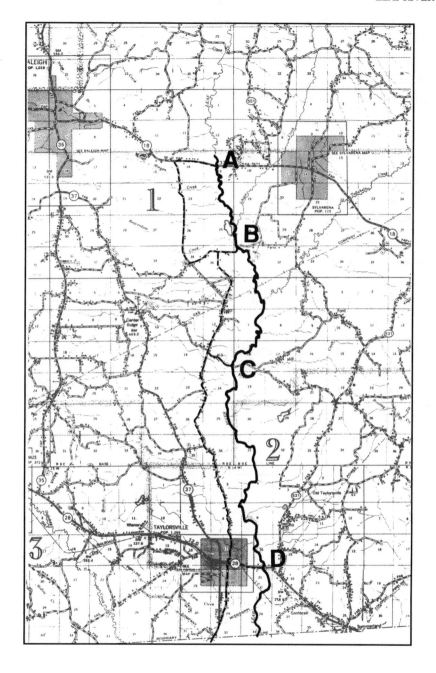

Section: MS 28 to county bridge at Moselle

Counties: Smith, Covington, Jones (MS)

USGS Quads: Taylorsville, Hot Coffee, Hebron, Moselle, Eastabuchie

Suitable for: Cruising, camping

Appropriate for: Families, beginners

Months Runnable: All

Interest Highlights: Scenery, wildlife, local culture

Scenery: Pretty in spots to beautiful in spots

Difficulty: Class I

Average Width: 60–100 ft.

Velocity: Slow to moderate

Hazards: Deadfalls

Rescue Index: Accessible to accessible but difficult

Source of Additional Information: Okatoma Outdoor Post, Sanford, MS; (601) 722-4297.

Access Points	Access Code	River Miles	Shuttle Miles
D–E	1357	10.4	10.7
E–F	1357	12.7	12.3
F–G	1357	6.1	7.0
G–H	1357	2.7	3.4
H–I	1357	3.3	4.5
I	1367		

Access Key:

1	Paved road	7	Clear trail,
2	Unpaved road	8	Brush and trees
3	Short carry	9	Launching fee charged
4	Long carry	10	Private property, need permission
5	Easy grade	11	No access, reference only
6	Steep incline		

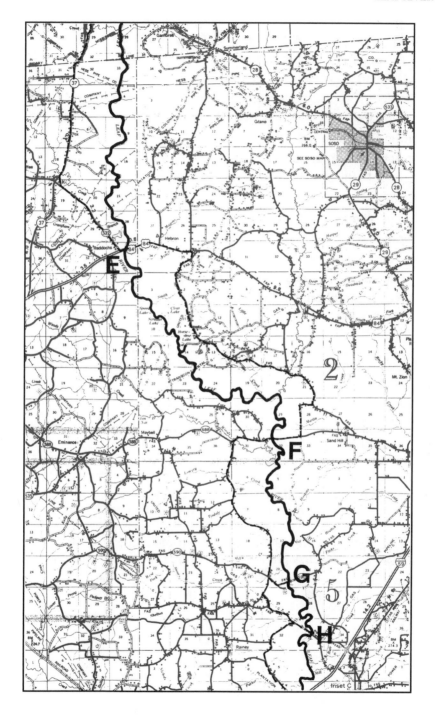

Section: County road at Moselle to National Guard landing

Counties: Jones, Forrest (MS)

USGS Quads: Eastabuchie, Hattiesburg, Carterville, McLaurin

Suitable for: Cruising, camping

Appropriate for: Families, beginners

Months Runnable: All

Interest Highlights: Scenery, wildlife

Scenery: Pretty in spots to pretty

Difficulty: Class I

Average Width: 100–200 ft.

Velocity: Slow

Hazards: None

Rescue Index: Accessible to accessible but difficult

Source of Additional Information: Mississippi Department of Wildlife Conservation, Fisheries Division, Hattiesburg Office, Hattiesburg, MS; (601) 264-8616.

Access Points	Access Code	River Miles	Shuttle Miles
I–J	1357	5.7	5.1
J–K	1357	9.5	7.7
K–L	1357	1.3	2.8
L–M	1357	8.0	6.5
M–N	1367	5.9	6.1
N	2357		

Access Key:

1	Paved road	7	Clear trail
2	Unpaved road	8	Brush and trees
3	Short carry	9	Launching fee charged
4	Long carry	10	Private property, need permission
5	Easy grade	11	No access, reference only
6	Steep incline		

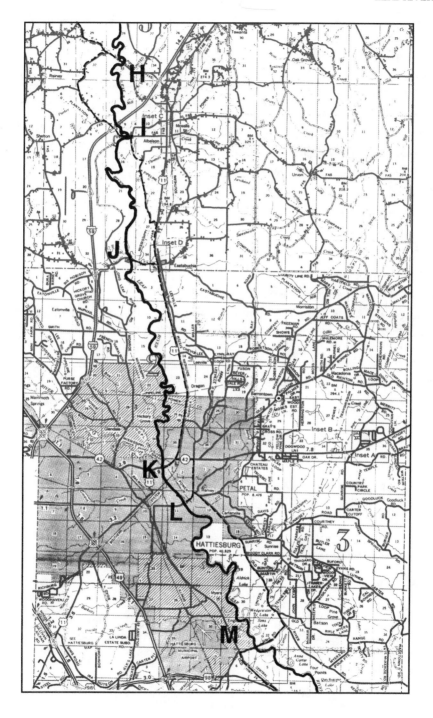

Section: National Guard landing to MS 596

Counties: Forrest, Perry, Greene, George (MS)

USGS Quads: McLaurin, New Augusta, Beaumont, Neely, McLain, Leakesville SW, Avent, Merrill

Suitable for: Cruising, camping

Appropriate for: Families, beginners

Months Runnable: All

Interest Highlights: Scenery, wildlife

Scenery: Pretty in spots to pretty

Difficulty: Class I

Average Width: 150–350 ft.

Velocity: Slow

Hazards: None

Rescue Index: Accessible but difficult

Source of Additional Information: Mississippi Department of Wildlife Conservation, Fisheries Division, Hattiesburg Office, Hattiesburg, MS; (601) 264-8616.

Access Points	Access Code	River Miles	Shuttle Miles
N–O	2357	6.1	7.2
O–P	1357	3.9	3.2
P–Q	1357	4.5	5.8
Q–R	1357	8.0	7.8
R–S	1357	11.6	9.7
S–T	1357	3.5	3.2
T–U[1]	1357	12.5	12.4
U[1]	1357		

[1] On the Pascagoula River

Access Key:

1	Paved road	7	Clear trail
2	Unpaved road	8	Brush and trees
3	Short carry	9	Launching fee charged
4	Long carry	10	Private property, need permission
5	Easy grade	11	No access, reference only
6	Steep incline		

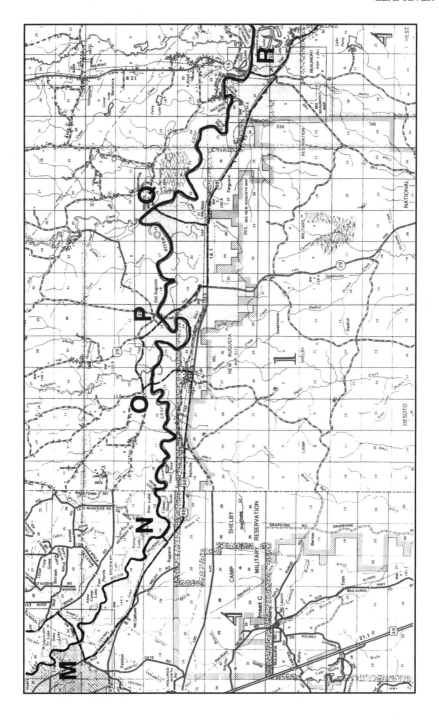

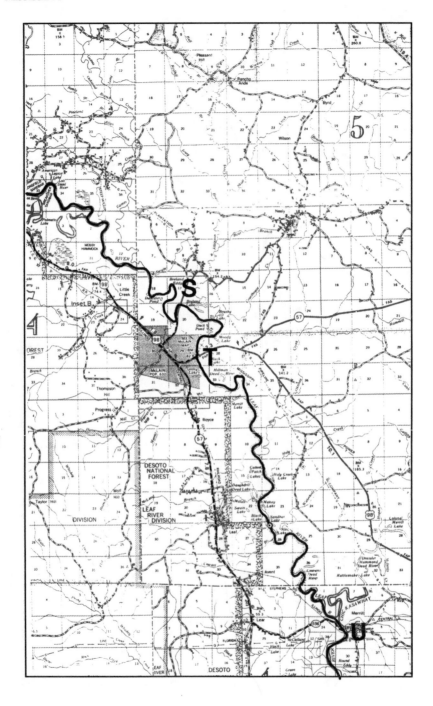

Black Creek

A designated National Wild and Scenic River, this classic canoe camping stream is born in south-central Mississippi in Jefferson County. With its dark, tannin waters and deep, cool pools, Black Creek is appropriately named. For most of its length, Black Creek flows through the DeSoto National Forest which creates a buffer for the stream and limits the amount of human encroachment. The National Guard's Camp, Shelby Military Reservation, borders the northern part of the middle sections of the stream. Infrequently, you hear the noise from their artillery. Otherwise, Black Creek is a superb canoe stream suitable for an overnight trip or an extended canoeing trip. During the summer months, the creek receives a lot of use by canoeists and organized groups.

It is not until Black Creek reaches the town of Purvis at the U.S. 11 bridge (access A) that canoeing is practical. The put-in downstream of the bridge on river left is the beginning of one of the true canoeing treasures of Mississippi. This first section is narrow (20 to 30 feet) and very twisty. There is no gauge to judge the water level; make sure that there is sufficient flow to carry a boat through the first few riffles. This section often has deadfalls that require pullovers. Because of the deadfalls and twisting nature of the stream, be cautious and avoid the segment at high water when the creek rises out of its banks. Because of the potential obstacles, this upper section is good primarily for day trips. This stretch is a good wilderness experience. After about 3.5 miles, the creek passes under the I-59 bridge. There is no access there. Continue on another 1.5 miles to the Browns bridge take-out (access B) on river right. This access is on a county road about 4 miles east of Purvis.

In the next section, access B–access C, Black Creek has recently been pressured by agricultural and livestock operations. Some clearing is evident from the creek, but because of few paddlers and adequate water quality, this section is still worth sampling. Be cautious just below Browns bridge; in the past, downed trees have formed large debris jams that required difficult pullovers or portages. After just over 5 miles, you reach the bridge (access C) on Churchwell Road at Camp Dantzler. This access is about 4 miles southwest of Paul B. Johnson State Park.

Below the access at Camp Dantzler, Black Creek flows approximately 4.5 miles through a mature pine forest before it reaches the Forest Service take-out at the Big Creek Landing (access D). The creek is unhindered by deadfalls and pullovers; however, there are very few prime camping spots in this section. The Big Creek Landing maintained by the Forest Service is just north of a county road, 5.5 miles west of Brooklyn. An excellent day trip of 5.5 miles begins at the Big Creek Landing. The creek is now within the DeSoto National Forest. Also at Big Creek Landing is the Black Creek Trail, a National Forest hiking trail that follows the creek for approximately 60 miles, ending at the Fairly bridge. There are a few small sandbars in this section. After some 4.5 miles past stands of large pines, you find the U.S. 49 bridge (access E). This is a very poor take-out and is not recommended. Continue for less than a mile further to reach a take-out (access F) a couple of hundred yards upstream and river right of the old U.S. 49 bridge in Brooklyn.

The 5.5-mile section of Black Creek from the old U.S. 49 bridge to Moody's Landing (access F–access H) is an easy day trip, or it can be combined with the next section to make a wonderful 14.5-mile overnight trip. In this section, there are more and larger sandbars. The remains of downed trees and limbs in the gravel riffles create a fun obstacle course. There is no developed access at Forest Service Road 308 (access G) 1 mile downstream of Brooklyn, but it can be used for emergencies. The take-out at Moody's Landing (access H) is at a sand beach on river left at the end of a dirt road a couple of hundred yards downstream of the picnic area. Moody's Landing is about 5.5 miles east of Brooklyn on Forest Service Road 301.

From Moody's Landing, Black Creek winds for 9.5 miles to the Janice Landing (access I). Magnolia and birch trees stretch out over the stream and a loblolly pine forest encompasses the creek, increasing the sense of solitude. The 20-mile section from Moody's Landing to Fairly bridge is a designated National Wild and Scenic River. This section has an adequate number of sandbars for choice camping spots and breaks for relaxing or swimming. The take-out at Janice Landing (access I) is a boat ramp on river left downstream of the MS 29 bridge. To find Janice Landing, travel about 10.5 miles east of Brooklyn on Forest Service Road 301 to MS 29. Then go south for 3 miles on MS 29 to the bridge crossing at Black Creek.

Below Janice Landing, the creek flows another 5.5 miles to Cypress Creek Landing (access J). In this section, there are numerous sandbars for camping. The Black Creek hiking trail follows closely along the creek. A mile below Janice Landing, Beaverdam Creek enters on river right. This is a very small, remote, twisting branch of Black Creek that is canopied by birches. Beaverdam Creek is boatable below Forest Service Road 308 at the Spring Branch Landing. This is approximately an 8-mile float, through a very dense forest, down to the confluence with Black Creek. There is good potential for downed trees on Beaverdam Creek, so be prepared for pullovers and quick stops. In the area around and below the junction of Beaverdam Creek, Black Creek flows by the small but scenic Black Creek Wilderness Area. Below the entrance of Beaverdam Creek, Black Creek meanders another 4.5 miles to the Cypress Creek Landing boat ramp on river left. This access has developed camping sites. To reach the landing, drive approximately 10.5 miles east of Brooklyn on Forest Service Road 301 to MS 29. Then turn left onto MS 29 for one-eighth of a mile and turn right on to Forest Service Road 305. Travel southeast for 3.5 miles to the gravel road on the right which leads 1.5 miles to the Cypress Creek Landing.

The 5.5-mile section from Cypress Creek Landing to Fairly bridge (access J–access K) is a nice day trip, but it is often combined with the section above (starting at Janice Landing) to make an excellent overnight camping trip. There are numerous sandbars to camp on, and you may catch a glimpse of the many deer and turkey that inhabit the national forest area. The boat ramp at Fairly bridge is downstream and on river right. Fairly Bridge (access K) is about 10.5 miles northeast of Wiggins on Forest Service Road 318.

From Fairly Bridge, Black Creek meanders through a deep forest of pine, with many good sandbars. The stark white sandbars and deep blackwater pools make exceptional summer swimming spots. After 8.5 miles, the creek reaches the MS 26 bridge (access L) where there is a boat ramp access. The MS 26 bridge is 12.5 miles east of Wiggins.

After MS 26, Black Creek flows some 18.5 miles through pine woods and pastures to the MS 57 bridge (access M). The scenery is similar to that in sections above, but the stream is no longer in the national forest, so be aware of private landowners' rights. The boat ramp at the MS 57 bridge is 8 miles south of Benndale.

The last section of Black Creek, from MS 57 to the take-out at the Wade bridge (access N) on MS 614, is very different in character from its upper segments. Here the creek meanders slowly through dense, swampy wetlands. Gone are the abundant sandbars found in the upper reaches. The pines are also replaced by a wonderful hardwood forest. This wild area is in the Pascagoula River Wildlife Management Area. Keep a watchful eye for the many deer and turkey here. Thirteen miles below the MS 57 bridge, Red Creek enters on river right. Now the stream is Big Black Creek and flows another 8 miles through remote wetlands to join the Pascagoula River. A flotilla of houseboats used by fishermen and hunters are anchored at the confluence with the Pascagoula. They are the signal that the wilderness experience is over. A short 3-mile paddle down the wide Pascagoula River to the take-out is quite a contrast to the intimate Black Creek. The boat ramp on river left at the MS 614 bridge is 3 miles southwest of the town of Wade.

Section: U.S. 11 bridge to Old U.S. 49 bridge at Brooklyn

Counties: Lamar, Forrest (MS)

USGS Quads: Purvis, Dixie, Rock Hill, Brooklyn

Suitable for: Cruising, camping

Appropriate for: Families, beginners

Months Runnable: All except during dry spells

Interest Highlights: Scenery, wildlife

Scenery: Pretty in spots to beautiful in spots

Difficulty: Class I

Average Width: 40–70 ft.

Velocity: Slow to moderate

Hazards: Deadfalls

Rescue Index: Accessible to accessible but difficult

Source of Additional Information: U.S. Forest Service, Black Creek Ranger District, Wiggins, MS; (601) 928-4422. Black Creek Canoe Rentals, Brooklyn, MS; (601) 582-8817.

Access Points	Access Code	River Miles	Shuttle Miles
A–B	1357	4.9	7.9
B–C	1357	5.2	5.1
C–D	1357	4.6	7.4
D–E	2357	4.4	4.6
E–F	11	0.9	1.1
F	1357		

Access Key:

1	Paved road	7	Clear trail
2	Unpaved road	8	Brush and trees
3	Short carry	9	Launching fee charged
4	Long carry	10	Private property, need permission
5	Easy grade	11	No access, reference only
6	Steep incline		

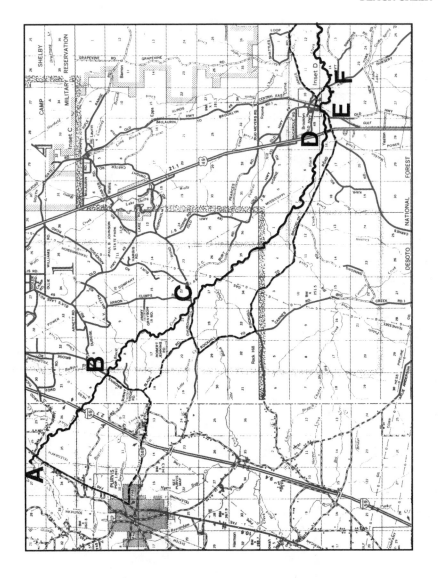

Section: Old U.S. 49 bridge to FairlyBridge

Counties: Forrest, Perry (MS)

USGS Quads: Brooklyn, Janice, Bond Pond, Barbara

Suitable for: Cruising, camping

Appropriate for: Families, beginners

Months Runnable: All

Interest Highlights: Scenery, wildlife, local culture

Scenery: Beautiful in spots

Difficulty: Class I

Average Width: 50–90 ft.

Velocity: Slow to moderate

Hazards: Deadfalls

Rescue Index: Accessible but difficult

Source of Additional Information: U.S. Forest Service, Black Creek RAnger District, Wiggins, MS; (601) 928-4422. Black Creek Canoe Rentals, Brooklyn, MS; (601) 582-8817.

Access Points	Access Code	River Miles	Shuttle Miles
F–G	1357	1.1	1.1
G–H	1367	4.3	5.0
H–I	1357	9.5	7.9
I–J	1357	5.3	7.4
J–K	2357	5.5	9.0
K	1357		

Access Key:

1	Paved road	7	Clear trail
2	Unpaved road	8	Brush and trees
3	Short carry	9	Launching fee charged
4	Long carry	10	Private property, need permission
5	Easy grade	11	No access, reference only
6	Steep incline		

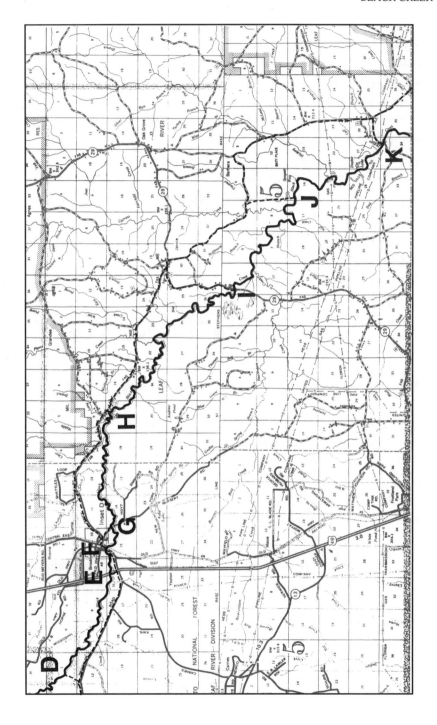

Section: FairlyBridge to MS 614

Counties: Perry, Stone, George, Jackson (MS)

USGS Quads: Barbara, Ramsey Springs, Benndale, Basin, Eason Hill, Vancleave

Suitable for: Cruising, camping

Appropriate for: Families, beginners

Months Runnable: All

Interest Highlights: Scenery, wildlife

Scenery: Pretty in spots to beautiful in spots

Difficulty: Class I

Average Width: 70–110 ft.

Velocity: Slow

Hazards: Deadfalls

Rescue Index: Accessible to difficult to remote

Source of Additional Information: U.S. Forest Service, Black Creek Ranger District, Wiggins, MS; (601) 928-4422. Black Creek Canoe Rentals, Brooklyn, MS; (601) 582-8817.

Access Points	Access Code	River Miles	Shuttle Miles
K–L	1357	8.4	9.1
L–M	1357	18.3	14.0
M–N	1357	21.9	16.8
N[1]	1357		

[1]On the Pascagoula River

Access Key:

1	Paved road	7	Clear trail
2	Unpaved road	8	Brush and trees
3	Short carry	9	Launching fee charged
4	Long carry	10	Private property, need permission
5	Easy grade	11	No access, reference only
6	Steep incline		

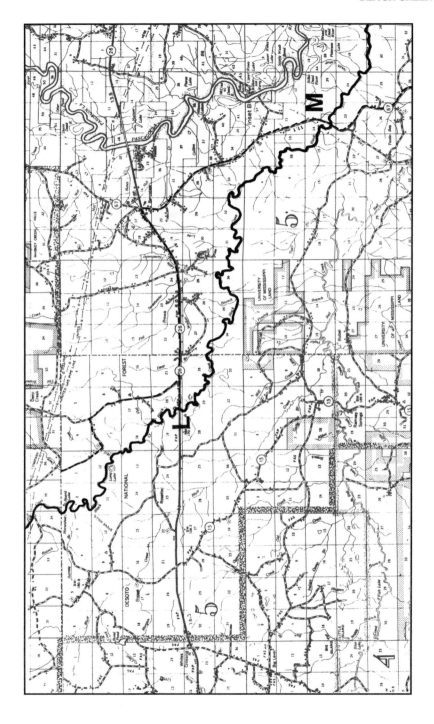

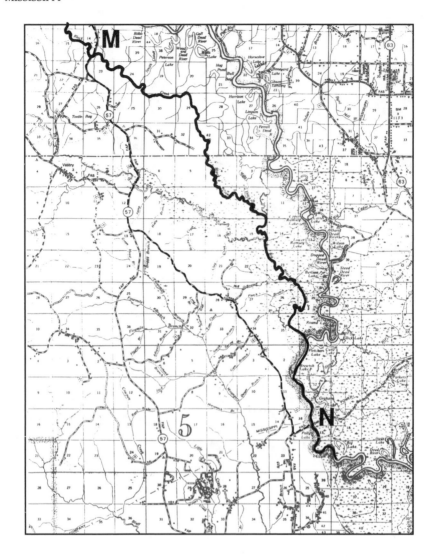

Red Creek

Originating in Lamar County in southern Mississippi, Red Creek has similarities to its northern sister, Black Creek. Fed by cool springs, Red Creek is a delight to float, especially in the summer. The creek flows through a primarily pine forest. The resulting reddish, tannin-colored waters in a shallow streambed account for the stream's name. Red Creek, with its winding, gravel riffles, deep pools, and generous sandbars, is one of the best overnight camping streams in Mississippi. Throughout its length, the creek flows through largely undisturbed land, giving it a sense of remoteness. In addition, Red Creek is not pressured by many floaters or anglers.

Red Creek is first consistently runnable at the MS 26 bridge (access A) about 3 miles west of Wiggins. Here the creek is larger because of the addition of several creeks just upstream that provide an adequate flow most of the year. The put-in at the MS 26 bridge is fairly steep and is on the river left side. Below MS 26, Red Creek starts off as only 20–30 feet wide, and is very meandering. Riffles created by gravel bars and deadfalls make maneuvering a canoe exciting. Within the first mile, a county road crossing (access B) provides an emergency take-out. In the upper part of this section, there are only a few small sandbars for camping. It is not until about halfway down it that you find larger, more numerous sandbars. After floating almost 9.5 miles from MS 26, you reach the bridge at U.S. 49 (access C) in Perkinston. There is a good take-out at the sandbar under the bridge on river left.

Below U.S. 49, the true character of the stream appears. There are large, brilliant white sandbars in dramatic contrast with dark, deep pools—Red Creek's trademark. This section is one of the better accesses to the beginning of one of the premiere canoe camping streams in the Southeast. From U.S. 49 down to City Bridge (access D), a county road crossing, Red Creek flows for 6.5 miles, making a relaxing day trip or, combined with lower sections, overnight trip. The access at City Bridge is a boat ramp downstream and river right of the new concrete bridge. City Bridge is about 8 miles east of Perkinston.

The section starting at City Bridge is a favorite for overnight camping.

139

The ideal trip is the 14 miles down to the Ramsey Springs bridge (access F) at MS 15, spending the maximum amount of time allowable soaking in the water. In the summer, plan on paddling for an hour or so, then playing, swimming, or eating for an equal amount of time, and camping about halfway through the trip. Along the creek, birch, willow, and bay laurel form a canopy over the stream that provides welcomed shade and creates an intimate setting. Between pools, Red Creek has some exciting gravel shoals to negotiate. The pine and mixed hardwoods surrounding the creek provide habitat for several threatened species, including the Mississippi and swallow-tailed kites. Sightings of these birds performing their aerial acrobatics, the fairly common great blue heron, and belted kingfishers are highlights of any trip.

For a leisurely day trip, float the 9.5 miles from City Bridge to the alternate take-out at the Cable Bridge Landing (access E). (There is no longer a bridge at this spot.) Cypress Creek pours its cold waters into Red Creek on river left just upstream of the access, making a wonderful lounging spot. Take out on river right near the power line crossing. To find the Cable Bridge Landing, go 1 mile south of Perkinston on U.S. 49 and turn east on a county road. Continue east and bear to the left on this road for 12 miles until you reach a gravel road on the left which leads 3.5 miles to the landing. The Ramsey Springs bridge (access F) is approximately 4.5 miles downstream of the Cable Bridge Landing. There is a new concrete bridge on MS 15 at Ramsey Springs. Take out on river right at the boat ramp upstream of the new MS 15 bridge. The Ramsey Springs access is about 26 miles north of Biloxi on MS 15.

The 15-mile section from Ramsey Springs bridge to the Vestry bridge (access F–access G) is another excellent overnight trip. The current weakens as the streambed deepens and the pools lengthen. This lower section is good for fishing, especially for catfish. Human encroachment continues to be limited in this segment, also. A steep take-out (access G) is downstream on river left of the Red Creek Road bridge at the small community of Vestry, 10 miles south of Benndale.

From Vestry, Red Creek flows slowly through pine forests with few sand bars. Hunting for deer and wild turkey is evidently good in these lower sections, witnessed by the many posted-for-hunting signs along the stream. After paddling almost 4 miles, there is a boat ramp (access H) on river left just downstream of the MS 57 bridge. The access at MS 57 is 13 miles north of the town of Vancleave.

Below MS 57, a 15.5-mile float trip covers the remaining miles of Red Creek and ends in the Pascagoula River. The character of Red Creek changes dramatically here. The forest begins as mixed pine and hardwoods and becomes almost all hardwoods. There are signs of recent clear-cutting in the upper part of this section that diminish the wild quality of the stream. Sandbars are infrequent in this segment with wetlands and swampy conditions predominating. The creek takes a slow, twisting path as it flows through the Red Creek Game Management Area and joins Black Creek 8 miles below MS 57 to form Big Black Creek. After paddling another 5 miles on Big Black Creek through the Pascagoula Wildlife Management Area, you find the confluence with the Pascagoula River. A 3-mile paddle on the wide Pascagoula brings one to the boat ramp at the Wade bridge (access I) on river left. The Wade bridge is on MS 614 3 miles southwest of the community of Wade.

Section: MS 26 to MS 15

Counties: Stone (MS)

USGS Quads: Wiggins, Whites Crossing, Ramsey Springs

Suitable for: Cruising, camping

Appropriate for: Families, beginners

Months runnable: All except during dry spells

Interest Highlights: Scenery, wildlife

Scenery: Beautiful in spots

Difficulty: Class I

Average Width: 40–80 ft.

Velocity: Slow to moderate

Hazards: Deadfalls

Rescue Index: Accessible to accessible but difficult

Source of Additional Information: U.S. Forest Service, Biloxi Ranger District, McHenry, MS; (601) 928-5291. Red Creek Market, Perkinston, MS; (601) 928-5365.

Access Points	Access Code	River Miles	Shuttle Miles
A–B	1357	0.9	1.6
B–C	1357	8.4	8.0
C–D	1357	6.5	8.4
D–E	1357	9.6	14.6
E–F	2357	4.5	8.3
F	1357		

Access Key:	1	Paved road	7	Clear trail
	2	Unpaved road	8	Brush and trees
	3	Short carry	9	Launching fee charged
	4	Long carry	10	Private property, need permission
	5	Easy grade	11	No access, reference only
	6	Steep incline		

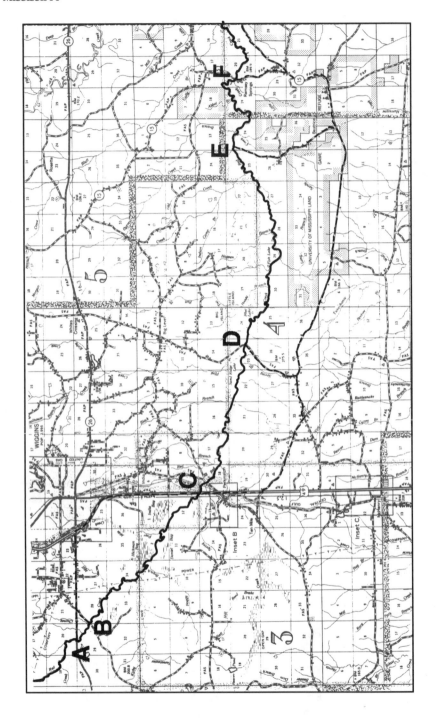

Section: MS 14 to MS 614

Counties: Stone, George, Jackson (MS)

USGS Quads: Ramsey Springs, Benndale, Vestry, Easen Hill, Vancleave

Suitable for: Cruising, camping

Appropriate for: Families, beginners

Months Runnable: All

Interest Highlights: Scenery, wildlife

Scenery: Pretty in spots to beautiful in spots

Difficulty: Class I

Average Width: 60–100 ft.

Velocity: Slow

Hazards: Deadfalls

Rescue Index: Accessible but difficult to remote

Source of Additional Information: U.S. Forest Service, Biloxi Ranger District, McHenry, MS; (601) 928-5291. Red Creek Market, Perkinston, MS ; (601) 928-5365.

Access Points	Access Code	River Miles	Shuttle Miles
F–G	1357	15.2	11.1
G–H	1357	3.8	4.0
H–I[1]	1357	15.8	11.1
I[1]	1357		

[1]On the Pascagoula River

Access Key:
1 Paved road
2 Unpaved road
3 Short carry
4 Long carry
5 Easy grade
6 Steep incline
7 Clear trail
8 Brush and trees
9 Launching fee charged
10 Private property, need permission
11 No access, reference only

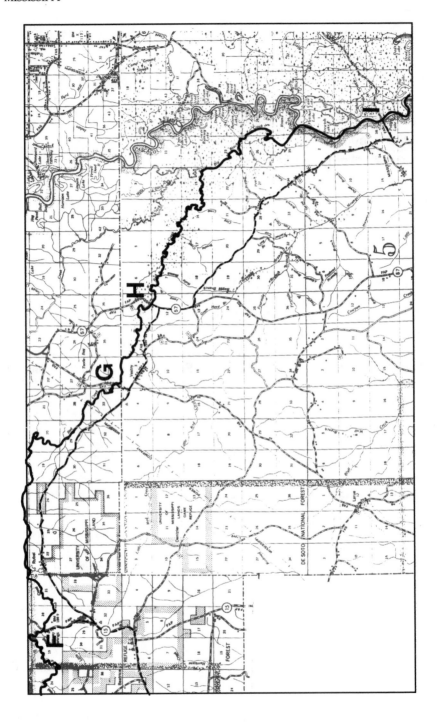

Pearl River

The Pearl River is born in Winston County and eventually grows into one of the major drainage basins in the state of Mississippi. In its upper reaches, the river is similar to most streams of the state, meandering between banks of 5 to 12 feet in height with a streambed width of approximately 50 feet. However, with the addition of several large tributaries, the river becomes a sizable waterway when it reaches the Ross Barnett Reservoir.

The uppermost put-in which has few pullovers is at MS 16 (access A) in Edinburg. This 8-mile float down to the Sunrise bridge (access B) makes a nice day trip. The primarily hardwood forest and lack of human intrusion enhance the experience. There may be some downed trees that cause pullovers in this section. Find the access at the Sunrise bridge by traveling 5 miles northeast of Carthage on MS 16 and turning right at the community of Sunrise. Then continue for a half mile to the county road bridge that crosses the Pearl.

Below Sunrise bridge, the Pearl twists another 10.5 miles to the MS 35 bridge at Carthage. Sandbars occur periodically in this segment, allowing for rest breaks or camping spots. These upper sections support good populations of bass and catfish. Take out on river left at the MS 35 bridge (access C) one half mile south of Carthage.

The next segment from Carthage to the old MS 13 bridge (access C–access D) is a convenient day trip. This is a 10-mile paddle through a broad floodplain. Cypress and hardwoods are plentiful. The section is generally free of pullovers and has many large white sandbars. Take out at the boat ramp on river left near the old MS 13 bridge (access D). The new MS 25 bridge (access E) immediately downstream does not have any access from the river.

Continuing downstream, the Pearl winds for another 8 miles to the Leake County Water Park (access F). In this section the river deepens and its current becomes more sluggish. You'll encounter motorized boats frequently. However, the scenery remains well worth the effort. The boat ramp at the Leake County Water Park is on river left. To reach the water park, travel 6 miles southeast on MS 25 from the junction with MS 16 to a paved county road on the right. Go west on this road for 1.5 miles to the intersection with another county road. Turn right on this road and proceed north 1.5 miles to the water park.

Below the water park, you encounter a low-head dam in less than 2 miles. Approach with caution and portage around on river left to continue downstream. (There is also a boat ramp (access G) on river left upstream of the dam that provides an alternate take-out.) By the time you reach Coal Bluff State Park in another 3 miles, the river is large enough to accommodate power boats, making canoeing less safe or pleasant. Take out on river left at the boat ramp (access H) in the park.

After Coal Bluff State Park, the Pearl flows slowly into the Ross Barnett Reservoir. There are many accesses around the reservoir if you wish to explore the area. Take caution by anticipating adverse conditions caused by wind, waves, or power boats.

Below the reservoir, the river continues through a forested floodplain adjacent to the city of Jackson. Bank erosion from fluctuating releases at the reservoir have deteriorated the river somewhat, but the trip from the reservoir spillway (access I) to MS 25 (access J) is a popular nearby summertime float for Jacksonians briefly escaping the city pressures. The river passes through a dense hardwood forest on the river left side and there are many sandbars to lounge on in this section. At the MS 25 bridge in Flowood, there is no good take-out, but the river left side provides the best options.

A mile below MS 25, is the LeFleur's Bluff State Park, but there is no access to the river there. Two miles below MS 25 is another low-head dam. This one was constructed by the city of Jackson for water supply. It should be approached with extreme caution and portaged on river right. Several unsuspecting people have died recently as a result of underestimating the hydraulic power below the dam.

After the dam, the river has been channelized as it flows past Jackson. In its lower reaches, it becomes much larger with fewer points of interest until it nears the Gulf, where its swamps and marshes provide wildlife habitat and places of great beauty.

Section: MS 16 to Coal Bluff State Park

Counties: Leake, Scott, Madison (MS)

USGS Quads: Edinburgh, McAfee, Carthage, Sharon, Jackson SE

Suitable for: Cruising, camping

Appropriate for: Families, beginners

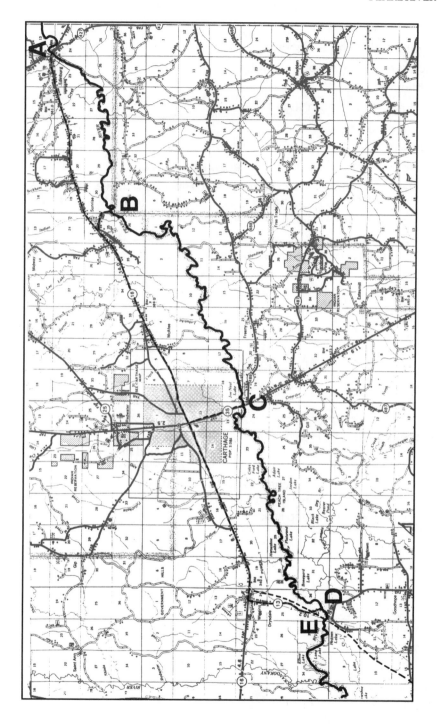

Months Runnable: All

Interest Highlights: Scenery, wildlife

Scenery: Pretty in spots to pretty

Difficulty: Class I

Average Width: 40–150 ft.

Velocity: Slow

Hazards: Deadfalls, power boats, low-head dam

Rescue Index: Accessible to accessible but difficult

Source of Additional Information: Pearl River Basin Development District, Jackson, MS; (601) 354-6301. Leake County Water Park; (601) 654-9359. Coal Bluff State Park; (601) 654-7726.

Access Points	Access Code	River Miles	Shuttle Miles
A–B	1357	8.1	7.2
B–C	1357	10.5	10.3
C–D	1357	10.2	10.7
D–E	1357	0.1	0.3
E–F	11	8.0	7.6
F–G	1357	1.7	4.1
G–H	1357	2.7	9.6
H	1357		

Access Key:

1	Paved road	7	Clear trail
2	Unpaved road	8	Brush and trees
3	Short carry	9	Launching fee charged
4	Long carry	10	Private property, need permission
5	Easy grade	11	No access, reference only
6	Steep incline		

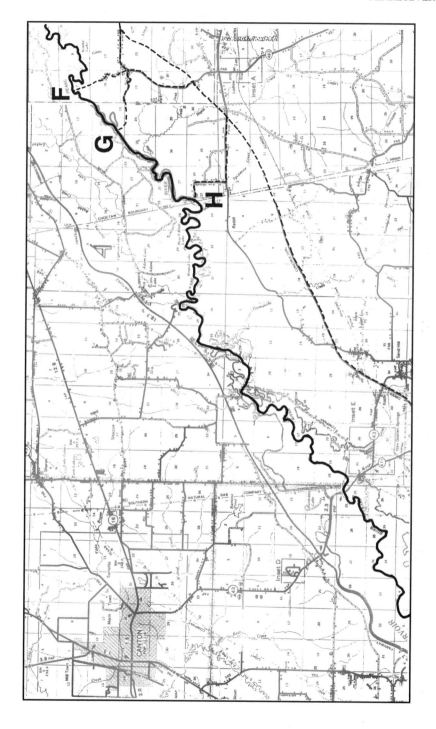

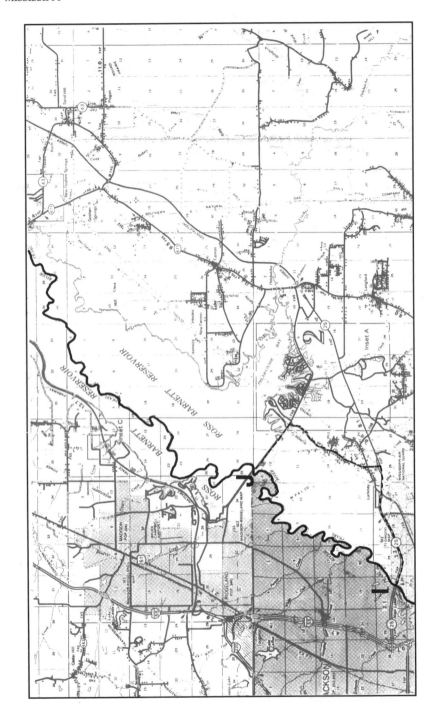

Section: Ross Barnett Reservoir Dam to MS 25

Counties: Hinds, Rankin (MS)

USGS Quads: Jackson SE, Jackson

Suitable for: Cruising, camping

Appropriate for: Families, beginners

Months Runnable: All

Interest Highlights: Scenery

Scenery: Pretty in spots

Difficulty: Class I

Average Width: 80–200 ft.

Velocity: Slow

Hazards: Deadfalls, dam

Rescue Index: Accessible to accessible but difficult

Source of Additional Information: Pearl River Development District, Jackson, MS (601) 354-6301. Leake County Water Park; (601) 654-9359. Coal Bluff State Park; (601) 654-7726.

Access Points	Access Code	River Miles	Shuttle Miles
I–J	1357	9.1	10.1
J	1367		

Access Key:

1	Paved road	7	Clear trail
2	Unpaved road	8	Brush and trees
3	Short carry	9	Launching fee charged
4	Long carry	10	Private property, need permission
5	Easy grade	11	No access, reference only
6	Steep incline		

Bear Creek

Flowing out of Alabama into Tishomingo County in the northeast corner of Mississippi, Bear Creek is a good example of a fringe Appalachian stream. The creek passes along gentle forested hills, then carves a small canyon out of the limestone and sandstone ridges in Tishomingo State Park. The creek is also a historical setting with Civil War and Indian artifacts to explore.

After being channelized by the Soil Conservation Service near Belmont, the creek regains its natural streambed and again becomes interesting to float near Dennis. The put-in just below the channelized section is found at an old iron bridge (access A) on a county road 2 miles east of Dennis. The access is on river right and upstream of the bridge. An excellent 6.5-mile day trip begins at the old iron bridge and ends at Tishomingo State Park (access C). Immediately below the iron bridge, Bear Creek begins a 2-mile horseshoe bend. Here the creek is about 60 feet wide with steep banks of 5–10 feet. Birch and maple trees provide shade over the creek. After the horseshoe bend, the creek passes under another iron bridge (access B) that can be used as an alternate or emergency take-out on river left.

Continuing on, the creek enters the boundary of Tishomingo State Park about 1.5 miles below the second iron bridge. The forest makes a significant change to hardwoods such as oak and hickory as it enters the park. Several shoals of gravel and sandstone provide excitement and require some maneuvering skills. Shortly after entering the park, boaters encounter the remains of a confederate bridge. Beyond the stone pillars of the bridge are heavily forested bluffs of sandstone. There are several scenic nature trails for short hikes in this, Mississippi's most rugged and beautiful park. A cable suspension bridge (access C) signals a good take-out point in the park on river left.

If a longer trip is desired, a paddler may float another 5.5 miles to the MS 30 bridge (access E) at the community of Mingo. There is a new concrete bridge (access D) on the Natchez Trace Parkway a mile below the suspension bridge, but there is no access there. Below the MS 30 bridge, Bear Creek flows back into Alabama on its way to the Tennessee River. Just before leaving Mississippi, there are some very impressive Indian mounds along Bear Creek on river right about 2 miles downstream of the MS 30 bridge.

Section: Dennis to MS 30

Counties: Tishomingo (MS)

USGS Quads: Belmont, Tishomingo

Suitable for: Cruising

Appropriate for: Families, beginners

Months Runnable: All except during dry spells

Interest Highlights: Scenery, wildlife, geology, historical locations

Scenery: pretty in spots to beautiful in spots

Difficulty: Class I

Average Width: 40–70 ft.

Velocity: Slow to moderate

Hazards: Deadfalls

Rescue Index: Accessible to accessible but difficult

Source of Additional Information: Tishomingo State Park, Dennis, MS; (601) 438-6914.

Access Points	Access Code	River Miles	Shuttle Miles
A–B	2357	2.6	1.4
B–C	1357	3.8	3.5
C–D	1357	1.2	2.3
D–E	1357	3.4	2.8
E	1357		

Access Key:
1 Paved road
2 Unpaved road
3 Short carry
4 Long carry
5 Easy grade
6 Steep incline
7 Clear trail
8 Brush and trees
9 Launching fee charged
10 Private property, need permission
11 No access, reference only

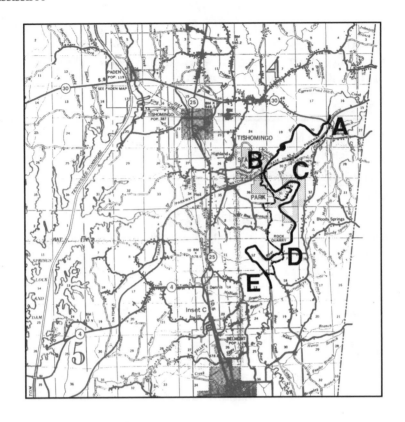

Bayou Pierre

Rising in Lincoln County, Bayou Pierre passes through Copiah and Claiborne counties to its junction with the Mississippi River. In its headwaters the stream is 30 feet wide and has heavily vegetated sandy banks. As it approaches the Mississippi, Bayou Pierre has a wide, shallow, sandy streambed. The stream presents many options for both day and canoe camping trips.

Bayou Pierre is first boatable at the community of Dentville, 12 miles northeast of Hazlehurst. The put-in (access A) is on a county road a half mile south of Dentville. River birch and willow hang out over the water, screening the sun. Twisting and shaded in its first miles, the stream soon begins to widen as sand and gravel bars become more frequent. After paddling a little over 11 miles, you reach the MS 18 bridge (access B) which is 8 miles southwest of Utica. There is a good take-out on river right upstream of the bridge.

A mile and a half downstream of MS 18, White Oak Creek, a boatable tributary, comes in on river right. Gravel bars are more frequent in this section. Rock hounds will want to spend time on these bars searching for geodes, petrified wood, and coral. Three and a half miles downstream of MS 18, Scutchalo Creek flows in on river right. There is a pretty 10-foot waterfall three-quarters of a mile up the creek that is worth the hike. The Carlisle bridge is 9 miles from MS 18 (access C) on river right. The old community of Carlisle is 14 miles southwest of Utica just north off MS 18.

Below the Carlisle bridge, Bayou Pierre widens dramatically. A combination of a shallow gravel bed and deadfalls requires a lot of maneuvering at lower water levels. As you approach its confluence with the Mississippi, the once rolling hills around the stream give way to marsh and swampland. Access to Bayou Pierre is adequate at most of the road crossings in the lower reaches. The take-out (access G) at the end of Bayou Pierre is where MS 552 terminates at the Mississippi River.

Section: County road near Dentville to Willows

Counties: Copiah, Claiborne (MS)

USGS Quads: Dentville, Dentville NW, Utica West, Carlisle, Willows

Suitable for: Cruising, camping

Appropriate for: Families, beginners

Months Runnable: All

Interest Highlights: Scenery, wildlife

Scenery: Pretty in spots to pretty

Difficulty: Class I

Average Width: 40–80 ft.

Velocity: Slow to moderate

Hazards: Deadfalls

Rescue Index: Accessible to accessible but difficult

Source of Additional Information: None known

Access Points	Access Code	River Miles	Shuttle Miles
A–B	1357	11.3	11.8
B–C	1357	8.8	6.3
C–D	1357	6.2	7.4
D	1357		

Access Key:

1	Paved road	7	Clear trail,
2	Unpaved road	8	Brush and trees
3	Short carry	9	Launching fee charged
4	Long carry	10	Private property, need permission
5	Easy grade	11	No access, reference only
6	Steep incline		

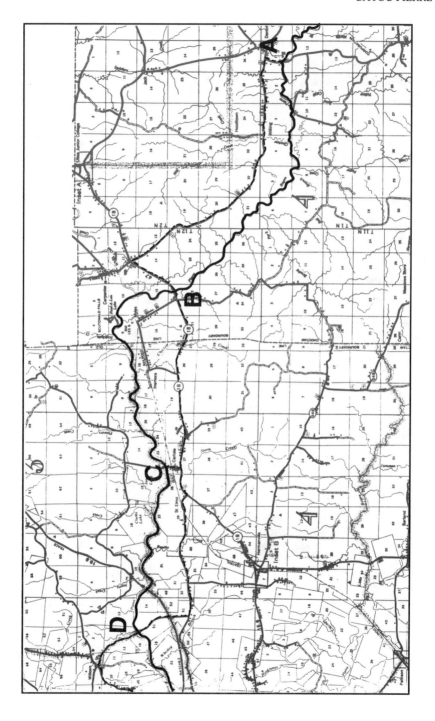

Section: Willows to MS 552

Counties: Claiborne (MS)

USGS Quads: Willows, Port Gibson, St. Joseph

Suitable for: Cruising, camping

Appropriate for: Families, beginners

Months Runnable: All

Interest Highlights: Scenery, wildlife

Scenery: Pretty in spots

Difficulty: Class I

Average Width: 70–120 ft.

Velocity: Slow

Hazards: Deadfalls

Rescue Index: Accessible but difficult

Source of Additional Information: None known

Access Points	Access Code	River Miles	Shuttle Miles
D–E	1357	6.5	7.9
E–F	1357	3.2	5.0
F–G[1]	1367	17.8	18.1
G[1]	1357		

[1]On the Mississippi River

Access Key:

1	Paved road	7	Clear trail
2	Unpaved road	8	Brush and trees
3	Short carry	9	Launching fee charged
4	Long carry	10	Private property, need permission
5	Easy grade	11	No access, reference only
6	Steep incline		

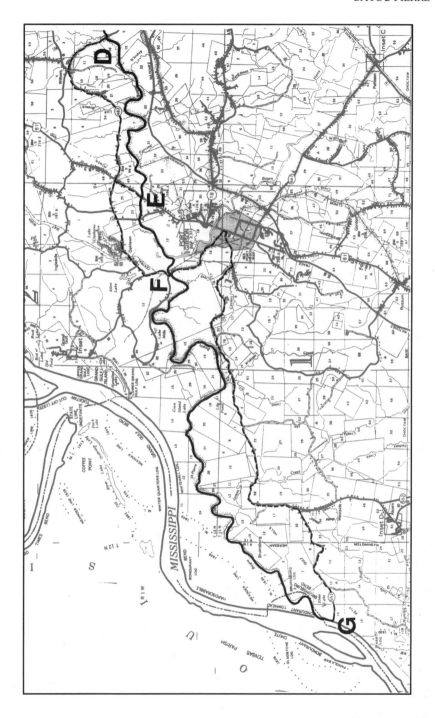

Homochitto River

Born in Copiah County in southwest Mississippi, the Homochitto River travels through the scenic woods of the Homochitto National Forest on its way to join the Mississippi. The river begins as a fairly narrow creek but dramatically expands to a quarter of a mile wide in its lower reaches. The primary characteristics of the Homochitto are its sandbars. These are small in the upper section, but become huge and lengthy in the bottom portions. There are no gauges for the river, and the extremely shallow nature of the stream makes judging water levels difficult.

The first reliable put-in is at the MS 550 bridge (access A). Here the stream is about 30 feet in width with fairly steep banks of 5 to 10 feet in height. The stream has a fairly steep gradient here, creating long gravel shoals. It is best to boat this section at moderate water levels following periods of local rain. During the summer and fall, boaters can expect to walk many of the shallow gravel shoals in the upper sections. There is an alternate put-in or emergency take-out at a county road (access B) 3 miles below MS 550. A good day trip covers the 6 miles down to a take-out on river right at a county bridge (access C). This access is 8 miles north of Eddiceton.

From MS 550 to U.S. 84, the river flows through portions of the Homochitto National Forest. The forest is a mixture of pine and hardwoods. Birch, hornbeam, and maple are common along the stream. Heavily vegetated banks and shallow pools provide habitat for bass, bluegill, and catfish. Signs of human activity are minimal in the publicly owned, upper segments. However, there is private property along the upper part of the stream, and some landowners are concerned about trespassing. The 8-mile section from access C to U.S. 84 (access D) is a fine day trip or can be combined with the sections above to make a good overnight camping trip. Be careful if you camp on the low gravel bars since heavy local rains can cause a sudden rise in the river. The take-out at U.S. 84 in Eddiceton is steep with an unclear trail. There is an alternate take-out (access E) at a county road crossing just south of Eddiceton.

Below U.S. 84 is a nice day trip of 7 miles down to U.S. 98. Extensive sandbars are found throughout this section. Boaters, be aware that private land surrounds this access, and there is a fee charged for access by a private water park south of the bridge. Also in this area, canoeing may conflict with all-terrain vehicle (3-wheeler) use. The private water park rents 3-wheelers, which use the huge, expansive, flat gravel bars and riverbed as a playground. The take-out at U.S. 98 (access F) is just south of Bude.

Leaving U.S. 98, the Homochitto flows 4 miles to a county bridge south of Meadville. The river continues to widen to several hundred feet across. The sandbars are large and flank the river banks. The forest previously surrounding the river gives way to farmland and pastures. The take-out for this section is at a county bridge (access G) about 3 miles south of Meadville.

The sections from the Meadville county road to MS 61 (access G–access I) are very similar and cover a total distance of just over 43 miles. This can make a long canoe camping trip or can be divided into two shorter overnight trips by using the access at MS 33 (access H). Water quality in these sections remains good; the river here flows through a wide plain of sand. Take care while wading around the sandbars or swimming in the river, since the river bottom is sometimes like quicksand. The take-out at U.S. 61 (access I) is approximately 11 miles south of Natchez.

Below U.S. 61, the Homochitto has been channelized by the U.S. Army Corps of Engineers. There, the river is referred to as the Abernathy Canal. It is a sterile sand ditch for the remaining 10 miles to the Mississippi River. Unless you have a desire to experience quicksand or view the ravages of channelization, avoid this artificial portion of the river.

Section: MS 550 to U.S. 98

Counties: Lincoln, Franklin (MS)

USGS Quads: Caseyville, McCall Creek, Union Church, Bude

Suitable for: Cruising, camping

Appropriate for: Families, beginners, intermediates

Months Runnable: All except during dry spells

Interest Highlights: Scenery, wildlife

Scenery: Pretty in spots to beautiful in spots

Difficulty: Class I

Average Width: 40–80 ft.

Velocity: Slow to moderate

Hazards: Deadfalls

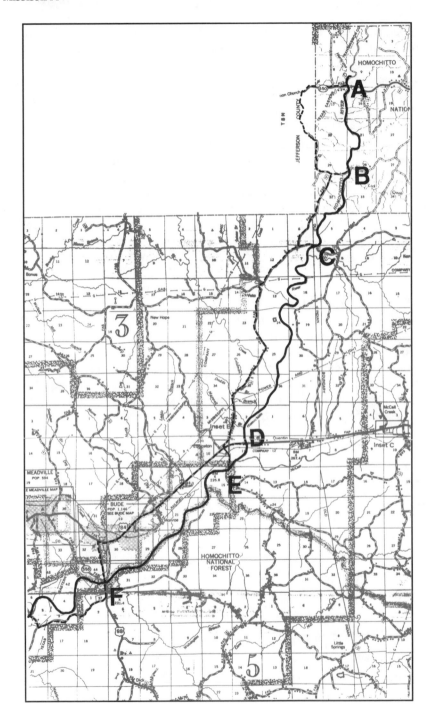

Rescue Index: Accessible to accessible but difficult

Source of Additional Information: U.S. Forest Service, Bude Ranger District, Meadville, MS; (601) 384-5876.

Access Points	Access Code	River Miles	Shuttle Miles
A–B	1357	3.0	4.8
B–C	1367	2.7	3.7
C–D	1357	8.1	8.9
D–E	1368	1.3	1.5
E–F	13579	5.6	7.2
F	1357		

Access Key:

1	Paved road	7	Clear trail
2	Unpaved road	8	Brush and trees
3	Short carry	9	Launching fee charged
4	Long carry	10	Private property, need permission
5	Easy grade	11	No access, reference only
6	Steep incline		

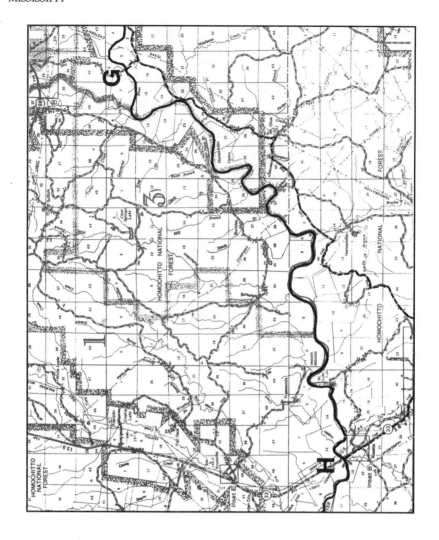

Section: U.S. 98 to U.S. 61

Counties: Franklin, Amite, Wilkinson, Adams (MS)

USGS Quads: Bude, Crosby, Kingston

Suitable for: Cruising, camping

Appropriate for: Families, beginners

Months Runnable: All

Interest Highlights: Scenery, wildlife

Scenery: Pretty in spots to pretty

Difficulty: Class I

Average Width: 100–200 ft.

Velocity: Slow to moderate

Hazards: None

Rescue Index: Accessible to accessible but difficult

Source of Additional Information: U.S. Forest Service, Homochitto Ranger District, Gloster, MS; (601) 225-4281.

Access Points	Access Code	River Miles	Shuttle Miles
F–G	1357	3.9	3.6
G–H	1357	22.2	21.5
H–I	1357	21.3	25.2
I	1357		

Access Key:

1	Paved road	7	Clear trail
2	Unpaved road	8	Brush and trees
3	Short carry	9	Launching fee charged
4	Long carry	10	Private property, need permission
5	Easy grade	11	No access, reference only
6	Steep incline		

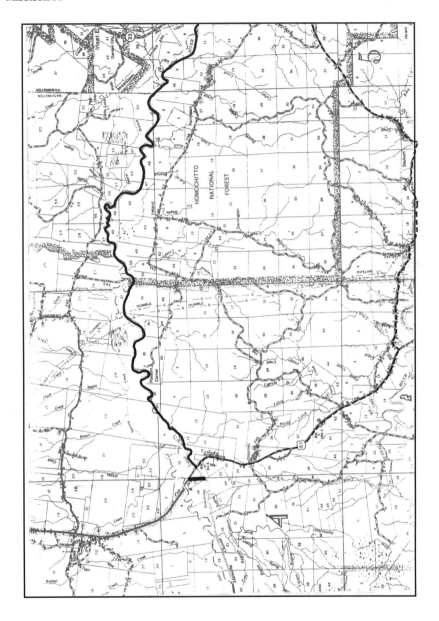

Chickasawhay River

Formed by the confluence of the Chunky River and Okatibee Creek in Clarke County, the Chickasawhay meanders through eastern Mississippi until it joins with the Leaf River to form the Pascagoula River. A variety of scenery from towering bluffs to wide, expansive sandbars makes the river interesting from top to bottom. In its upper reaches, the Chickasawhay passes through, and thus exposes, many different geological formations containing a wide variety of fossils. While there are no gauges, paddling below Enterprise is generally possible in all but drought conditions.

At its beginning in the town of Enterprise, the Chickasawhay is about 60 feet wide with steep clay banks. There is a good put-in (access A) on river left at the new MS 513 bridge. An access road just past the bridge on the east side leads down to a convenient launching area with plenty of parking space. An alternate put-in is approximately 1 mile below MS 513 on river right (west side of river) at a public boat ramp (access B) next to Buckley's Canoe Rental. Besides the concrete boat ramp, the access has a picnic area and space for parking vehicles. Though the river passes through urban areas around Enterprise and Stonewall, the steep banks and vegetation along the river help to isolate it. This float makes a nice half-day introduction to the river. It is a 2-mile paddle from Buckley's Canoe Rental down to the county bridge (access C) in Stonewall where a public boat ramp is located.

The 16-mile section from Stonewall to MS 512 (access C–access D) can be a full day trip but is generally made as a leisurely overnight trip. Occasional sandbars are found, but there are also wooded areas for camping. The forest in this section consists primarily of hardwoods and pines. Look for signs of deer, turkey, and beaver, which are plentiful in this area. Unusual bluffs of clay and limestone attract most of the attention in the upper sections. King's Bluff, a particularly large one of nearly 90 feet, is located about 10 miles downstream of Stonewall on river right. The take-out (access D) is a boat ramp at the MS 512 bridge on the west side of Quitman.

Below Quitman, there is a good day trip of 10 miles down to a county bridge (access F) near DeSoto. Approximately a mile downstream of MS 512, Souinlovey Creek, a major tributary, flows into the Chickasawhay on river right. Steep bluffs of clay and limestone continue in this section. There is an alternate access or emergency take-out at the U.S. 45 bridge (access E) 1 mile south of Quitman. Another scenic bluff worth exploring is Doby's Bluff, 2 miles downstream of U.S. 45 on river right. The take-out at DeSoto (access F) is fairly steep. An alternative is the access on river right at Gappy's Fish Camp, downstream of the county bridge. There is a charge for using the private access.

Another excellent day trip covers the 14 miles of river from DeSoto to MS 510 (access F–access H). Clay and limestone bluffs are around almost every bend. Shoals of gravel and clay outcropings keep paddlers alert at the end of flatwater stretches. Ten miles downstream of DeSoto, another major tributary, Shubuta Creek comes in on river right. A county road crossing (access G) 10.5 miles downstream of DeSoto provides an emergency take-out. The boat ramp (access H) at MS 510 is just east of the town of Shubuta.

From Shubuta, the river meanders another 24 miles to the U.S. 84 bridge (access K) near Waynesboro. This section is a good length for an overnight camping trip. Just over a half mile below Shubuta, another U.S. 45 bridge (access I) is encountered and could be used as an emergency access, though the banks are steep. Below, the section is unpredictable in its scenic quality. The river passes both forest scenes of exceptional beauty then pastureland cleared to its banks. However, there are still wonderful limestone bluffs along the river. Filled with fossils such as sharks' teeth and mollusks (marine snails and clams), the bluffs are an open book sure to be enjoyed by those curious about the earth's natural history. An interesting segment of the river is approximately 3.5 miles above the U.S. 84 bridge. The river has cut a perfectly straight channel through the limestone for nearly a mile. Perhaps following a geologic fault, the river is hemmed in by 30–40 foot high limestone walls crowned with lush ferns. Immediately below, there is an access at a county bridge (access J) just northwest of Waynesboro. However, it is best to continue another 1.5 miles to the boat ramp (access K) at the U.S. 84 bridge 1 mile west of Waynesboro.

Leaving U.S. 84, the Chickasawhay travels 5 miles to MS 63 (access L). This is a very nice section if you only have time for a half-day trip, or it can be combined with the above section to make a lengthier trip. A number of bluffs are encountered on this section also, but they are not as extensive as those in the upper sections. The limestone outcroppings create some fun shoals to negotiate. A boat ramp (access L) at the MS 63 bridge 1 mile south of Waynesboro provides the take-out for the section.

Below Waynesboro, the Chickasawhay flows through an alluvial plain more characteristic of Mississippi rivers. No longer contained by the clay and limestone formations, the river widens as it meets more erodible sandy soils.

Large sandbars are formed in these lower sections along with more deep pools that provide excellent fishing opportunities. The Chickasawhay eventually joins with the Leaf River, forming the Pascagoula River at Merrill.

Section: MS 513 to MS 510

Counties: Clarke (MS)

USGS Quads: Stonewall, Wautubee, Quitman, DeSoto, Shubuta

Suitable for: Cruising, camping

Appropriate for: Families, beginners

Months Runnable: All

Interest Highlights: Scenery, wildlife, geology

Scenery: Pretty in spots to beautiful in spots

Difficulty: Class I

Average Width: 50–80 ft.

Velocity: Slow to moderate

Hazards: Deadfalls

Rescue Index: Accessible to accessible but difficult

Source of Additional Information: Out-N-Under, Meridian, MS; (601) 693-5827. Buckley Canoe Rental, Enterprise, MS; (601) 659-9185. Gappy's Fish Camp, DeSoto, MS; (601) 776-5710.

Access Points	Access Code	River Miles	Shuttle Miles
A–B	1357	1.0	0.9
B–C	1357	2.4	2.4
C–D	1357	16.1	11.6
D–E	1357	4.5	3.1
E–F	1367	5.5	3.4
F–G	1367	10.6	10.4
G–H	1367	3.2	1.9
H	1357		

Access Key:

1	Paved road	7	Clear trail
2	Unpaved road	8	Brush and trees
3	Short carry	9	Launching fee charged
4	Long carry	10	Private property, need permission
5	Easy grade	11	No access, reference only
6	Steep incline		

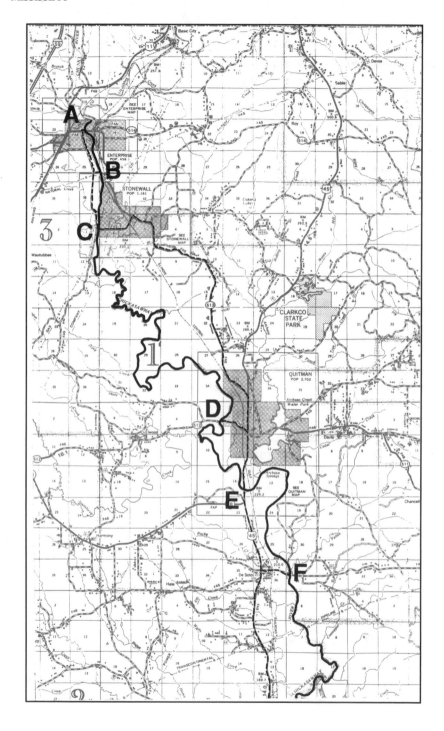

Section: MS 510 to MS 63

Counties: Clarke, Wayne, (MS)

USGS Quads: Shubuta, Waynesboro

Suitable for: Cruising, camping

Appropriate for: Families, beginners

Months Runnable: All

Interest Highlights: Scenery, wildlife, geology

Scenery: Pretty in spots to beautiful in spots

Difficulty: Class I

Average Width: 60–100 ft.

Velocity: Slow to moderate

Hazards: None

Rescue Index: Accessible to accessible but difficult

Source of Additional Information: Out-N-Under, Meridian, MS; (601) 693-5827. Buckley Canoe Rental, Enterprise, MS; (601) 659-9185. Gappy's Fish Camp, DeSoto, MS; (601) 776-5710.

Access Points	Access Code	River Miles	Shuttle Miles
H–I	1357	0.7	1.6
I–J	1367	21.9	13.8
J–K	1367	1.5	2.4
K–L	1357	5.1	4.7
L	1357		

Access Key:

1	Paved road	7	Clear trail
2	Unpaved road	8	Brush and trees
3	Short carry	9	Launching fee charged
4	Long carry	10	Private property, need permission
5	Easy grade	11	No access, reference only
6	Steep incline		

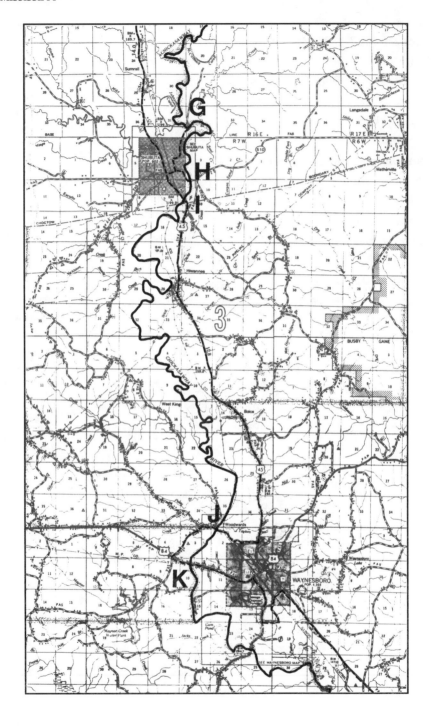

Section: MS 63 to Knobtown

Counties: Wayne, Green (MS)

USGS Quads: Waynesboro, Denham, Buckatunna, Knobtown, Clark

Suitable for: Cruising, camping

Appropriate for: Families, beginners

Months Runnable: All

Interest Highlights: Scenery, wildlife

Scenery: Pretty in spots to pretty

Difficulty: Class I

Average Width: 80–150 ft.

Velocity: Slow

Hazards: None

Rescue Index: Accessible but difficult

Source of Additional Information: Out-N-Under, Meridian, MS; (601) 693-5872. Buckley Canoe Rental, Enterprise, MS; (601) 659-9185. Gappy's Fish Camp, DeSoto, MS; (601) 776-5710.

Access Points	Access Code	River Miles	Shuttle Miles
L–M	1357	13.6	15.1
M–N	1367	14.8	12.0
N–O	1367	5.2	5.2
O	1357		

Access Key:

1	Paved road	7	Clear trail
2	Unpaved road	8	Brush and trees
3	Short carry	9	Launching fee charged
4	Long carry	10	Private property, need permission
5	Easy grade	11	No access, reference only
6	Steep incline		

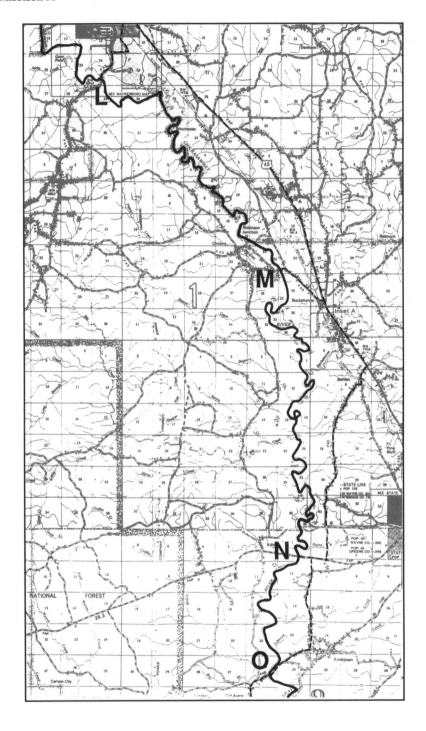

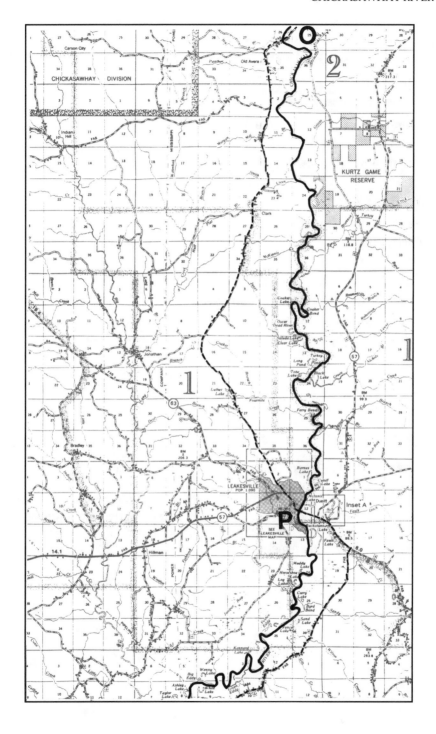

Section: Knobtown to MS 596

Counties: Greene, George (MS)

USGS Quads: Clark, Leakesville, Vernal, Leakesville SW, Merrill

Suitable for: Cruising, camping

Appropriate for: Families, beginners

Months Runnable: All

Interest Highlights: Scenery, wildlife

Scenery: Pretty in spots to pretty

Difficulty: Class I

Average Width: 100–200 ft.

Velocity: Slow

Hazards: None

Rescue Index: Accessible but difficult

Source of Additional Information: None known

Access Points	Access Code	River Miles	Shuttle Miles
O–P	1357	22.1	17.4
P–Q	1357	21.9	17.9
Q–R[1]	1368	5.5	7.4
R[1]	1357		

[1]On the Pascagoula River

Access Key:

1	Paved road	7	Clear trail
2	Unpaved road	8	Brush and trees
3	Short carry	9	Launching fee charged
4	Long carry	10	Private property, need permission
5	Easy grade	11	No access, reference only
6	Steep incline		

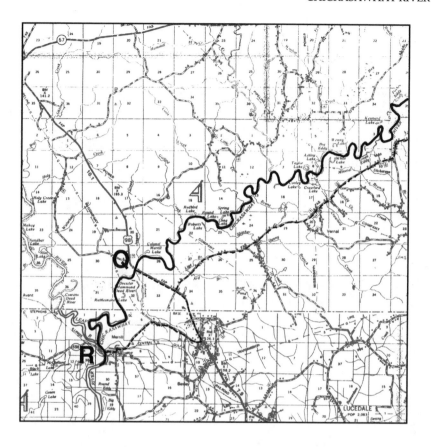

Chunky River

The Chunky River has its headwaters in Newton County and flows through parts of Lauderdale and Clarke counties before joining with Okatibbee Creek to form the Chickasawhay River near Enterprise. Though named a river, the Chunky resembles a creek in size. Its width ranges from 30 to 120 feet. Because of the convenient location of accesses, many fun shoals, and exceptional scenery, including a waterfall, the Chunky offers a popular day trip.

The most upstream put-in is 1.5 miles west of the town of Chunky at the U.S. 80 bridge (access A). Here, there are three bridges, close together, that cross the Chunky River floodplain. The main flow of the Chunky goes under the middle bridge. Access is down a fairly steep highway embankment downstream and on river right of the middle bridge. Parking is limited to the shoulder of the road, but there are more protected areas nearer the town of Chunky. At the put-in, the Chunky is only 30 to 60 feet wide. You are likely to encounter several downed trees in the first mile before the creek widens. For this reason, only boaters experienced in tight maneuvering and in dealing with obstructions should float this section. The stream is fairly shallow but has a steady current. It meanders for about 6.5 miles through the pastures and woods south of the town of Chunky before returning to U.S. 80 east of the town.

A county road crossing (access B) just south of the town of Chunky could be used for an alternate or emergency access. The old iron bridge here deteriorated and has been closed. Though locals may still use the bridge, it is not advised. The take-out on river right is best suited for emergency use only since it is not convenient and has limited parking space. At this point the stream is approximately 75 feet wide and is lined by oaks, cypress, and birch.

Just east of the town of Chunky at the second U.S. 80 bridge crossing the Chunky, there is a good boat launching area (access C) with plenty of parking space. At this point the Chunky is wider and has a clear channel, making this access a more reasonable place to start a Chunky River trip. To get to the put-in, proceed east from the bridge and take the first paved road to the right. Travel one-tenth of a mile and turn right onto a dirt road leading to the concrete boat ramp upstream of the bridge. Here the river flows north of the highway making a 3-mile loop, locally called Seven Mile Bend, and again crosses U.S. 80. A public boat ramp (access D) adjacent to Boyette's Fish Camp is just downstream and river right of the bridge. This is the third U.S. 80 bridge the Chunky passes under. The concrete boat ramp provides an excellent access and there is ample room for parking. Since the shuttle for the put-in and take-out for this section are only a quarter of a mile apart, the segment is a favorite for half-day floats or fishing trips.

Below this last U.S. 80 bridge, the Chunky travels for 9 miles down to Stuckey's bridge, an old iron county bridge (access F). This makes a nice day trip through a mixed hardwood and pine forest. In the fall, oak and hickory trees put on a beautiful display of colors. The Chunky has broadened to almost 120 feet when it reaches an alternate take-out (access E) at Point bridge, a county bridge 2.5 miles downstream of the last U.S. 80 bridge. Access is on county right-of-way along a washed out trail on river right immediately downstream of the bridge. There is limited parking here. Another access on river left (east side) and upstream of the bridge is a short steep pitch down to the river but has more parking space.

A popular day trip begins at Stuckey's bridge (access F) 4 miles upstream of the I-59 bridge. Stuckey's bridge is closed for safety reasons, but access to the river there is still possible. The best launching spot is on river right. This 10- to 11-mile river trip that ends on the Chickasawhay River has several shoals to keep the paddler alert. The historic Dunn's Falls area is also in this section, approximately 5.5 miles below Stuckey's Bridge.

In the mid-1800s, John Dunn built a clothing factory at this site. A waterfall of nearly 40 feet that provided the power for the mill flows into the river from a diverted tributary. The state established a park here and built a replica of the old mill just above the falls. Below Dunn's Falls, the Chunky's banks become weathered clay walls, home to maidenhair fern and other water-loving plants that enjoy the continuous groundwater seeps.

Three miles downstream of Dunn's Falls is the U.S. 11 bridge (access G) 1 mile north of Enterprise. This is a very steep and difficult take-out. There is a better take-out 1.5 miles downstream to the new MS 513 bridge on the Chickasawhay River. Or keep going to the public boat ramp at Buckley's Canoe Rental, which is 2.5 miles below the U.S. 11 bridge on river right. Except for the area around Dunn's Falls, the Chunky flows through private land. Be especially mindful of posted property along the river if you plan to camp overnight.

One mile downstream of U.S. 11, the Chickasawhay River is born at the confluence of the Chunky River and Okatibbee Creek. The Chunky's smaller sister stream, Okatibbee Creek, is also runnable by canoe. A good day trip with several fun shoals can be made on lower Okatibbee Creek from a county bridge just east of U.S. 11 near Basic City down to the junction with the Chunky. As with the lower section of the Chunky, the take-out is on the Chickasawhay River on river left at the new MS 513 bridge, or 1 mile farther at the public boat ramp at Buckley's Canoe Rental on river right. Boaters who wish to extend a Chunky River trip into the Chickasawhay should consult the preceding description of the Chickasawhay.

Section: U.S. 80 near Hickory to MS 513

Counties: Newton, Lauderdale, Clarke (MS)

USGS Quads: Chunky, Meehan, Stonewall

Suitable for: Cruising, camping

Appropriate for: Families, beginners

Months Runnable: All except during dry spells

Interest Highlights: Scenery, wildlife, historical locations

Scenery: Pretty in spots to beautiful in spots

Difficulty: Class I

Average Width: 40–80 ft.

Velocity: Slow to moderate

Hazards: Deadfalls

Rescue Index: Accessible to accessible but difficult

Source of Additional Information: Out-N-Under, Meridian, MS'(601) 693-5827. Buckley Canoe Rental, Enterprise, MS; (601) 659-9185. Dunn's Falls Water Park, Enterprise, MS; (601) 655-8550.

Access Points	Access Code	River Miles	Shuttle Miles
A–B	1367	5.3	3.2
B–C	2457	1.2	1.0
C–D	2357	2.7	0.8
D–E	1357	2.6	2.7
E–F	1367	5.8	7.4
F–G	2357	8.5	7.3
G–A[1]	1467	1.3	1.8
A[1]	1357		

[1]On the Chickasawhay River

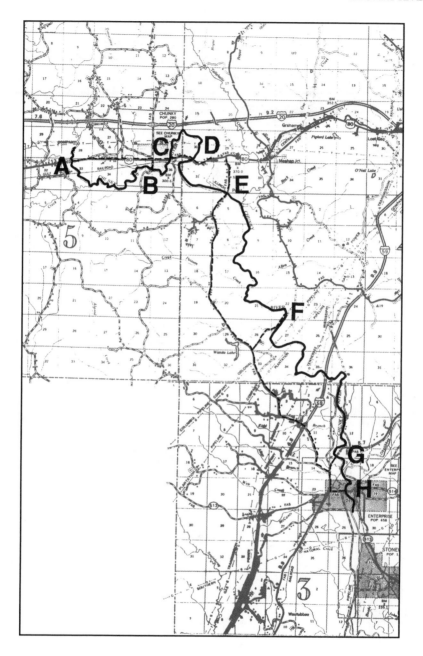

Access Key:

1	Paved road	7	Clear trail
2	Unpaved road	8	Brush and trees
3	Short carry	9	Launching fee charged
4	Long carry	10	Private property, need permission
5	Easy grade	11	No access, reference only
6	Steep incline		

Part Three

ALABAMA

Escatawpa River

The Escatawpa River, the most southwesterly of Alabama waterways, is shared with Mississippi. It is a river of two faces. The Alabama portion is considered a prime example of a Southern "blackwater" stream, being relatively shallow and swift-running with water the color of strongly brewed tea. The banks are heavily forested, while at the waters' edge, beachlike sandbars abound. There is little public access or encroachment and it has been considered for designation as a Wild and Scenic River. On the contrary, in Mississippi, in the last 123 miles before its confluence with the Pascagoula River, it is so heavily industrialized that in a recent best-selling novel a character remarked on the ugliness and ruin of this once beautiful stream!

The Escatawpa "makes up" in eastern Washington County within 2 miles of the Mississippi-Alabama state line. It is the recipient of the runoff from dozens of tributary streams that drain this area between the Chickasawhay River in Mississippi and the Tombigbee River in Alabama and is over 90 miles long. The first good access is off C.R. 96 west of Citronelle in northern Mobile County. There is a possible access 11 miles upstream at Deer Park, but it is on private property and the stream itself is not always canoeable from that point.

From the C.R. 96 access, the river continues for 22 miles in Alabama, flowing into Mississippi just below the U.S. 98 access. It continues for another 45 miles until its confluence with the Pascagoula River. This 22-mile section lends itself to a lazy float trip with lots of stops to examine the tracks on the sandbars, look for interesting driftwood, or just relax. Campsites are abundant and firewood is plentiful.

The woods along the banks consist of second generation hardwoods, cypresses, and some stands of pine. Wax myrtle line the edges of the stream, and sweetgum and poplar trees make a spectacular show of color in the fall. There is very little human encroachment other than rural bridges and a couple of gas pipelines that cross the riverbed. The entire area is widely hunted for deer and wild turkey, and signs of those familiar Southern natives—racoon, opossum, and armadillo—are evident. Although few wading birds are observed, songbirds are prolific, as are birds of prey such as hawks and owls. Overall, the Escatawpa River offers a remote and private atmosphere on an easily canoeable stream.

The 3-mile section from C.R. 96 to Lotts Road (access A–access B) is moderately difficult. From Citronelle, Alabama, travel west on C.R. 96 for about 9 miles to the bridge across the Escatawpa. Access is on the northwest side of the bridge.

At this access point, the river is about 100 feet wide and very shallow with small sandbars on both sides. The banks behind the sandbars are 6 to 10 feet high and heavily wooded. Just before reaching Lotts Bridge, there are 15- to 20-foot-tall sand and clay bluffs on river right. The current is lively through this section, and there are a number of downed trees in the stream creating obstacles. This results in the need for moderate maneuvering skills on the part of the canoeist.

The next 7 miles, from Lotts Road to C.R. 88 (access B–access C), is an easy paddle. From Citronelle, travel west on C.R. 96 for about 9 miles to the bridge across the Escatawpa. Cross the bridge and continue for 1 mile to the junction of Lotts Road on the left. Turn left (south), and travel for 3 miles to the bridge across the Escatawpa. Access is from a small "woods road" on the left (north) just before reaching the bridge.

This access at Lotts Road is also called the "Granny Hole" by local people and is used as a starting point for most canoe trips on the river. From here to C.R. 88, the stream continues to alternate between very wide sections with shallow water and numerous sandbars and narrower stretches with high banks. Some of these banks are an interesting orange and deep red color with water draining from under the sand ledges into the river. When this occurs, the river takes on a more golden hue. Landmarks on this section include a gas line crossing the river about 1 mile downstream from Lotts bridge and the confluence of Puppy Creek on river left just above the C.R. 88 bridge. Puppy Creek is also a canoeable stream whose access is reached from S.R. 217.

From C.R. 88 to U.S. 98 (access C–access D) is an easy 12-mile section. From Lotts Road (access B) cross the river and travel east about one mile to the intersection with C.R. 21. Turn right (south) and continue for approximately five miles until it deadends at C.R. 88 on the Escatawpa River. The access is on the southeast side of the bridge. This access can also be reached by traveling northwest on C.R. 88 from the community of Georgetown.

The river continues its characteristic widening and narrowing with huge white sandbars in the curves. A power line crosses the stream about 1.5 miles below C.R. 88 and a gas line crosses under the river bed about 4 miles downstream from this access. Brushy Creek, another canoeable tributary, enters from river right about 2 miles upstream of the U.S. 98 bridge.

To reach the take-out from Mobile, travel west on U.S. 98 for about 27 miles to the Escatawpa River. Access is on the northeast side of the bridge.

Section: C.R. 96 to U.S. 98

Counties: Mobile (AL)

USGS Quads: Deer Park, Wilmer

Suitable for: Cruising, camping

Appropriate for: Families, beginners, intermediates

Months Runnable: All

Interest Highlights: Scenery, wildlife, remoteness

Scenery: Superb

Difficulty: Class I

Average Width: 60-100 ft.

Velocity: Slow to moderate

Hazards: Deadfalls

Rescue Index: Accessible to accessible but difficult

Source of Additional Information: Bob Andrews, Sunshine Canoes, 5460 Old Shell Road, Mobile, AL 36608; (205) 344-8664.

Access Points	Access Code	River Miles	Shuttle Miles
A-B	1367	3.0	4.0
B-C	2357	7.0	7.5
C-D	2357	12.0	22.0
D	1357		

Access Key:

1	Paved road	7	Clear trail
2	Unpaved road	8	Brush and trees
3	Short carry	9	Launching fee charged
4	Long carry	10	Private property, need permission
5	Easy grade	11	No access, reference only
6	Steep incline		

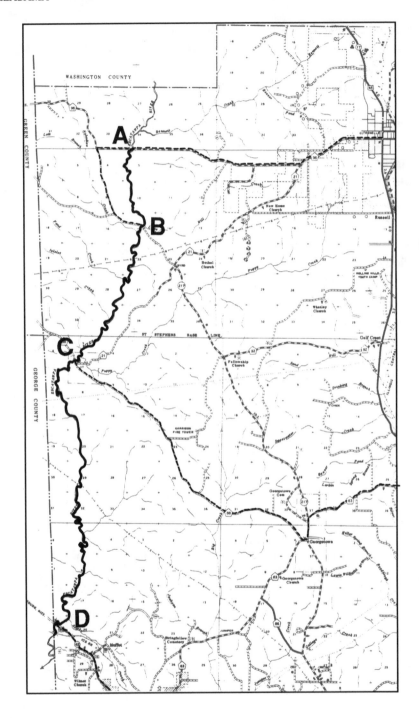

Little River

This remote stream serves as the county line between Baldwin and Monroe counties. Although it runs through the Little River State Park, it is a tiny, swampy creek at that point and is not canoeable. At its other end, Little River flows into the mighty Alabama River near Dixie Landing. Above its confluence with the Alabama, it becomes swampy again and fingers out into numerous channels. As a result, the middle section, from Monroe C.R. 1 to S.R. 59 is the portion most preferred by canoeists.

This middle section is a stream of surprising beauty. A typical blackwater river, it is very clear, shallow, and fast running. It is sharply curving with a multitude of large gravel bars and many downed trees in the waterway. This combination of fast current and obstacles results in the need for maneuvering skills on the part of the canoeist.

The banks are heavily forested, and there is little encroachment or public access. Forestation includes pine, cedar, and upland hardwoods. The gravel bars are covered with interesting rocks and with the remains of very large trees that attest to the power of this stream when it is flooded. There are also relics of two gravel quarries in the lower section, but they are no longer active, and frequent flooding has smoothed out the scars of these man-made disturbances.

The 8-mile section from Monroe C.R. 1 to S.R. 59 (access A–access B) is a moderately difficult paddle through superb scenery. From Bay Minette, travel north on S.R. 59 for about 36 miles to the bridge across Little River. (This will be the take-out point.) Cross the bridge and continue for 1.5 miles to the intersection with C.R. 2. Turn right on C.R. 2 and travel for about 6 miles to the first paved road to the right: C.R. 1. Turn right on C.R. 1 and continue for 2 miles to the bridge across Little River. Access is on the southwest side of the bridge.

At this access, the stream is 30 to 40 feet wide with generous white gravel bars and sandbars on both sides. Less than 1 mile downstream is a small rapid with a drop of 1 to 2 feet. For the first 4 miles, the combination of lively current, small sandstone rapids, and downed trees in the water leads to a fast and technical trip. At about the halfway point, a power line crosses the river. Below the power line the stream gradually narrows, becomes deeper, and there are higher banks and fewer sandbars.

To reach the take-out, return to the bridge at S.R. 59.

Section: Monroe C.R. 1 to S.R. 59

Counties: Baldwin, Monroe (AL)

USGS Quads: Uriah West, Chrysler

Suitable for: Cruising, camping

Appropriate for: Intermediates

Months Runnable: All

Interest Highlights: Scenery, wildlife, remoteness

Scenery: Excellent to superb

Difficulty: Class I–II

Average Width: 30–40 ft.

Velocity: Moderate to fast

Hazards: Downed trees, sharp turns

Rescue Index: Accessible but difficult

Source of Additional Information: Bob Andrews, Sunshine Canoes, 5460 Old Shell Road, Mobile, AL 36608; (205) 344-8664.

Access Points	Access Code	River Miles	Shuttle Miles
A–B	1357	8.0	10.0
B	1357		

Access Key:

1	Paved road	7	Clear trail
2	Unpaved road	8	Brush and trees
3	Short carry	9	Launching fee charged
4	Long carry	10	Private property, need permission
5	Easy grade	11	No access, reference only
6	Steep incline		

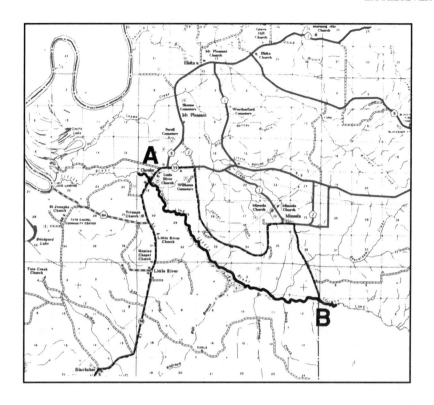

Styx River

The Styx River is named for the river in Greek mythology over which Charon, the ferryman, ferried the souls of the dead. The old bridge on U.S. 90 had a sign that read, "River Styx, Charon retired." The new bridge doesn't even give the name of the river! Despite being overlooked by the road department, the Styx is a very beautiful canoeing stream that is readily accessible for travelers on U.S. 90 or I-10. It is a classic blackwater stream, meaning that the water is not black at all, but a range of colors from pale gold to cola, depending on the degree of tannin contained in the runoff from surrounding swamps. It is a tributary of the Perdido River, which is the state line dividing Alabama and Florida. At the point where these two streams combine, they are both wide, frequented by large boats, and affected by the tide from nearby Perdido Bay.

Some adventurous paddlers start canoeing on the Styx at Truck Trail 17 off S.R. 112 and bushwack their way for 6 miles down to Baldwin C.R. 64. This upper access is narrow and overgrown and may have a number of pullovers depending on the water level. It definitely should not be attempted during periods of dry weather. It is also possible to begin a Styx River trip on Hollinger Creek by paddling 4 miles down to the confluence just above C.R. 64. Most canoeists prefer to start their trip at C.R. 68.

C.R. 68 to C.R. 64 (access A–access B) is a short 2-mile stretch of easy paddling. From Loxley, Alabama, travel east and north on C.R. 68 for just over 8 miles to the bridge across the Styx River. This route will lead east from Loxley, then north over I-10, then east and north again to the river. Access is on the northwest side of the bridge. Do not use the access on the southwest side; it is on private property.

At this access, the Styx is 40 to 60 feet wide and is shallow and clear with white sandbars on both sides. Forestation is scanty with only a thin corridor of wax myrtle and second growth hardwood right at the water's edge. About 10 yards downstream is a small sandstone rapid, a drop of 2 to 3 feet over a distance of 15 to 20 feet. It is best run on the far left or can be portaged on the right. An access road leads from C.R. 68 to this point, and some canoeists choose to start their trip below the rapid. Between this point and the confluence of Hollinger Creek there are several small islands. They have white sandbars and young cypress trees and make attractive campsites.

C.R. 64 to C.R. 87 (access B–access C) is another easy 5-mile section. From Loxley, travel east and north on C.R. 64 for about 10 miles to the bridge across the Styx River. This route will lead east from Loxley, north over I-10, then east and north to the river. Access is on the southeast side of the bridge.

The stream continues to be clear and shallow with a good current. The band of vegetation on the banks is narrow with some stretches of flat, treeless areas bordering the river. There are numerous "woods roads" providing access to the stream, and some cottages and mobile homes are scattered along the banks. In this section, the river flows so near I-10 that one is never out of hearing range of rather heavy traffic sounds. The beautiful water and nice sandbars make this a pleasant section for swimming and picnicking, and it is an easy paddle for novice canoeists.

The 12-mile section of river from C.R. 87 to U.S. 90 (access C–access D) flows through Baldwin (AL) and Escambia (FL) counties. From Loxley, travel south and east on U.S. 90 for about 13 miles to the intersection with C.R. 87. Turn left (north on C.R. 87) and continue for about 6 miles to the bridge across the Styx River. Access is on the northeast side of the bridge.

Below C.R. 87, the river maintains its shallow, clear character with white sandbars for the first few miles. It becomes increasingly wide and deep as it nears its confluence with the Perdido River, and the length of this section makes it somewhat tedious for a one-day trip. It continues to parallel I-10 until it flows under this divided highway 3.5 miles downstream from the put-in at C.R. 87. About 3 miles north of U.S. 90 it becomes very wide and is used by large motorboats.

To reach the take-out, from Loxley travel south and east on U.S. 90 for about 23 miles to the bridge across the Styx River. Access is on the west side of the bridge, on either side of the road, and is very poor on both sides since it is steep and eroded.

It is about 1 mile from U.S. 90 to the confluence of the Styx River with the Perdido River. Just below the confluence is an access off a graded road that turns east off C.R. 91. The Perdido River is as wide as a small lake at that point and is frequented by very large boats. It is also affected by tides from Perdido Bay.

Section: Baldwin C.R. 68 to U.S. 90

Counties: Baldwin (AL), Escambia (FL)

USGS Quads: Steelwood Lake, Gateswood, Elsanor, Seminole

Suitable for: Cruising, camping

Appropriate for: Families, beginners

Months Runnable: All

Interest Highlights: Scenery, wildlife

Scenery: Good

Difficulty: Class I

Average Width: 40–60 ft.

Velocity: Slow to moderate

Hazards: Deadfalls; powerboat traffic

Rescue Index: Accessible

Source of Additional Information: Bob Andrews, Sunshine Canoes, 5460 Old Shell Road, Mobile, AL 36608; (205) 344-8664.

Access Points	Access Code	River Miles	Shuttle Miles
A–B	1357	2	9
B–C	1357	5	6
C–D	1357	12	14
D	1468		

Access Key:
1 Paved road
2 Unpaved road
3 Short carry
4 Long carry
5 Easy grade
6 Steep incline
7 Clear trail
8 Brush and trees
9 Launching fee charged
10 Private property, need permission
11 No access, reference only

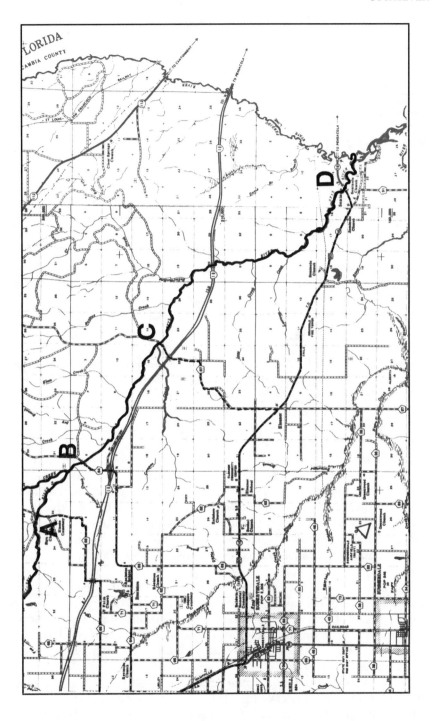

Perdido River

The Perdido River originates in south Alabama with the confluence of Dyas Creek and Perdido Creek. It serves as the state line separating Alabama and Florida, and is about 15 miles from Pensacola. The Spanish name, which means *lost*, probably resulted from the hidden nature of Perdido Bay which is formed by the Perdido River before it reaches the Gulf of Mexico.

Except for the upper section near Dyas Creek, a very strenuous trip, the Perdido is considered an easy and relaxing canoeing river. It is located in a remote area and runs through deep forests with banks lined with juniper and cypress trees as well as other upland hardwoods. The stream alternates between straight sections with modest banks 3 to 5 feet high to long curves with generously-sized gravel and sandbars on the insides of almost every bend.

There are a number of small streams that drain into the Perdido; its major tributary is the Styx River that flows in from Alabama. The Alabama side of the river is primarily the property of private hunting clubs. On the Florida side, La Floresta Perdido Wildlife Management Area, a cooperative public hunting area managed by the Florida Game and Fresh Water Fish Commission, runs for many miles. Guns and dogs should not be taken on the river and the canoe camper should be careful to observe posted and no trespassing signs.

Because of the limited access and protected wildlife areas, the forests along the Perdido are heavily populated with deer and turkey as well as wild hogs and bears. Local people also report an occasional sighting of a Florida panther along with the usual raccoons, opossums, and beavers. The observant canoeist may also see otters and alligators and anglers may catch bream and catfish.

In periods of normal rainfall, the Perdido is a shallow river and the water will vary from being very clear to a tannish yellow color in areas where there is more siltation. There is no industrial development of any kind on its banks and very little agricultural activity. There are a number of excellent swimming holes as well as ample white sandbars for sunning and picnicking.

The upper part of the Perdido River, from Dyas Creek to the section called Three Runs is very remote and inaccessible. It is also almost unnavigable because of the many logjams and pullovers that occur. These logjams are caused by the somewhat unusual characteristics of the red cedar tree which is abundant in this area. These trees have a multitude of closely spaced branches that break off to a stiletto sharpness. Furthermore, the juniper tree is easily blown over because of its shallow but widespread root system; both tree branches and tree roots become buried in the sandy banks on either side of the river. Since the red cedar is noted for its durability, once down it seems to stay there forever.

Below U.S. 90, the Perdido becomes tidal and begins to finger off into sloughs and bayous. It is frequented by large motorboats as well. Perdido Bay is a large body of water that is subject to waves and high winds and is not advisable for canoeing. The recommended canoe trail is from Three Runs to U.S. 90, a distance of about 34 miles.

The 5-mile section from Jackson Springs Road to Old Water Ferry Landing (access A–access B) is an easy paddle. From Pensacola, travel north on S.R. 29 to the junction with S.R. 182. Turn left (west) on S.T. 182 and proceed to S.R. 99. Turn right (north) on S.R. 99 and continue to the junction with S.R. 97A. Turn left (west) and continue for 3 miles until the paved road makes an abrupt turn to the right (north). Turn right, and travel for 1.5 miles to the first intersection with a graded road. Turn left (west) on this road and continue to the river.

This is the most northern point recommended for a canoe trip on the Perdido. The river is 50 feet wide with heavily forested banks 6 to 8 feet high. The water tends to be shallow and there may be some obstructions, but it is an easy section and maneuvering is not difficult. There are large gravel bars on the insides of most of the curves. The forests on either side are hunting preserves, and it is a remote area with no public access. Schoolhouse Branch enters from the east about midway between Three Runs and Old Water Ferry Landing.

The next section is 10 miles long, from Old Water Ferry Landing to Barrineau Park (access B–access C). It is also easy to maneuver. Follow the directions for section A–B to the point where S.R. 97A is reached. Turn left (west) on S.R. 97A and travel for 3 miles until the point where the paved road makes an abrupt turn to the right. Turn left (south) instead, onto a graded road. Follow this graded road to the river, a distance of about 2 miles.

Greatly similar to section A–B, the river continues to be remote, and varies between straight sections with clearly defined banks to gentle curves. Several creeks including West Fork of Boggy Creek and McDavid Creek flow in from the east and the river becomes wider. The hunting preserves continue on both sides and there are frequent sandbars and gravel banks.

For paddlers, the 9 miles from Barrineau Park to Muscogee Landing (access C–access D) is a simple trip. Follow the directions for section A–B up to the point where S.R. 182 crosses S.R. 99. Turn left (south) on S.R. 99 and continue to the junction with S.R. 97. Turn right (west) onto the graded road and travel one-quarter mile to the bridge across the river. Access is on the northeast side of the bridge.

The Perdido retains its shallow, winding characteristics with sandbars on the insides of turns alternating straight sections with deeper water. There is more frequent access to the river from the east side and this is a popular section for canoeing and fishing. There are a number of places where the

---

Section: Jackson Springs Road to Barrineau Park

Counties: Escambia (FL)

USGS Quads:

Suitable for: Cruising, camping

Appropriate for: Families, beginners, intermediates

Months Runnable: All, except in very dry weather

Interest Highlights: Scenery, wildlife, remoteness

Scenery: Superb

Difficulty: Class I

Average Width: 25–50 ft.

Velocity: Slow to moderate

Hazards: Deadfalls

Rescue Index: Accessible but difficult

Source of Additional Information: Adventures Unlimited/Perdido; (904) 968-5529. West Florida Canoe Club: (904) 587-2211

Access Points	Access Code	River Miles	Shuttle Miles
A–B	2357	5	5.5
B–C	2357	10	12

Access Key:
1 Paved road
2 Unpaved road
3 Short carry
4 Long carry
5 Easy grade
6 Steep incline
7 Clear trail
8 Brush and trees
9 Launching fee charged
10 Private property, need permission
11 No access, reference only

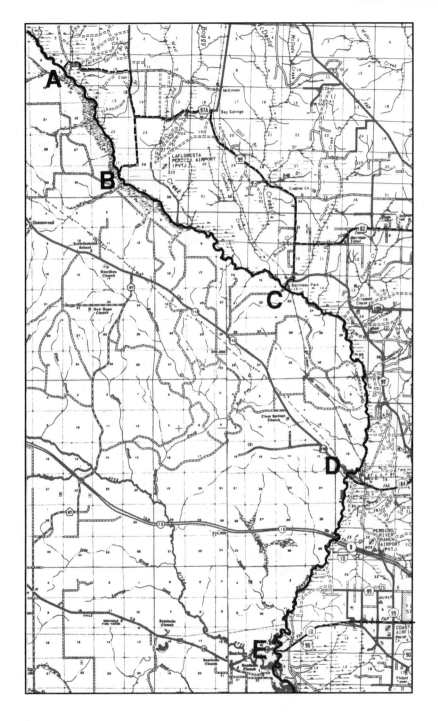

presence of old pilings in the river indicates the location of former bridges. Just before reaching Muscogee Landing, there is an island in the river and a series of closely spaced pilings. The river narrows at this point and runs swiftly through the pilings giving a touch of excitement to the run.

The 10-mile section from Muscogee Landing to U.S. 90 (access D–access E) is an easy to moderate run. From Cantonment, travel west on S.R. 184 to the concrete bridge across the Perdido River. Access is on the northeast side of the bridge.

There is a very large sandbar on the north side of the river at Muscogee Landing (S.R. 184) which is a popular swimming and sunbathing area for local people. This is the last of the campsite-sized sandbars, as the river becomes deeper and wider with either clearly defined banks, or swampy areas on either side. There are some sites that could provide space for two or three tents, but they are scattered along this 10-mile section.

It is just over 2 miles from Muscogee to I-10. Just below the south lane of the interstate is a drop where water rushes through a group of old stumps and pilings. If you have moderate maneuvering skills, stay to the middle right and follow the current. If you are unsure, scout from the left side and carry around if you choose.

An exception to the generally wider and deeper nature of the river occurs about one half mile below the interstate highway. There is often a formidable logjam there as the river narrows and flows swiftly through the more confined area. An island divides the river just below this point and it is possible to paddle on either side. The island appears to have been used for camping.

Below the island, the river becomes much wider, the obstructions disappear, and the current slows considerably. Motorboat traffic increases with the advent of the deeper water and lack of obstructions. Hardwood forests line the banks, and some swampy areas and small sloughs make an appearance.

To reach the take-out via road vehicle from Pensacola, travel due west on U.S. 90 for about 15 miles. There is no public access to the river from the bridge on U.S. 90, but there is a privately owned boat launch on the northeast side of the bridge. There is a fee for launching.

From U.S. 90 to Perdido Bay, the river continues to become wider, tidal, and subject to wind. It is 8 miles to Hurst Landing, the last public access before reaching Perdido Bay.

Section: Barrineau Park to U.S. 90

Counties: Escambia (FL)

USGS Quads:

Suitable for: Cruising, camping

Appropriate for: Families, beginners, intermediates

Months Runnable: All

Interest Highlights: Scenery, wildlife

Scenery: Excellent

Difficulty: Class I

Average Width: 40–60 ft.

Velocity: Slow to moderate

Hazards: Deadfalls, motorboats

Rescue Index: Accessible

Source of Additional Information: Adventures Unlimited/Perdido; (904) 968-529. West Florida Canoe Club (904) 587-2211.

Access Points	Access Code	River Miles	Shuttle Miles
C–D	2357	9	10
D–E	1357	10	10
E	1469		

Access Key:

1	Paved road	7	Clear trail
2	Unpaved road	8	Brush and trees
3	Short carry	9	Launching fee charged
4	Long carry	10	Private property, need permission
5	Easy grade	11	No access, reference only
6	Steep incline		

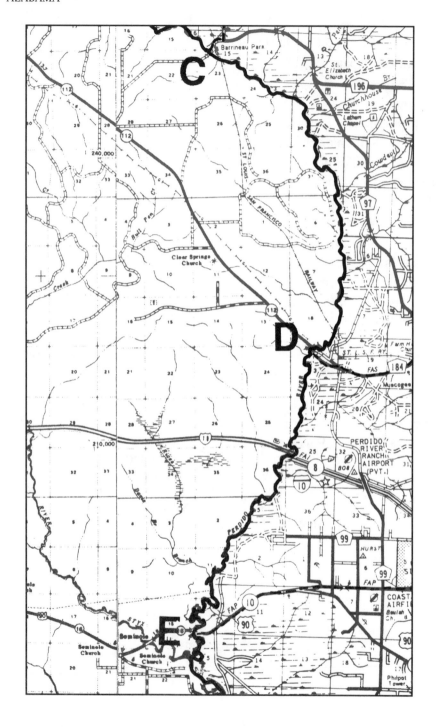

Big Escambia Creek

Big Escambia Creek flows for over 30 miles from Monroe County into Conecuh County, and through Escambia County, Alabama, before joining the Conecuh River in Escambia County, Florida. It has hundreds of tributary creeks and streamlets and a gradient of up to 5 feet per mile. It is a very fine example of a Southern blackwater stream, being fast and clear with beautiful white sand and gravel bars. The banks are heavily wooded with pine, cypress, small hardwoods, wax myrtle, and Atlantic white cedar. There is little encroachment except for the marring of the landscape by gravel mines. Some of these are still active, while others have been almost obliterated by flooding. The large number of sand-gravel bars provide an abundance of scenic campsites.

From Gressett bridge to Escambia C.R. 27 (Sardine bridge) (access A– access B) is a moderately difficult 9-mile section. From Flomaton, Alabama, travel north on S.R. 113 for about 15 miles until it passes over I-65. Continue for 1.5 miles to a graded road that turns left (west). Turn left and travel for about 2 miles to Gressett bridge. The access is on the southwest side of the bridge via a large gravel bar.

At Gressett bridge, Big Escambia Creek is 30 to 40 feet wide, shallow, and has a gravel bottom and a good current. The banks are from 3 to 6 feet high and heavily wooded. There are a multitude of large white sand-gravel bars appropriate for picnicking or camping, and the water is almost clear with a slight tannin stain. The gradient in this section is a little more than 3 feet per mile, resulting in a steadily flowing current. The stream does twist and turn throughout these 9 miles, and there are numerous obstructions such as downed trees in the streambed. Combined with the current and the frequent gravel bars, this results in moderately technical canoeing.

This is a very pretty section of river, quite remote and pleasant to paddle. Just before reaching the Sardine bridge at C.R. 27, there is a small shoal with a drop of 8 to 10 inches. From that point, the water cascades for another mile with continuous sets of small shoals and mini-rapids.

The next section, the 12 miles from C.R. 27 (Sardine bridge) to U.S. 31 at Flomaton (access B–access C) is an easy paddle with excellent scenery. From Flomaton, travel north on C.R. 27 and S.R. 113 for about 10 miles to Stanley Crossroads. At that point, C.R. 27 separates from S.R. 113 and veers to the west. Follow C.R. 27 for less than 2 miles to the bridge across Big Escambia Creek.

For the first mile below the Sardine bridge, the creek is flowing very fast over a series of small shoals and flat rock ledges. In the second mile, a lovely canopied stream, Sizemore Creek, flows in from the west and just below this confluence is a chute of cascading water.

At another point, the remains of a large gravel-mining operation have formed a huge gravel-sand bar on the west bank, and the stream has cut a channel to the east, making an island. The banks vary from these large bars to narrower spots where there are beautiful rock ledges. Except for the marring of the landscape by the gravel mines, this is a very scenic section. It is easy to paddle, has ample camping and picnic spots, and the stream is shallow and clear.

The take-out is on U.S. 31 at Flomaton. Access is on the northwest side of the bridge.

Section: Gressett bridge to U.S. 31 at Flomaton

Counties: Escambia (AL)

USGS Quads: Barnett Crossroads, Flomaton (AL)

Suitable for: Cruising, camping

Appropriate for: Families, beginners, intermediates

Months Runnable: All

Interest Highlights: Scenery, wildlife

Scenery: Beautiful to very pretty

Difficulty: Class I, II

Average Width: 30–40 ft.

Velocity: Moderate

Hazards: Deadfalls

Rescue Index: Accessible

Source of Additional Information: West Florida Canoe Club (904(587-2211

Access Points	Access Code	River Miles	Shuttle Miles
A–B	2357	9.0	10.0
B–C	1357	12.0	13.0
C	1357		

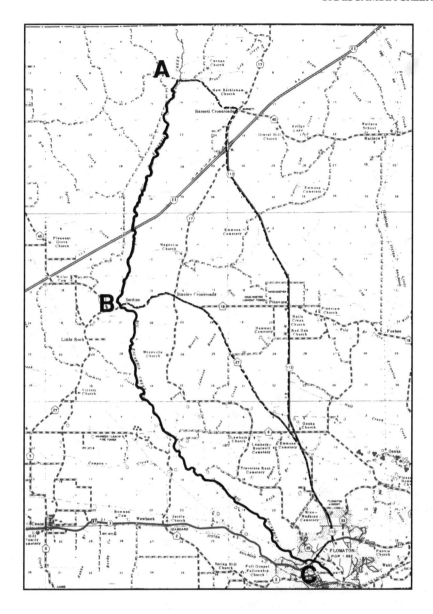

Access Key:

1	Paved road	7	Clear trail
2	Unpaved road	8	Brush and trees
3	Short carry	9	Launching fee charged
4	Long carry	10	Private property, need permission
5	Easy grade	11	No access, reference only
6	Steep incline		

Murder Creek

Murder Creek marks the beginning, traveling from west to east, of the Alabama streams that are not totally blackwater in nature. While it still has some sections with clear water and white sandbars, it also has deep banks and limerock ledges. It begins in Conecuh County near Evergreen and flows for nearly 30 miles to its confluence with the Conecuh River just north of East Brewton. Its grisly name is the result of an incident that occurred in 1788. A Colonel Kirkland and his party of travelers were murdered on the banks of this creek near the settlement of Kirkland. Of the three murderers, only one was caught; but he was hanged—on the banks of Murder Creek.

This stream has a drop and pool nature with frequent rocky shoals. The gradient can be up to 5 feet per mile, and there are long stretches of cascading water. The banks are heavily wooded with second-growth hardwoods, such as river birch, sycamore, and some scattered cypress. Further down there are yellow clay bluffs and large sandbars. A distinctive characteristic of the creek is the brightly colored orange, purple, and red colorations on the banks. This is a result of the mineral content of the water that seeps down the banks, but its bloodlike appearance lends credulity to the name, Murder Creek!

From a bridge near Castleberry to a bridge near Kirkland (access A–access B) is a moderately difficult 9-mile section that flows through Conecuh and Escambia counties. From Brewton, travel north on S.R. #3 / U.S. 31, for about 14 miles to Castleberry. In Castleberry, at the intersection of S.R. 3/U.S. 31 and C.R. 6, turn right (east) on C.R. 6. Continue across the railroad tracks and turn right (south). Continue on this unmarked road for about 1 mile, bear left (east) and continue for less than 1 mile to the creek. Access is on the southwest side of the bridge.

At this access, Murder Creek is about 50 feet wide with banks from 6 to 8 feet high. The banks are heavily wooded, and the stream is shallow and sandy-colored with a sand and gravel bottom. It has a drop and pool nature with frequent rocky shoals that, combined with a nice gradient, result in long stretches of cascading water. Oxbows in the streambed create sections that are narrow, swift, and strewn with fallen logs and debris. In the bends of the creek, there are frequently nice sand and gravel bars that are suitable for picnicking or camping.

One mile above the bridge, at Kirkland, a limerock ledge results in a drop of 18 inches to 2 feet with a small rocky island in midstream. Scouting can be done from this island, and the drop can usually be run from either side. Just below this small rapid there is a large sandbar on river right that is suitable for camping.

From a bridge near Kirkland to S.R. 41 at Brewton (access B–access C) is an easy 8-mile paddle through excellent scenery in Escambia County. From Brewton, travel north on S.R. 3/U.S. 31 for about 6 miles to the junction of C.R. 7. Turn right (east) on C.R. 7 and continue for about 2 miles to the crossroads of a graded road. Turn left (east), cross the railroad tracks, and continue one-fourth mile to the bridge. Access is on the southwest side of the bridge down a rough trail.

A large sandbar across the stream from the access at the Kirkland bridge is suitable for camping. Vehicles can be driven into that area as well. For the first mile below this access, there is an abundance of large sandbars. In the second mile, the banks become higher with yellow clay bluffs of up to 50 feet tall on the east side of the river. The confluence of a small creek from the east side marks the beginning of a section of stream that has clay walls, 6 to 8 feet high on both sides. These clay walls are in striking colors of yellow, red, and purple and are very beautiful, making this a most scenic section to paddle.

The drop and pool characteristics of the stream continue through this section with large sand and gravel bars on most of the bends. About 4 miles north of the take-out, Cedar Creek enters from the east. Murder Creek becomes wider below this point and continues to be 60 to 70 feet wide, deeper, and with less current to the end of this run.

The take-out is at the S.R. 41 bridge in the city of Brewton.

Section: Bridge near Castleberry to S.R. 41 at Brewton

Counties: Conecuh, Escambia (AL)

USGS Quads: Castleberry, Brewton North, Brewton South

Suitable for: Cruising, camping

Appropriate for: Beginners, intermediates

Months Runnable: All

Interest Highlights: Scenery, wildlife, geology, historical

Scenery: Beautiful to very pretty

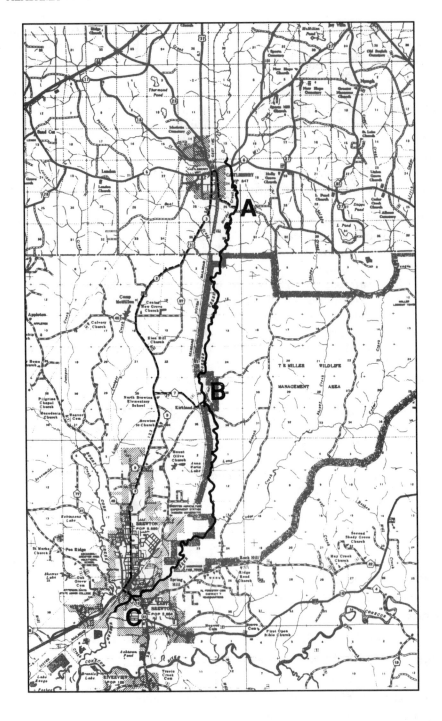

Difficulty: Class I, II

Average Width: 50–60 ft.

Velocity: Moderate

Hazards: Deadfalls

Rescue Index: Accessible

Source of Additional Information: West Florida Canoe Club (904)587-2211

Access Points	Access Code	River Miles	Shuttle Miles
A–B	2357	9.0	13.0
B–C	2357	8.0	7.0
C	1357		

Access Key:

1	Paved road	7	Clear trail
2	Unpaved road	8	Brush and trees
3	Short carry	9	Launching fee charged
4	Long carry	10	Private property, need permission
5	Easy grade	11	No access, reference only
6	Steep incline		

Sepulga River

Maps show a tiny stream called the Sepulga River flowing for miles from the northeast corner to the southwest corner of Conecuh County. It is a small waterway until it is joined by Persimmon Creek just south of I-65. The 5 or 6 miles of river from that point to U.S. 31 is said to be canoeable, but access is over dirt roads that are difficult to find. As a result, most paddlers begin their Sepulga trip at U.S. 31. Some 35 miles later, the Sepulga joins the Conecuh River. The Conecuh becomes the Escambia River when it crosses the Florida line and flows on to form Escambia Bay at Pensacola.

The Sepulga is the first of the southwestern Alabama rivers, when moving from west to east, that is not a blackwater stream at all. The high banks that have been noted only occasionally on the streams to the west are its primary characteristic. It has beautiful smooth rock walls colored by the minerals in the water that seep down them and that are dripping with lush fern falls. Since the land bordering the Sepulga is primarily owned by large paper companies, it boasts a deep corridor of heavy forestation on each side, and there is little access to the river.

This is a drop and pool river with long pools that have little current, broken by drops of up to 2 feet high followed by stretches of rocky shoals. There are occasional small sandbars on the upper section and further down, where tributary streams flow into the river. Campsites are scarce however, due to the high banks and the limited number of suitable sandbars.

Pigeon Creek flows into the Sepulga 7 miles below U.S. 84. It is also a canoeable stream, but it has a 2-foot drop followed by a rock garden of ledges and boulders only one-quarter mile upstream from the confluence with the Sepulga. As a result, Pigeon Creek is very swift at the confluence and difficult to paddle into.

In the section of river below the bridge at Paul, the relic of an old mill stands at the confluence of Robinson's Mill Creek. The bulwark across the creek is made of stone, and it still holds back the creek and produces an   8-

212

foot waterfall as the creek spills into the river. This is a very scenic spot for picnicking or camping.

It is 7 miles from the last access to the Sepulga to the confluence with the Conecuh, and another 3 miles to an access below that point.

U.S. 31 (Travis bridge) to U.S. 84 (access A–access B) is a moderately difficult 7-mile section of river. From River Falls, travel west on U.S. 84 for about 15 miles to the intersection of Conecuh C.R. 47. Turn right (north) on C.R. 47 and continue for about 1.5 miles to the intersection of C.R. 71. Turn left (northwest) on C.R. 71 and continue for about 3 miles to the point where C.R. 24 branches off to the left. Turn left on C.R. 24 and continue for one-half mile to the junction with U.S. 31. Turn left (west) and travel for about one-quarter mile to Travis bridge. The access is on the southeast side of the bridge.

The river is about 60 feet wide at this point with heavily wooded banks 4 to 6 feet high. Within the first one-quarter mile of the put-in, you encounter two sets of shoals. The second set has a drop of 1 foot and should be approached cautiously. This section is a series of drops and pools with several pretty islands in the stream. Just before reaching U.S. 84, the stream flows through a long shoal with one-half mile of rocky ledges to be maneuvered. By this point, the banks have become rocky and are covered with beautiful fern falls.

The 12-mile section in Conecuh County, from U.S. 84 to Paul (access B–access C) is moderately difficult and passes through excellent scenery. From River Falls, travel west on U.S. 84 for about 15.5 miles to the bridge across the Sepulga River. Access is on the southwest side of the bridge.

Less than one half mile below U.S. 84 is a large shoal with a 2-foot drop. This drop can be scouted and portaged on the left if necessary. The river continues its drop and pool pattern, but the pools are shorter and the drops more frequent. The banks continue to be high for the first few miles, but when the river takes an easterly turn, sandbars appear in the bends. This turn to the east occurs about 2 miles above the confluence with Pigeon Creek and marks the last opportunity to camp on a sandbar for about 6 miles.

The confluence with Pigeon Creek is 7 miles downstream from U.S. 84 and is clearly identifiable since it is a large, very fast flowing stream. There is a good campsite on Pigeon Creek about 100 yards from the confluence on the west bank. It is in the woods but has easy access to the stream and, being the remains of an old roadbed, it is partially cleared. From Pigeon Creek to the bridge at Paul is a distance of 5 miles with no adequate campsites. The banks are very high and sheer with heavy forestation. The river is a long, slow pool to the first set of shoals, but is very beautiful as it flows through these high walls.

The next 7 miles, from Paul to C.R. 42 (Brooklyn) (access C–access D) is an easy paddle with excellent to superb scenery. From River Falls, travel west on U.S. 84 for about 15.5 miles to the bridge across the Sepulga River. Cross the river and continue for about 1 mile to the intersection of C.R. 39. Turn left (south) on C.R. 39 and travel for just under 2 miles to the junction within C.R. 43. Turn left (south) on C.R. 43 and continue for about 7 miles to the community of Paul. A paved road, C.R. 8, intersects from the right just south of Paul. After passing C.R. 8, continue for 1 mile to the next graded road on the left. Turn left (east) on this road and continue to the bridge across the Sepulga, a distance of about 1.5 miles. Access is on the northwest side of the bridge.

For the first mile below the Paul bridge, the river is very narrow as it runs between rock boulders on either side. One mile downstream, the relic of an old mill at the confluence of Robinson's Mill Creek makes a good rest stop. The stone bulwark is still in place and the mill creek drops 8 to 10 feet over it, making an impressive waterfall. The small sandbar may not be level enough for a campsite, but the area on top of the bank is adequate for several tents. A long shoal begins at that spot also, and downstream, on river right, are beautiful red rock walls with fern falls.

Just over 1 mile downstream from this spot, Hart Creek flows in on river left. It has cut deeply into the rock walls at its confluence and makes a pretty waterfall with a little pool at the bottom. There is also a small sandbar there.

Below Hart Creek the river makes a westerly turn and flows almost due west as it approaches the bridge at Brooklyn (C.R. 42). This is a very scenic part of the river and is easier to maneuver than the upper sections.

The take-out is on C.R. 42 at Brooklyn. Follow the directions for section access C–access D to the community of Paul. Do not turn off C.R. 43, but continue on that road for about 5 miles to its intersection with C.R. 42. Turn left on C.R. 42 and continue to the first paved street to the left. Turn left and follow this road to the river. It becomes a dirt road before reaching the river.

Section: U.S. 31 (Travis bridge) to C.R. 42 (Brooklyn)

Counties: Conecuh, Covington, Escambia (AL)

USGS Quads: Old Town, Brooks, Loango, Dixie

Suitable for: Cruising, camping

Appropriate for: Beginners, intermediates

Months Runnable: All

Interest Highlights: Scenery, wildlife, geology, historical

Scenery: Beautiful to superb

Difficulty: Class I, II

Average Width: 60–80 ft.

Velocity: Moderate

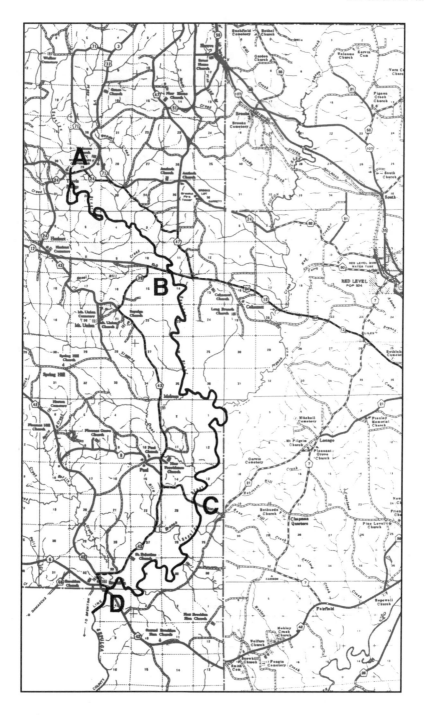

Hazards: Deadfalls, rock ledges, small waterfalls (2-ft–4-ft. drops)

Rescue Index: Accessible

Source of Additional Information: West Florida Canoe Club (904)587-2211

Access Points	Access Code	River Miles	Shuttle Miles
A–B	1357	7.0	7.0
B–C	1357	12.0	9.0
C–D	2367	7.0	6.0

Access Key:

1	Paved road	7	Clear trail
2	Unpaved road	8	Brush and trees
3	Short carry	9	Launching fee charged
4	Long carry	10	Private property, need permission
5	Easy grade	11	No access, reference only
6	Steep incline		

Pigeon Creek

Pigeon Creek is the largest tributary of the Sepulga River. It begins in a swamp in northwestern Covington County and flows for about 17 miles to its confluence with the Sepulga just above the community of Paul. From S.R. 55 to the confluence, the stream has a gradient of more than 6 feet per mile. It is a heavily forested stream with a preponderance of cypress, catalpa, willows, and river birch, as well as larger hardwoods such as oak and magnolia. Access is limited, and it provides a remote and intimate atmosphere. The drop and pool streambed with its many rocky ledges provide an interesting and mildly technical canoeing experience.

From S.R. 55 to U.S. 84 (access A–access B) is an easy 8-mile paddle. From Red Level, travel north and northwest on S.R. 55 for about 5.5 miles to the bridge across Pigeon Creek. Access is on the northwest side of the bridge.

At the put-in, the stream is shallow and swift, about 35 feet wide with a rocky bottom. The banks are 6 to 8 feet high with heavy forestation of cypress, catalpa, willows, and river birch trees. The banks are frequently limerock with an abundance of rich green lichen and ferns growing on them. There are a number of little wooded islands and small rocky shoals in the section.

Less than a mile upstream from the C.R. 82 bridge, there is an access by road to the river that leads to a cleared area that has been used for camping. There is a nice ledge across the stream at this point that lends a little excitement but is easily navigated. From C.R. 82 to U.S. 84, a distance of about 3 miles, the stream has a nice gradient, resulting in a series of shoals. These too are easily navigated.

From U.S. 84 to Paul (graded road off Conecuh C.R. 43) (access B–access C) is a moderately difficult 11-mile section. From Red Level, travel south on Covington C.R. 7 for 2 miles to the intersection with U.S. 84. Turn right (west) on U.S. 84, and continue for 3 miles to the bridge across Pigeon Creek. Access is on the northeast side of the bridge.

For the next 6 miles, to the confluence with the Sepulga River, the stream is a constant drop and pool. The banks continue to be high and heavily wooded. The first 2 miles below U.S. 84 are very twisting, and the many downed trees in the water require some technical canoeing. The water is shallow and clear, with a number of sandbars in this section.

One-quarter mile above the confluence with the Sepulga, the creek pools and drops over a 2- to 4-foot horseshoe-shaped ledge. This is a nice drop that requires some skill in maneuvering. Even more skill is needed for the next quarter mile as the stream flows through a rock garden of ledges and boulders.

At the confluence with Pigeon Creek, the Sepulga is 50 to 75 feet wide and very heavily wooded with high banks. The next 5 miles, to the take-out at Paul, is a series of long pools with an occasional small ledge. The high rock walls and the beautiful fern falls make this a most scenic section.

To reach the take-out, from Red Level, travel south on Covington C.R. 7 for 2 miles to the intersection with U.S. 84. Turn right (west) on U.S. 84 and continue for 3 miles to the bridge across Pigeon Creek. Continue on U.S. 84 for just over 4 miles to the junction with Conecuh C.R. 39. Turn left (south) on C.R. 39, and travel for just under 2 miles to the junction with C.R. 43. Turn left (south) on C.R. 43 and continue for about 7 miles to the community of Paul. A paved road, C.R. 8, will enter from the right. After passing Paul and C.R. 8, continue for 1 mile to the next graded road to the left. Turn left (east) on this road and continue to the bridge across the Sepulga River, a distance of about 1.5 miles. Access is on the northwest side of the bridge.

Section: S.R. 55 to Paul (graded road off C.R. 43)

Counties: Covington, Conecuh (AL)

USGS Quads: Red Level, Loango (AL)

Suitable for: Cruising, camping

Appropriate for: Intermediates

Months Runnable: All

Interest Highlights: Scenery, wildlife

Scenery: Excellent

Difficulty: Class I, II

Average Width: 35–50 ft.

Velocity: Moderate

Hazards: Deadfalls, rocky ledges

Rescue Index: Accessible to accessible but difficult

Source of Additional Information: None known

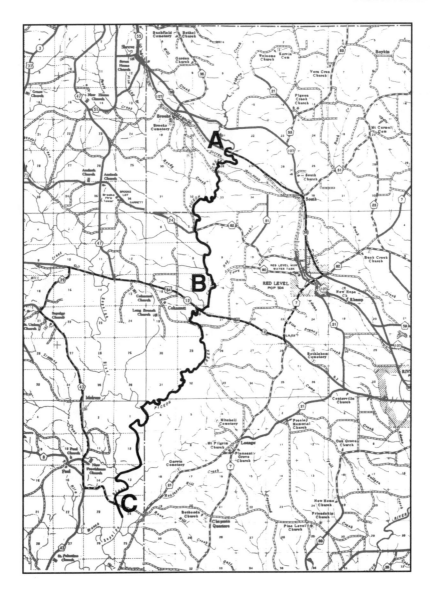

Access Points	Access Code	River Miles	Shuttle Miles
A–B	1357	8.0	9.0
B–C	1367	11.0	13.0
C	2367		

Access Key:

1	Paved road	7	Clear trail
2	Unpaved road	8	Brush and trees
3	Short carry	9	Launching fee charged
4	Long carry	10	Private property, need permission
5	Easy grade	11	No access, reference only
6	Steep incline		

The Yellow River Basin

The Yellow River drains the highest point in Florida and is fed by nearly 100 small streams and creeks as well as the Shoal River. It begins in south Alabama in the Conecuh National Forest and ends on the boundaries of the Eglin Air Force Base.

It is a swift-flowing river that traverses a sparsely settled area, providing over 50 miles of wilderness canoe camping and touring. The Yellow is generally not as clear as the neighboring streams in the Blackwater Forest. The sand along the banks and the river bottom has more of a tan hue than white, resulting in the yellow appearance of the water. There is also more aquatic vegetation than in the rivers to the west; there are fish, alligators, turtles, and water birds.

Other wildlife that might be seen include deer, turkeys, raccoons, and bobcats. Beavers are extremely active on this river and evidence of their handiwork is everywhere. A private hunting preserve shelters a large herd of Sika (Japanese deer) that may be glimpsed behind a high wire fence.

The trees along the river include river birch, willows, spruce pines, and many varieties of hardwoods. Lush vines, some with flowers, are frequently seen woven among the tree limbs.

With the confluence of the Shoal River, the Yellow turns almost due west and becomes much wider. It continues to flow for another 30 miles to Blackwater Bay but is broad and heavily used by motorboats and is of little interest to most canoeists.

The Yellow River

The 13 miles from S.R. 55 to S.R. 4 (access A–access B) is a moderately difficult paddle with excellent scenery. From Florala, Alabama, travel northwest on S.R. 55 to Watkins bridge, which crosses the Yellow River. Access is from the northeast or northwest side of the bridge.

This is the furthest point at which the Yellow River can be run with any degree of ease. This section is winding with occasional banks up to 20 feet high. There are numerous sandbars on the curves, and the deeper water on the outside of the bends provides good swimming holes.

About 6 miles downstream, Five Runs Creek enters from the west bank and the river widens considerably as a result. It soon narrows again, and there is a rocky shoal below that point that can create a diversion at low water. Less than a mile from the Alabama S.R. 4 bridge, the river narrows, picks up speed, and flows through a series of strainers that may require a pullover or carry-around. The strong current, deep water, and lack of maneuvering space make this a potentially hazardous spot for the novice paddler.

The next 10 miles, from S.R. 4 to Florida S.R. 2 (access B–access C), is similarly scenic and also of moderate difficulty. From Florala, Alabama, travel west on S.R. 4 until Givens bridge which crosses the Yellow River. There is access on either side.

Just below the S.R. 4 access are several fishing-hunting camps. In this section, the winding nature of the river continues with many bends, sandbars, and some high banks. The strong current lends assistance to the paddler, but some maneuvering skill is needed to manage some of the tighter curves. There are numerous woods roads (just tracks through the woods made by vehicles) that come down to the river. These are used by fishermen and local people for swimming and picnicking. However, there is no public access during this run, and, overall, the river retains a remote atmosphere.

The next 17 miles fall entirely within Florida's Okaloosa County, from Florida S.R. 2 to U.S. 90 (access C–access D). The section continues to flow through excellent scenery still at a moderately difficult pace.

From Crestview, travel north on S.R. 85 to the junction with S.R. 2. Turn left (west) on S.R. 2 and continue to the bridge across the Yellow River. Access is from a paved boat ramp on the northeast side of the bridge.

This is the beginning of the Florida Canoe Trail. The river becomes deeper and cloudier as it flows toward U.S. 90. The variation from steep banks to low sandbars with some swampy areas continues, with the sandbars becoming smaller and less frequent during the first 15 miles. Bluffs up to 40 feet high are occasionally seen on the east side and may continue for one-quarter mile or more along the bank. There are myriad streams feeding the river from both sides, and campsites are scarce until a few miles above U.S. 90.

Brightly colored markers on the trees indicate the placement of bushhooks (baited lines attached to the lower limbs of trees to catch catfish; they can be dangerous to boaters who are unaware that there are fishhooks hidden under the water on the ends of the lines). Boats with small motors may occasionally be encountered.

Silver Lake Landing, an improved access off a private road, occurs just over halfway down this section. There are several houses along the east bank at this point.

A very tall, yellow bluff marks the beginning of 2 miles of sturdy fence on the east bank. This is the boundary for a hunting preserve that protects a herd of Sika. This fence is rigorously patrolled. There is a good campsite across the river on the west bank opposite the end of the fence. About 2 miles above U.S. 90, the large sandbars resume, and ample camping space is available on most of them.

The section from U.S. 90 to Gin Hole Landing (access D–access E) is 10 miles of similar difficulty but far less scenic interest. From Milligan, travel east on U.S. 90 to the Yellow River bridge. Access is from a graded road that turns off U.S. 90 about one-quarter mile southwest of the bridge.

The Yellow divides immediately south of the U.S. 90 bridge at a large island. At the southern end of the island is the Louisville and Nashville Railroad trestle that crosses the river. At one time the Yellow River was considered a navigable stream from Blackwater Bay up to this point, which was called Barrows Ferry.

The sandbars decrease again below U.S. 90 as the riverbanks become much lower and more heavily wooded. I-10 crosses the river about 4 miles below U.S. 90, but there is no access. From I-10, it is less than 3 miles to the confluence with the Shoal River. Just above this confluence, the Yellow River splits into several swift-flowing runs and the Shoal, flowing in from the east, is not easily identifiable. After the Shoal joins the Yellow, it turns west and becomes much broader.

From this point on, the left (south) bank of the river is the property of Eglin Air Force Base and usage is restricted. Much of the property on the right bank is privately owned and posted. Groupings of houses and cabins occur on the north bank at regular intervals from this point to the take-out, but the roads that lead to them are not open to the public. With the advent of the deeper water and broader river, one encounters an increasing number of motorboats, and the trip becomes less interesting. There are several access points on the south bank that are frequently used by the public at this time. They are on the military reservation, however, and access may be closed in the future.

To reach the take-out (access E), from Crestview, travel south on S.R. 85 for 4 miles to the bridge across the Shoal River. Continue across the river for three-quarters of a mile to the first graded road turning right (west). Turn right, and continue for 4.5 miles to a poorly maintained dirt track turning right. A sign, M.P. CAMP, CH 17, will be seen at that point. Turn right and follow this track for about a half mile to the river.

The Yellow River from Gin Hole Landing to S.R. 189 is easily accessible to motorboats and not particularly desirable to the canoeist. For those wishing to canoe this section, it is 9 miles long and the access can be reached as follows: From Crestview, travel west on U.S. 90 to the junction with S.R. 189 at the town of Holt. Turn left (south) on S.R. 189, and continue for 3 miles to the river.

The Yellow River Delta, the 30-mile section from S.R. 189 to Blackwater Bay, is a maze of saw grass and tidal flats. It is often difficult to locate the main channel of the river. Blackwater Bay is a large body of water subject to high winds and waves.

Section: Alabama S.R. 55 to Gin Hole Landing

Counties: Covington (AL), Okaloosa (FL)

USGS Quads: Libertyville, Watkins Bridge, Wing (AL); Oak Grove (FL)

Suitable for: Cruising, camping

Appropriate for: Families, beginners, intermediates

Months Runnable: All

Interest Highlights: Scenery, wildlife

Scenery: Beautiful to superb

Difficulty: Class I

Average Width: 30–60 ft.

Velocity: Moderate

Hazards: Deadfalls, strainers

Rescue Index: Accessible to accessible but difficult

Source of Additional Information: None known

Access Points	Access Code	River Miles	Shuttle Miles
A–B	1357	13.0	12.0
B–C	1357	10.0	12.0
C–D	1357	17.0	26.0
D–E	2357	10.0	15.0
E	2357		

Access Key:	1	Paved road	7	Clear trail
	2	Unpaved road	8	Brush and trees
	3	Short carry	9	Launching fee charged
	4	Long carry	10	Private property, need permission
	5	Easy grade	11	No access, reference only
	6	Steep incline		

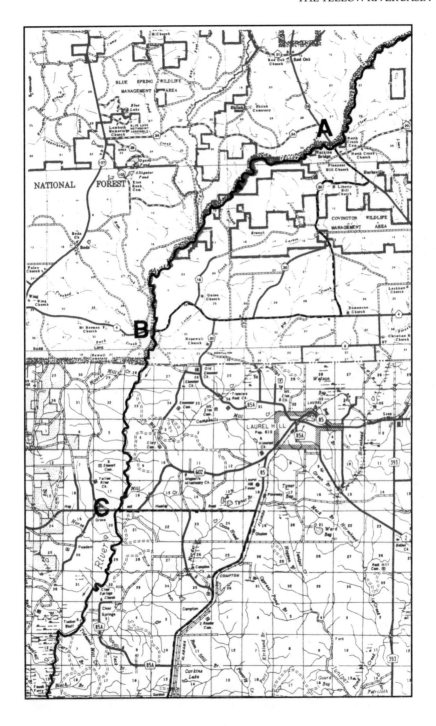

Pea River

The Pea River is one of south Alabama's finest touring rivers since it is both long enough and varied enough to be of interest for canoe trips of several days' duration. It is the major tributary of the Choctawhatchee River, and the two streams are close neighbors as they traverse southern Alabama. The Pea flows for more than 125 miles before it joins the Choctawhatchee at Geneva, but only 85 miles of that distance is canoeable. After the two rivers merge, the Choctawhatchee continues for nearly 60 miles into Florida, where it is the major source of Choctawhatchee Bay. The two streams provide 145 miles of excellent canoe trails.

On this long journey, the Pea River flows through a wide variety of terrain. It changes constantly from high limerock walls to low swampland, to heavily forested banks, to wide sandbars. It also has many, many rocky shoals, ledges, drops, and some modest "whitewater." Hazards include deadfalls in the river, and there is a large dam below Elba that must be portaged.

Forestation on the river ranges from second growth hardwoods and river birch to cypress stands and some high pine woods. In the spring, dogwood, mountain laurel, wild azalea, wild wisteria, and other flowering plants are prolific on some sections. Wildlife here includes raccoon, opossum, deer, wild turkey, and beaver.

Since the Pea River flows through an agricultural area, it is usually a tannish yellow color. In sections where there are many shoals, the siltation may have been strained, and it will be a clear green color. During very dry seasons when the water is low, it may have the tea-colored blackwater appearance seen more frequently in streams to the west.

U.S. 231 (Veterans Memorial Bridge) to Coffee C.R. 36 (access A–access B) is an easy 5-mile paddle through Dale and Coffee counties. From Ozark, travel north on U.S. 231 for about 20 miles to the Veterans Memorial Bridge across the Pea River. Access is on the northeast side of the bridge.

There are two bridges at this access, the new U.S. 231 bridge and the very graceful and beautiful Veterans Memorial Bridge built in 1920–21. It is thought to be the first reinforced concrete bridge built in Alabama and is registered on the Alabama Register of Landmarks and Heritage of the Alabama Historical Commission. This crossing is also the site of an old resort of which only the swimming pool remains.

The river is about 75 feet wide at this point with banks from 2 to 6 feet high that are sloping and heavily wooded. Looking upstream from U.S. 231, the river seems open and inviting. This is misleading, since a storm in the 1970s pushed so many trees into the stream between S.R. 10 and this point that it is no longer canoeable.

At normal to low water levels, there is a moderate current through this section. There are also many downed trees in the riverbed, which result in the need for some maneuvering skill. On the curves in the river, there is an abundance of sandbars that make good campsites.

C.R. 36 (Lurleen B. Wallace Bridge) to C.R. 60 (Coles Bridge) (access B–access C) is another easy stretch of 4 miles. From Ozark, travel north on U.S. 231 for about 20 miles to the bridge across the Pea River. Cross the bridge, and turn left at the first road, Coffee C.R. 82. Continue on C.R. 82 for less than 1 mile to the intersection with C.R. 73. Turn left (south) on C.R. 73, and travel 2 miles to the intersection with C.R. 79. Turn left (south) on C.R. 79, and travel for 1 mile to the junction with C.R. 36. At C.R. 36, turn left and continue for less than 1 mile to the bridge.

At this access, there are rock walls on either side of the river, but it is only a short distance before the sandbars resume. Less than 1 mile downstream from the bridge, an unnamed streamlet flows in on river left. Paddle or wade up it for about 100 yards to see a very pretty waterfall. The water pours over four broad ledges, dropping for about 5 feet.

Just before reaching the C.R. 60 bridge, the sandbars stop and the river flows through rock walls again. The remains of an old dam stretch across the river here, producing a drop of about 1 foot at normal water levels.

The next 5 miles from Coles Bridge to S.R. 167 (Folsom Bridge) (access C–access D) are similarly easy. Follow the directions from Ozark to access B, but do not turn left on C.R. 36. Stay on C.R. 79 and continue to the junction with C.R. 60. Turn left on C.R. 60 and travel for one half mile to the bridge.

Below this access there is a large sandbar that appears to be a popular swimming spot in the summer. Also, about 200 yards downstream from the bridge is a 2-foot drop that extends across the river. It should be run just to the left of the cut in the rocks. There is another, smaller drop about one-quarter mile further downstream. The river begins to have steep banks that are 8 to 12 feet tall and heavily wooded. The sandbars have been left behind, and campsites are scarce.

From Folsom Bridge to C.R. 43 (Weeks Bridge) (access C–access E) is 6 easy miles in Coffee County. Travel north on S.R. 167 from Enterprise for about 11 miles to the bridge across the Pea River.

The river is straight through this section, and the current is usually lively. The high rock walls continue for about 2 miles below the access, but a sizable

227

sandbar on river left about 1 mile above Roe Bridge usually makes a good campsite. Access to the river from Roe Bridge may be poor since it is often steep and slippery. There are several sandbars on curves in the river below this bridge before the high banks resume, and there is a pretty island in the river just above the access at C.R. 43.

The 8-mile section between Weeks Bridge and U.S. 84 at Elba (access E–access F) is an easy to moderate paddle through excellent scenery. From Enterprise, travel north on U.S. 84 for about 8 miles to the intersection of C.R. 43. Turn right on C.R. 43 and continue for about 2 miles to the bridge across the river. This section is a popular day trip because of the swift current, the number of rocky shoals and chutes, and the presence of an interesting rapid.

Below the C.R. 43 bridge is an obvious change in the character of the river as it becomes deeper and straighter. About 1 mile below the access there is a large shoal, some 300 feet wide, that stretches across the river. Within one-quarter mile downstream a curve to the right reveals a rather impressive rapid. There is a trail on river right that can be used for scouting or portaging. The rapid consists of a shelf of rock extending across the river with a drop of 2 to 3 feet. There are two chutes that flow through the ledge. Both of them can be run, but care should be taken if the canoe is heavily loaded.

Below this rapid, the river turns sharply to the right and flows over another shoal. There are several more shoals and cascading "roller coasters" in the next half mile. Downstream from these shoals, the river becomes calm again but the current is still lively. A number of small streams flow in, creating little "canyons" and waterfalls that are very picturesque. Whitewater Creek, a canoeable stream, flows into the Pea River on river right at the town of Elba. Access is from S.R. 125.

The 4-mile stretch from U.S. 84 at Elba to the Elba Dam (access F–access G) includes easy to strenuous paddling through less impressive scenery. This section should not be run at very high water levels or at floodstage because of the difficulty in crossing the river to portage the dam.

At Elba, the access is located on the south side on the U.S. 84 bridge in a park. There is a boat ramp there.

While this is a nice section of river, it is often very slow paddling because of the backup from the dam. If the river is high and running fast, it is dangerous to paddle because of the difficulty in taking out to portage the dam and the possibility of being swept over. Either way, the dam must be portaged, a rather strenuous feat.

Those who choose to paddle this section can portagethe dam on either side. There is an access on river right just above the dam. Carry around and down a two-rut road to a path that leads to the river, a steep and poor access. On river left, the access is partially on a sandbar and is easier to manage, but may not be an option if the river is high.

The dam itself is an abandoned power plant that has fallen into ruin. It has three levels of cascading waterfalls and is a very scenic spot.

The section from the dam below Elba to S.R. 134 (Ballard Bridge) (access G–access H) is 8 miles. From Elba, travel south on S.R. 189 for 4 miles. Turn left on the first graded road to the left and continue for less than one half mile to the Elba Dam. The access is down a very steep two-rut road to the right.

This section of river flows almost due south with few bends or curves. The banks are high and heavily wooded. The river borders a U.S. military reservation about 1 mile below the dam. Sandbars for camping are not abundant, but a nice one is located at the confluence of Kimmy Creek, about 1 mile above Ballard Bridge. Pages Creek flows in on river right just a few yards above the bridge. It can also be used as an access to the river.

From Ballard Bridge to C.R. 6 (access H–access I) is an easy 4-mile section. From Elba, travel south on S.R. 189 for about 6 miles. At the junction with C.R. 9, bear left and continue for just over 4 miles to the intersection with S.R. 134. Turn left on S.R. 134, and travel just over 1 mile to the bridge across the river. Access is on the northwest side of the bridge down a woods road and is steep. This same woods road leads to Pages Creek where there is also an access that can be used to reach the river.

The river continues to flow straight and due south for 2 miles below this access, resulting in high, heavily wooded banks. As the river curves to the west, a power line crosses; just below this point is the only sandbar of any size to be found in this section. This is less than 1 mile from the access at   C.R. 6.

The 13-mile section of river from C.R. 6 (Kingston Landing) to S.R. 52 at Samson (access I–access J) is an easy paddle through excellent scenery, in both Coffee and Geneva counties. From Enterprise, travel west on S.R. 27 for about 4 miles to the junction with C.R. 14. Turn right onto C.R. 14 and continue for 9 miles to the intersection with C.R. 25. Turn left on C.R. 25, and travel for about 4 miles to the junction with C.R. 6. Turn right on C.R. 6, and continue for 2 miles to the river. Kingston Landing, on the northeast side of the bridge, is a very pretty picnic area with a paved parking lot, tables, and a boat ramp.

This is a long section of river with no access. The stream begins to curve again and is characterized by high rock walls with beautiful fern falls and colorful lichens. A number of creeks flow into the river in this section, and several of them make pretty little waterfalls. The high banks make campsites scarce, but there are a few sandbars on the bends that are suitable for camping. Two miles above the S.R. 52 access, a railroad crosses the river. There is no public access at that point, but just below there, a set of steps has been cut into the side of the rock wall.

The 5-mile section from S.R. 52 to C.R. 17 (access J–access K) lies in Geneva County and is similarly easy but slightly less scenic, as are the remaining sections of this river. From Samson, travel west on S.R. 52 for 3 miles to the Pea River. Access, on the northeast or southeast side of the bridge, is very poor; it's steep and difficult to manage.

The river continues to alternate between high rock walls and bends with sandbars. An old railroad trestle crosses 2 miles below S.R. 52, but there is no access at that point. Just before reaching C.R. 17, note the high pinelands on river right.

From C.R. 17 to S.R. 87 (access K–access L) is a 10-mile paddle. From Samson, travel west on S.R. 52 for about 1 mile to the intersection with C.R. 17. Turn left on C.R. 17 and continue for 4 miles to the river. The access is on the northeast side of the bridge and has a paved parking lot, picnic tables, and a boat ramp.

After a 2-mile stretch that leads due south, the river bends at the confluence with Flat Creek. This is one of the major tributaries of the Pea and is a sizable stream on river right. It can be reached from S.R. 153 as an optional access to the Pea River. After passing Flat Creek, the terrain becomes more swampy than has previously been encountered. Two miles below the confluence of Flat Creek, a power line crosses overhead, and, just below this point, the river splits into two forks. The left fork is usually blocked with debris and the right has a very swift current and many obstacles that may be challenging. One paddler observed that this is the point where all of the garbage thrown into the Pea River from over a dozen bridges upstream ends up! There is also a washed-out bridge in this area to add to the excitement. Just after the two forks on the river rejoin, a double power line crosses overhead. The current becomes slow and the river is shallow. It is about 3.5 miles to the S.R. 87 bridge.

From S.R. 87 to the city park at Geneva (access L–access M) is 13 miles. Travel west on S.R. 196 from Geneva just to the edge of town where it intersects with C.R. 4. Turn left on C.R. 4 and continue for about 8 miles to the junction with S.R. 87. Turn left on S.R. 87 and go south for less than 1 mile to the river. The access is on the northeast side of the bridge, down a little road to the river.

This access is in a very swampy area, and this type of terrain continues for the next 2 miles. The river is flowing almost due east and dips into Florida for about 1 mile. After leaving the swamp, rock walls and high banks resume. S.R. 27 crosses the river at mile 11, but there is no access at that point. It is only 2 more miles to the city park at Geneva where there is an excellent boat ramp. At the confluence with the Choctawhatchee, it is possible to take out on river left, up a slight bank where there is a trail to the parking area. Or, the paddler can turn left (north) onto the Choctawhatchee and paddle for 200 yards or so upstream to the boat ramp.

To reach the take-out in the town of Geneva, travel east on S.R. 52 to the last paved street on the right before reaching the bridge across the Choctawhatchee River. Turn right and follow the city streets that lead to the park. This is a well-developed area with picnic tables, covered pavilions, portable water, and primitive toilet facilities. The boat ramp is on the Choctawhatchee River about 200 yards north of the confluence with the Pea. It is also possible to take out right at the confluence and carry up a short trail to the parking area.

Section: U.S. 231 (Veterans Memorial Bridge) to city park at Geneva

Counties: Dale, Coffee, Geneva (AL)

USGS Quads: Brundidge, New Brockton, Elba, Ino, Kinston, Sellersville, Samson, Darlington, Hobbs, Crossroads, Geneva West (AL)

Suitable for: Cruising, camping

Appropriate for: Beginners, intermediates

Months Runnable: January, February, March, April, all after rainfall

Interest Highlights: Scenery, wildlife

Scenery: Excellent to very good

Difficulty: Class I, II

Average Width: 60–100 ft.

Velocity: Mild to moderate

Hazards: Deadfalls, rock ledges, drops, old power dam

Rescue Index: Accessible

Source of Additional Information: The Canoe Livery, Rt. 2, Box 222-C, Newton, AL 36352; (205) 299-3888.

Access Points	Access Code	River Miles	Shuttle Miles
A–B	1357	5.0	5.0
B–C	1357	4.0	6.0
C–D	1357	5.0	4.0
D–E	1357	6.0	7.0
E–F	1357	8.0	9.0
F–G	1357	4.0	4.0
G–H	2468	8.0	9.0
H–I	2468	4.0	7.0
I–J	1357	13.0	10.0
J–K	1468	5.0	3.0
K–L	1357	10.0	11.0
L–M	1357	13.0	11.0
M	1357	13.0	11.0

Access Key:

1	Paved road	7	Clear trail
2	Unpaved road	8	Brush and trees
3	Short carry	9	Launching fee charged
4	Long carry	10	Private property, need permission
5	Easy grade	11	No access, reference only
6	Steep incline		

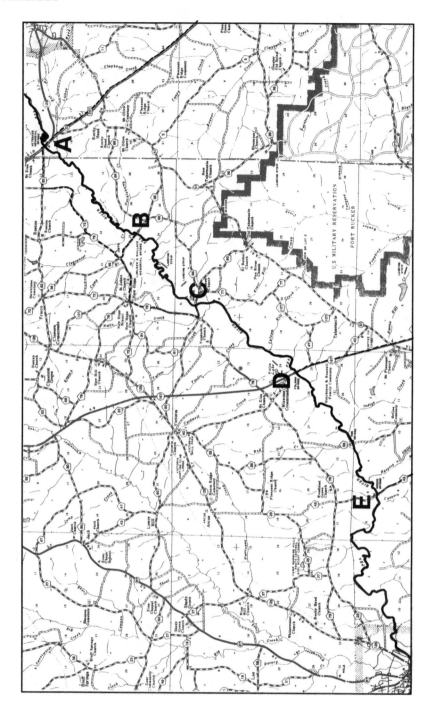

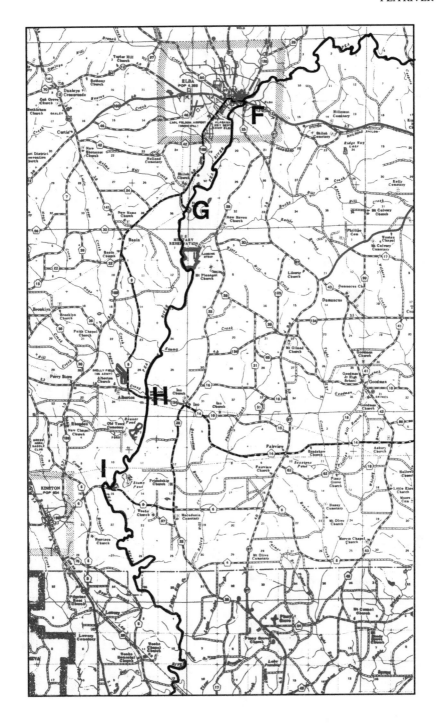

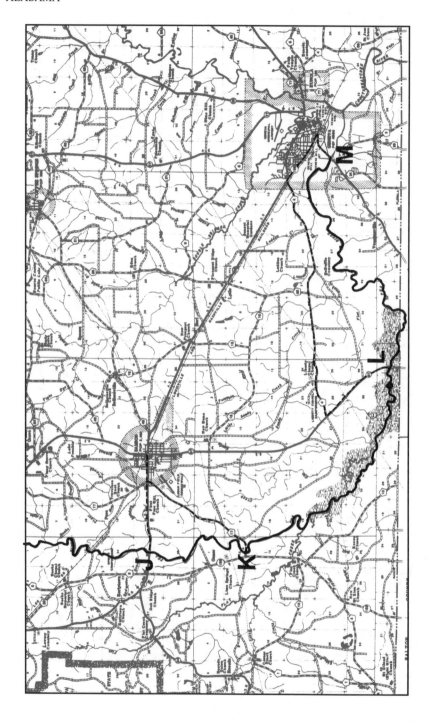

Choctawhatchee River

The Choctawhatchee River is over 170 miles long from its headwaters in Barbour County, Alabama, to the Choctawhatchee Bay near Fort Walton Beach, Florida. Of this length, there are over 100 miles of excellent canoeing, making it one of the finest touring rivers in south Alabama and northwest Florida. Not only is it a scenic river of high ecological significance, it is also very remote, has limited access, and offers an unusual opportunity for an extended wilderness experience.

The Choctawhatchee is a broad, shallow river that is usually yellow in color. It has an annual flooding pattern that is primarily responsible for the lack of development along its banks. The upper sections are characterized by high limestone banks, rocky shoals and drops, and sections of cascading water. After entering Florida, the river is calmer but more remote and has huge sandbars. The terrain varies from floodplain forests with upland hardwoods and pine hammocks to marshes and swampy wetlands. Wildlife is plentiful and a wide variety of animals indigenous to north Florida may be sighted along the banks. Beavers, in particular, have made an astounding comeback on the Choctawhatchee.

Major tributaries of the Choctawhatchee in Alabama include Judy Creek, the East Fork of the Choctawhatchee, the Little Choctawhatchee, and the Pea River. In Florida, Wright Creek, Holmes Creek, and several springs including Blue Spring and Morrison Spring feed the river.

Dale C.R. 36 to Alabama S.R. 27 (access A–access B) is a moderately difficult 6-mile paddle. From Midland City, Alabama, travel north on C.R. 59 to the intersection with C.R. 36. Turn left (west) and continue for one half mile to the West Fork of the Choctawhatchee. Access is on the southwest side of the bridge.

At the put-in on C.R. 36, the river is about 35 feet wide, shallow, and has a moderate current. It soon widens to 50 feet, and at normal or slightly less than normal water there are a series of rocky shoals that stretch across the

235

entire width of the stream. These shoals will require some skill in maneuvering to keep from running aground. The river is a drop-and-pool waterway with the short pools having a modest current followed by a stretch of faster water over the shoals.

Judy Creek enters the river about 3.5 miles downstream. This creek is an alternate access to the Choctawhatchee at normal to high water and has several interesting drops in its 2-mile run from C.R. 36 to its confluence with the river.

Below Judy Creek, the river bottom becomes sandier and shallow, but there are still shoals across the river. Just above S.R. 27, there is a 2-foot drop over a rocky ledge that may be troublesome to the novice paddler. It should be run on the extreme left and may be portaged if necessary. It is 2.5 miles from Judy Creek to S.R. 27.

The 9-mile stretch from S.R. 27 to S.R. 123 (Newton, Alabama) (access B–access C) is of similar difficulty. From Midland City, Alabama, travel north on C.R. 59 to the intersection with C.R. 27. Turn left (west) on C.R. 27 and continue to the bridge across the West Fork of the Choctawhatchee. A poor access is on the southwest side of the bridge.

The shoals increase below the S.R. 27 bridge and are frequently in sight of each other down to the confluence with the East Fork of the Choctawhatchee. The bridge from Bagwells Crossroads crosses the river about 3 miles down from the put-in, but this access is very poor. It is another mile to the confluence with the East Fork. There is a strong current at that point, and the river widens to 100 feet.

The drop and pool characteristic ends, and the river proceeds with a constant current. There are a few small shoals below this point and a few houses begin to appear. The banks are 10 to 15 feet high with an occasional sandbank where livestock come down to the water. It is 1 mile from the confluence of the East Fork to U.S. 231. This is a dual-lane bridge, and access from this road would be very difficult.

Just below U.S. 231, on the south bank, a stream has cut a deep crevasse in the limestone as it enters the river. It is possible to paddle into this opening for a short distance and to look overhead at a beautiful fern fall.

One mile further downstream, a large sandbar occurs on the south bank. This bar used to be an island; it is the result of a change of direction in the flow of the river. It is an excellent campsite for a large party of campers. A very pretty stream flowing into the river at the east end of this site is worth a short walk to see.

About 1.5 miles further downstream, a railroad trestle crosses the river. Just downstream of it is a large sandbank on the northwest side that is heavily used as an access point.

It is another 1.5 miles to the S.R. 123 bridge; access to the river is very poor here, but a canoe livery just above the bridge offers canoe rentals, shuttle service, and launching facilities for a fee.

S.R. 123 to S.R. 92 (access C–access D) is an easy 8-mile paddle. From Midland City, Alabama, travel north on S.R. 134 to the town of Newton. At this point, S.R. 123 will have joined S.R. 134. Continue north until crossing the Choctawhatchee River. Access from the canoe livery is reached via Waterford Road, the first graded road to the right after crossing the bridge. Access from S.R. 123 is on the northwest side of the bridge and is a poor access.

Just below the S.R. 123 bridge are the pilings from an old mill that can be troublesome depending on the water level. Approach with caution, and watch for debris that may have been caught, creating a strainer. There is usually a clear passage on the northwest side.

This section is a pleasant trip with high vertical banks and a good current. Little maneuvering skill is needed after passing the site of the old mill. Because of the high banks, campsites are scarce. There are two points where modest sandbanks line the river, and a small party could camp but they might have to share facilities with livestock from nearby pastures.

S.R. 92 to S.R. 167 (access D–access E) is another easy stretch of 9 miles which crosses into Geneva County. From Midland City, Alabama, travel north on S.R. 134 to the town of Newton. Just before reaching Newton, S.R. 123 will merge from the left (west). Turn left (west) on S.R. 123, and continue for about 8 miles until it intersects with S.R. 92. Turn right (north) on S.R. 92, and continue to the bridge across the Choctawhatchee River. Access is on the west side of the bridge on either side of the road.

A nice sandbar at the put-in is popular with swimmers and sunbathers on warm weekends. In the next 3 miles to U.S. 84, the banks are sloping and heavily wooded. A possible campsite lies at the point where the Little Choctawhatchee enters the river about 1.5 miles downstream from U.S. 92.

At U.S. 84 is an access to the river from a boat ramp on the northwest side of the bridge. There is another large, popular sandbar at this access, and for the next 2 miles there are numerous spacious and high sandbanks suitable for camping. The confluence with Pates Creek introduces sloping, heavily wooded banks again and an end to the sandbars.

Three miles further downstream Claybank Creek enters from the northwest. Just up this creek, and in sight of the river, is a large sandbar that would provide camping space for several tents. About 1 mile below Claybank Creek the bridge at S.R. 167 is reached.

The next 12 miles, from S.R. 167 to Geneva, Alabama (access E–access F), continue through Geneva County. From Dothan, Alabama, travel west on S.R. 52 through the town of Hartford to the intersection with S.R. 167. Turn right (north) on S.R. 167 and continue to the bridge across the Choctawhatchee River. Access is on the southwest side of the bridge.

The banks of the river become higher at S.R. 167, and shortly below this access, there is a high, wooded bluff on the southeast side that follows the river for about one-quarter mile. It becomes lower as the river bends to the left revealing a large sandbar, suitable for camping, on the left bank. This is the only good campsite for the next 2 miles as the banks continue to be high down to Bellwood Bridge. There is no access to the river at Bellwood Bridge.

Shortly below this bridge, the river begins a long loop to the west. At the end of the loop is a large sandbar on the north bank with an almost vertical bank on the south side. Although there are several more sandbars in the following miles, they are very low and a rise in water level would make them doubtful campsites.

About 6 miles downstream from the put-in, there is a bend to the east in the river and the relics of two old docks can be seen on the east bank. Some low pastures on the right bank could be used for camping with permission from the owners, but they would probably have to be shared with livestock.

As the river turns south, the banks become very high with pastures on top. You will observe a rock bluff on the west bank, followed one half mile downstream by a boat ramp on the east bank. The access to the ramp is from Highfalls, a small community located on Geneva C.R. 41.

Shortly below this access, there are several large sandbars suitable for camping. These bars have access from a road, however, and may be used for swimming and sunbathing. Downstream from these sandbars is another high, well-wooded bluff on the west bank.

As the river bends to the east, sheer rock walls 15 feet high, begin to appear with beautiful fern falls dripping down. This type of terrain continues almost to S.R. 52. One-half mile downstream from S.R. 52 is an old railroad bridge that swings on the center piling. This indicates that it was probably built in the early 1900s when steamboats still used the river. The pilings for the bridge are made of brick, and the center piling has an unusual wooden structure built around it to protect it from floating trees during floods. There is a boat ramp at the park at the river junction about one half mile below this bridge. Double Bridges Creek, a canoeable stream, flows into the Choctawhatchee River on river right at the town of Geneva. Access to this creek is from C.R. 65 or C.R. 40.

The easy 8-mile paddle from Geneva, Alabama, to Florida S.R. 2 (access F–access G) crosses into Florida's Holmes County. There is a boat ramp in the park located at the point where the Pea and Choctawhatchee rivers join, just south of Geneva. Turn west at the red light and then south on the first paved street to the left (one block). Continue for three blocks, cross the railroad tracks, and turn left on the first paved street. Continue for about 1.5 miles to the park and boat ramp.

Just below the park, the Pea River joins with the Choctawhatchee. A sizable river itself, the Pea flows through south Alabama to the north of and almost parallel to the Choctawhatchee. It is a beautiful river, excellent for canoe touring.

After the confluence with the Pea, the Choctawhatchee widens to some 300 feet and remains wide over the next few miles, gradually narrowing to its customary 150-foot width. The banks continue to be high and heavily wooded, with large sandbars in the curves. It is about 5 miles from the put-in at S.R. 52 to the Florida state line.

S.R. 2 to Camp Meeting Bay (access G–access H) is an easy 11-mile section that runs through Holmes County only. From Bonifay, travel west on U.S. 90 to the intersection with S.R. 177A, turn right (north) on S.R. 177A, and continue to the intersection with S.R. 2. Turn left (west) and continue for 4.5 miles to the bridge across the Choctawhatchee. There is not an adequate access at this bridge, but there are accesses used by local fishermen on the east side of the bridge, both to the north and to the south. These are rough tracks that run beside the river for one half mile in either direction.

For the next 10 miles, the river is broad, shallow, has a good current, and at low to normal water levels has some of the largest sandbars found on any north Florida waterway. Sandbars of 10 to 15 acres in size are not uncommon. These sandbars are frequently covered with tracks of the various birds and animals that inhabit this area. Of particular interest is the evidence of the beaver population. Practically driven to extinction by trappers in the early part of the century, they are obviously alive and well on the Choctawhatchee! The overnight camper on one of these large sandbars will often have a unique opportunity to see or hear beavers going about their business of dragging willow branches to the water, feeding, stripping the bark of river birch, or slapping their tails on the water.

This section of the river is very remote, and it is unusual to see another boat. The few encountered will be small fishing boats, many of which do not carry motors but are propelled by sculling.

There is a concrete landing at Curry Ferry, about 2 miles downstream from S.R. 2 on the east bank, and another landing on the west side at the end of a graded road opposite Dead River Lake, 3 more miles downstream.

Some 5 miles below this last landing is Cork Island. This is only an island at high water, since at low water the east channel is blocked by sand. On the west bank, just opposite the island, is Blue Spring. This is the most northwest spring in Florida and is accessible only by boat. It is a deep, clear blue hole suitable for swimming. Considering its remoteness and the swampy, inaccessible area around it, this water is probably safe for drinking if needed. Just over 1 mile below Blue Spring is Camp Meeting Bay.

Camp Meeting Bay to U.S. 90 (access H–access I), also in Holmes County, is a similarly easy 6-mile paddle. From Westville, travel north on S.R. 179A for 3 miles to an intersection where the road on the left (west) will be paved, and the road on the right (east) will be graded. Turn right (east) on the graded road, and continue for 1 mile to the river. Access is from a concrete ramp.

Camp Meeting Bay is a small community of cottages located on the top of a high, sandy bluff. Despite the height, most of the houses are built on pilings.

Three miles downstream from this put-in is the site of a former island. Annual flooding has washed away all but its northern tip, and the channel that went around it to the east now has trees growing in it. The channel to the west may also be obstructed with trees, but is navigable.

One mile below this point is Wrights Creek Landing on the east bank. The landing is about one-half mile above the confluence of Wrights Creek and is reached from S.R. 179. There is a small settlement of houses there. With the confluence of Wrights Creek, the river widens noticeably, the sandbars cease, and the current slows—this is less than 2 miles above U.S. 90.

U.S. 90 to Hinsons Cross Roads (access I–access J) is 12 miles of easy paddling through Holmes and Washington counties, still in Florida. From Caryville, travel west on U.S. 90 for less than 1 mile to the river. Access is from a concrete boat ramp on the southeast side of the bridge.

At U.S. 90, the Choctawhatchee is about 100 yards wide, shallow, with little current. This continues for 2 miles; in this section are the last of the large sandbars suitable for camping.

I-10 crosses the river 1 mile below U.S. 90. There is no access to the interstate from the river. About 1 mile below the interstate highway is an island whose west passage is blocked by trees. The east passage is partially obstructed with the debris caught up by old pilings. A large sand strip leads off to the east and evidently is a part of the river when the water is high. This is the last sandbar. Just below this point, the river narrows to 50 yards, and the current picks up. The banks are low, but very heavily wooded. Willows and river birch often hang off the banks into the waterway, and occasionally the banks are very swampy.

Five miles downstream from U.S. 90 is a rapid at Gum Creek. The main river flows to the right—a portion flows off to the left, over a drop, through an obstructed area, and rejoins the river on the other side of a small island. The fast water can be heard as it is approached, but scouting is difficult. Even though the run is only 15 yards long, it has a standing wave and a crosscurrent as well as the complication of downed trees. If in doubt, follow the main channel to the right.

In this area, the river begins to make wide oxbow bends that create islands. On one of these bends to the west are red reflectors nailed to the trees indicating an access at Old Creek. This access is reached from S.R. 181 out of Westville and cannot be seen from the river.

Shortly below this point, there is another long loop to the west with a group of houses on the high bank on the right side. The river begins to widen again, and the current slows as the landing at Hinsons Cross Roads nears. Just above the landing is an island; the landing is on the east bank at the end of the island.

Hinsons Cross Roads to the Boynton Cutoff boat ramp (access J–access K) is a 15-mile section of easy paddling through Holmes, Washington, and Walton counties. From Bonifay, travel south on S.R. 79 to the intersection with S.R. 280. Turn right (west) on S.R. 280, and continue to its junction with S.R. 170. Turn right (west), and continue for less than 1 mile to the community of Hinsons Cross Roads. Continue west on this road after the pavement ends for 2 miles to a concrete boat ramp on the river. (See map on page 00.)

The river continues to be wide at this point with a good current. The banks continue to be heavily wooded, some 4 to 6 feet high. The run from Morrison Spring enters the river from the west about 2 miles below this put-in. It is 1 mile up this run to the spring, which is a 250-foot pool containing three cavities in the bottom. One of the cavities is said to be 50 feet deep, another is 100 feet deep, and a third is 300 feet deep. All three terminate in a large underground cavern of unknown dimensions. This is a popular spot for swimming and picnicking as well as for diving. There's a concession, pumps for air tanks, and a boat ramp.

A mile below the confluence of the spring run, a large power line crosses the river, resulting in a partially cleared high area. There is also a dirt track on the west bank for about a half mile below the power line. This is one of the only high, cleared areas on this section of the river.

Below Morrison Spring, the river makes several large oxbow bends. Sandy Creek enters from the west side midway down one of the straighter sections. This creek is fed from Ponce de Leon Springs some 5 miles to the north. Just below Sandy Creek, there's a group of large houses on the west bank with no public access.

Less than one half mile below the houses is a large island. The best run appears to be to the east, but the shortest route is west. Below the island small bayous begin to appear along with an occasional hunting-fishing camp. About 3 miles below the island, the river takes a sharp turn to the south and begins a long, straight run. These long straights, broken by a few bends, will continue to just above Boynton Cutoff. The frequency of houses increases, although they tend to be set well back from the river.

At Boynton Cutoff, the main river goes west, to the right, but is narrower than the cutoff. To follow the cutoff, make a turn east. The water is always very swift in the cutoff. Just around the first bend is an old logging bridge that is usually a catch-all for large logs and other debris. This bridge should be approached with caution as the water is swift, and it may be difficult to find an opening. Around the next bend on the left is the take-out at a boat ramp on the east side of the river.

To reach the take-out (access K), from Bonifay, travel south on S.R. 79 to the intersection with S.R. 280. Turn right (west) on S.R. 280 and continue to its junction with S.R. 170. Follow S.R. 280/170 to Hinsons Cross Roads. Follow S.R. 284 south from Hinsons Cross Roads for 7 miles to the point where S.R. 284 turns due east, but S.R. 284A continues south. Stay on S.R. 284A for just under 3 miles. Turn right (south) on a graded road, and continue to the boat ramp. If you miss this turn, the S.R. 284A will continue for one-half mile to Shell Landing, a boat ramp on Holmes Creek.

When the Boynton Cutoff rejoins the Choctawhatchee River, the river becomes very broad and is frequented by large motorboats. It is 7 miles downstream to the bridge at S.R. 20.

Section: Dale C.R. 36 to Boynton Cutoff boat ramp

Counties: Dale, Geneva (AL); Holmes, Washington, Walton (FL)

USGS Quads: Skipperville, Clapton, Ewell, Pinckard, Daleville, Clayhatchee (FL); Geneva West (AL)

Suitable for: Cruising, camping

Appropriate for: Families, beginners, intermediates

Months Runnable: All

Interest Highlights: Scenery, wildlife

Scenery: Excellent

Difficulty: Class I, II

Average Width: 60–100 ft.

Velocity: Mild to moderate

Hazards: Deadfalls

Rescue Index: Accessible to accessible but difficult

Source of Additional Information: The Canoe Livery, Rt. 2, Box 222-C, Newton, AL 36352; (205) 299-3888.

Access Points	Access Code	River Miles	Shuttle Miles
A–B	2357	6.0	5.0
B–C	2368	8.0	7.0
C–D	2369	8.0	10.0
D–E	1357	9.0	9.0
E–F	1357	12.0	13.0
F–G	1357	8.0	12.0
G–H	2468	11.0	14.0
H–I	2357	6.0	8.0
I–J	1357	12.0	13.0
J–K	2357	15.0	12.0
K	2357		

Access Key:

1	Paved road	7	Clear trail
2	Unpaved road	8	Brush and trees
3	Short carry	9	Launching fee charged
4	Long carry	10	Private property, need permission
5	Easy grade	11	No access, reference only
6	Steep incline		

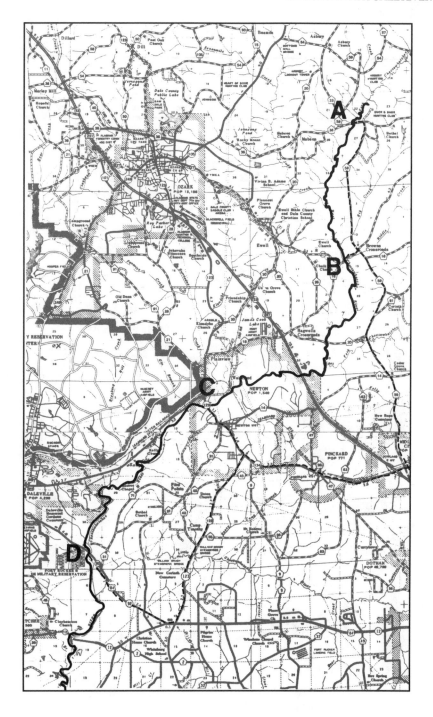

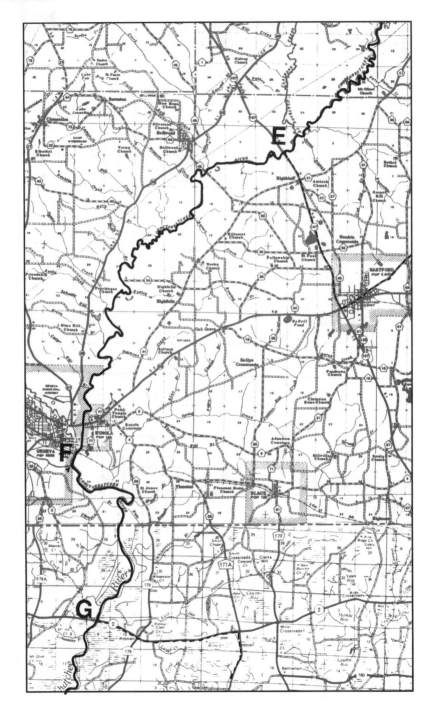

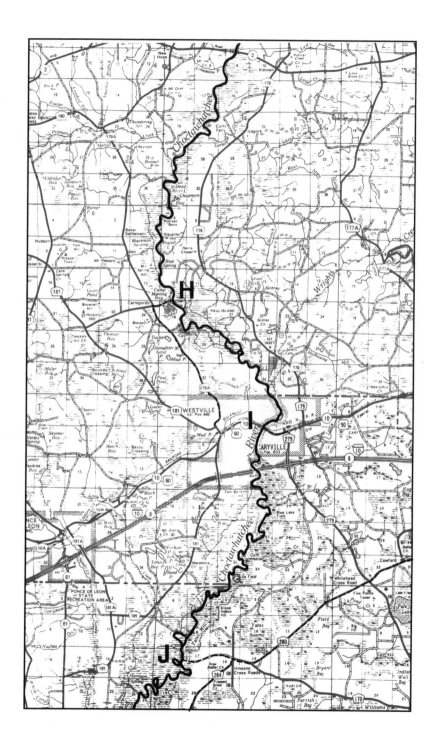

245

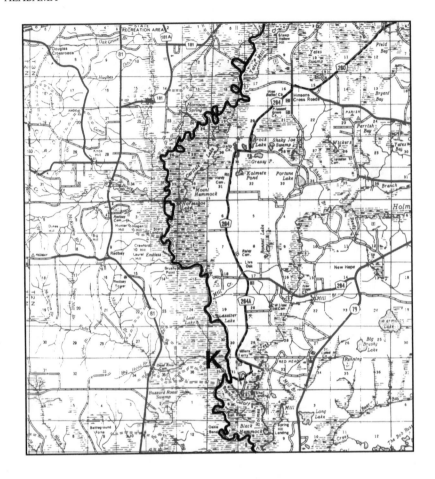

Omusee Creek

Omusee Creek originates near Dothan and ambles for more than 20 miles in a southeasterly direction toward the town of Columbia and the Chattahoochee River. It is a major drainage basin for the area, and dozens of feeder streams pour into it. At least two efforts to harness its energy have left relics that are now of scenic interest only.

The canoeable part of the creek begins at Henry C.R. 55 and continues to the confluence with the Chattahoochee, a distance of nearly 12 miles. It begins in a swampy area with large hardwoods and ends deep in high limerock walls. In between there is a gradient of more than 5 feet per mile, rocky ledges, cascading water, the two old structures, and spectacular walls of varying hues.

Access to the creek is poor, and there is very little encroachment. It is heavily forested and, in the spring, gardenlike with the variety of blooming trees and shrubs along the banks. There is a good boat ramp, with camping as well, at Omusee Creek Recreation Area.

C.R. 55 to C.R. 63 (access A–access B) is a 4.5-mile moderate to strenuous paddle through characteristically excellent scenery in Henry County. From Columbia, travel west on S.R. 52 for just over 1 mile to the junction of Houston C.R. 22. Turn right on C.R. 22, and continue for 7 miles to the junction with Henry C.R. 55. Turn right (north) on C.R. 55, and continue for just under 2 miles to the bridge across Omusee Creek. Access is on the northwest side of the bridge. An alternative access can be reached by turning left onto a graded road about 200 yards before reaching the bridge.

At this access, the creek is 30 to 40 feet wide with banks 2 to 4 feet high. The area right around the bridge is high and wooded, but it soon slips into an extensive swamp. The stream is clearly defined but may have many obstructions such as downed trees. There are large cypress and other hardwoods along the banks. The stream alternates between moderate banks and swamp with one very congested section where clear-cutting has pushed a number of trees into the creek.

About 1 mile above C.R. 63, the confluence of Armstrong Creek on river left signals the beginning of high rocky walls and some small shoals in the creek. This section is less than 5 miles long with a gradient of more than 20 feet, but it is very slow paddling because of the many obstructions.

C.R. 63 to Omusee Creek Recreation Area (access B–access C) is a moderate 7-mile paddle with some superb scenery. From Columbia, travel west on S.R. 52 for just over 1 mile to the junction of C.R. 22. Turn right on C.R. 22 and continue 4.5 miles to the junction with C.R. 63. Turn right (north) on C.R. 63 and continue for 2.5 miles to the bridge across Omusee Creek. Access is on the southwest side of the bridge.

Although this is a difficult access, the beauty of the stream from this point on is well worth the effort. Within 1 mile of the put-in, Jump and Run Creek flows over a series of ledges and into the Omusee on river left. Just over a mile downstream, the Southern Railroad trestle crosses the creek. Beware of the concrete slabs and iron bars under the trestle! The best path is usually on the extreme right, but be prepared to brace to avoid rocks at the end of the run. The middle path looks good but at low water levels it may have iron bars sticking out of the water. Within a few yards of the trestle, Hurricane Creek, a canoeable stream, flows in from the right. There are a series of rock ledges here that may be too shallow to paddle over. Stay to the left, and ride the roller coaster downstream. The creek drops 10 feet in this mile from the trestle to the old cotton factory.

The remains of the factory are on river right, an unfinished and abandoned brick edifice that has now become a part of the forest. There may be a drop of up to 2 feet here depending on water level. The best spot for crossing is on the right, about 10 feet from the right bank. Very high walls predominate now with beautiful fern falls and oak-leaf hydrangea growing on them.

The second edifice is an old dam and is a very large affair that appears to be in midstream. Follow the river to the right, and go around it since the left chute goes into the dam. At high to normal water levels, it is possible to paddle around the dam on the right and down a series of ledges into a flume that culminates in a roller coaster. A very exciting ride! At low water it may be necessary to carry around the ledges or to line the canoe through them. Scout from the right side of the dam, on river left. At very high water levels this is a Class III rapid complete with surfing holes.

Once the dam is passed, the current slows considerably. The scenery is even more beautiful, however, as small waterfalls flow over very high rock walls. There is no public access at S.R. 52, but it is less than 2 miles to the boat ramp at the recreation area. The section from S.R. 52 passes under another railroad trestle and an abandoned iron bridge. The water may be completely still depending on the amount of backup from the Chattahoochee River, but it is still very pretty.

To reach the take-out, from Columbia, travel west on S.R. 52 for about 1 mile to the junction with C.R. 95. Turn left (south) on C.R. 95, and continue for 1 mile to the sign indicating the Omusee Recreation Area. Turn left, and continue to the park. There are potable water, rest rooms, and campsites at the park.

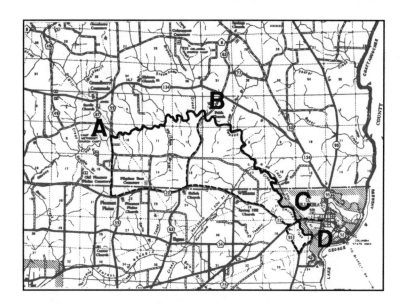

Section: C.R. 55 to Omusee Creek Recreation Area
Counties: Henry, Houston (AL)
USGS Quads: Sigma, Columbia
Suitable for: Cruising
Appropriate for: Intermediates
Months Runnable: Winter, spring—after heavy rainfall
Interest Highlights: Scenery, geology
Scenery: Beautiful to superb
Difficulty: Class I, II
Average Width: 30–40 ft.
Velocity: Mild to moderate
Hazards: Deadfalls, dams
Rescue Index: Accessible

Source of Additional Information: Aplachee Canoe Club; P.O. Box 4027; Tallahassee, FL 32315. Tri-State Paddler's Association; P.O. Box 8142; Dothan, AL 36304.

Access Points	Access Code	River Miles	Shuttle Miles
A–B	1357	4.5	4.0
B–C	1468, 10	7.0	8.0
C	1357		

Access Key:

1	Paved road	7	Clear trail
2	Unpaved road	8	Brush and trees
3	Short carry	9	Launching fee charged
4	Long carry	10	Private property, need permission
5	Easy grade	11	No access, reference only
6	Steep incline		

Abbie Creek

Abbie Creek is a product of the high, rolling ridges that spread westward from the Chattahoochee River. Beginning as a small streamlet in Barbour County, it flows south into Henry County, gathering the flow from dozens of smaller brooks and branches. Some 10 miles north of Columbia, the creek turns in an easterly direction and, cutting its way through high limerock walls, falls 70 feet in under 10 miles. The result is a rippling, cascading waterway of unusual beauty and canoeing excitement.

Development of the land along the banks of the creek has been discouraged by its location in a deep ravine. This also limits access to the stream for the canoeist and makes put-ins and take-outs challenging. The creek becomes very shallow during dry seasons, and heavy rainfall over a short period of time can cause flash flooding. Because it drains a large agricultural area, the waters of the creek are usually a tannish yellow color.

Plants native to the Appalachian Mountains are prolific along the high banks of Abbie Creek. In the spring, wild azalea, Alabama minus rhododendron, hairy laurel, coral honeysuckle, and graceful silver bell trees are among the wide variety of flowering plants that make the creek banks resemble a garden. In the summer, oak-leaf hydrangea and magnificent fern falls line the rock walls.

The high banks and scarcity of sandbars make camping on Abbie Creek difficult. Henry County maintains a recreation area at the confluence of Abbie Creek with the Chattahoochee River that offers primitive camping in a beautiful, wooded setting. Potable water is available from a hand pump.

C.R. 53 to C.R. 65 (access A–access B) is a moderate 3-mile paddle through Henry County. From Columbia, travel north on S.R. 95 for 1 mile to the junction with C.R. 53. Turn left on C.R. 53, and continue for about 10 miles to the bridge that crosses Abbie Creek. Access is on the southeast side of this bridge.

The first mile below this access can be tedious, since the stream is broad and shallow with many deadfalls of trees and debris in the water. At high water levels, these obstacles will hardly be noticed, but in low water they can lead to a number of pullovers. The effort is worthwhile, however, since the gradient beyond this point is almost 7 feet per mile, and there are several spectacular rock bluffs. Rock ledges, limerock boulders, and fast water combine to make this an interesting and exciting run. Just before reaching the C.R. 65 bridge, the Etheridge Gin Branch flows into Abbie Creek from the west, creating a pretty waterfall.

C.R. 65 to C.R. 97 (access B–access C) is a 9-mile section of moderate difficulty. From Columbia, travel north on S.R. 95 for 1 mile to the junction with C.R. 53. Turn left on C.R. 53, and continue for about 8 miles to the intersection with C.R. 26 at Browns Crossroads. Turn right on C.R. 26, and continue for 1 mile to the junction of C.R. 65. Turn left on C.R. 65, and continue to the bridge that crosses Abbie Creek. Access is on the northwest side of this bridge and is steep and difficult.

This section of Abbie Creek flows under two bridges: one on S.R. 95, and the other an old iron bridge on a graded road. There is no public access to the creek from either of these points.

This stretch of waterway has a fast current, bends in the stream, and downed trees that require skill in maneuvering a canoe. There is also a continuation of the impressive rock walls. Peterman Creek and Geneva Branch flow into Abbie Creek from the west and both enter through deep canyons that have beautiful fern falls and rock formations.

After the confluence of Geneva Branch, Abbie Creek begins to flow in a more southerly direction, and after passing under the old iron bridge, the current becomes slower. As Whetstone Branch flows in from the east, the creek becomes a wider, more shallow stream once more. The take-out at C.R. 97 is over a rock ledge and may take considerable agility, depending on the water level.

C.R. 12 and 97 to Abbie Creek Recreation Area (access C–access D) is a short (1.5-mile) easy paddle, though of less scenic interest. From Columbia, travel north on S.R. 95 for about 10 miles to the junction of C.R. 12 at Haleburg. Turn right, and continue on this road for about 3.5 miles to the bridge across Abbie Creek. Access is on the northwest side of the bridge. This short section is characterized by a broader, more shallow creek bed and banks that are low and swampy. Its primary attraction is that it enables canoeists to take out at an easily accessible boat launch.

To reach the take-out, from Columbia, travel north on S.R. 95 for about 5 miles to the junction with C.R. 97. Turn right on C.R. 97, and continue for about 3 miles to the junction with a paved road that turns right. A sign should indicate that this is the road to Abbie Creek Recreation Area. Turn right, and follow this road to the recreation area. The Chattahoochee River is on the right.

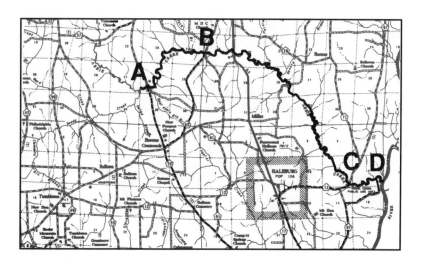

Section: C.R. 53 to Abbie Creek Recreation Area

Counties: Henry (AL)

USGS Quads: Haleburg, Columbia

Suitable for: Cruising

Appropriate for: Beginners, intermediates

Months Runnable: All, except in extremely dry periods

Interest Highlights: Scenery, wildlife, flowers, geology

Scenery: Superb

Difficulty: Class I, II

Average Width: 40–60 ft.

Velocity: Mild to moderate

Hazards: Deadfalls, rock ledges

Rescue Index: Accessible

Source of Additional Information: Applachee Canoe Club, P.O. Box 4027, Tallahassee, FL 32315; Tri-State Paddler's Association, P.O. Box 8142, Dothan, AL 36304.

Access Points	Access Code	River Miles	Shuttle Miles
A–B	1357	3.0	5.0
B–C	1368	9.0	8.0
C–D	1368	1.5	3.0
D	1357		

Access Key: 1   Paved road   7   Clear trail,
                  2   Unpaved road   8   Brush and trees
                  3   Short carry   9   Launching fee charged
                  4   Long carry   10   Private property, need permission
                  5   Easy grade   11   No access, reference only
                  6   Steep incline

The Cowikee Creeks

The three forks of Cowikee Creek—the South, Middle, and North—drain a large area of rolling hills and high ridges just north and west of Eufaula, Alabama. It feeds into the Chattahoochee River at the Walter F. George Reservoir, also known as Lake Eufaula. Since the lake is a dam-controlled facility, the lower sections of the Cowikee Creeks are greatly influenced by the water level of the reservoir.

The South and Middle forks flow almost due east at interesting gradients of up to 15 feet per mile. This results in swift-running water, rocky shoals and ledges, and some small drops in the streambed. The banks are generally high, and access to the streams is limited. In places, beautiful rock walls, smoothed to a glassy surface by the action of the water, provide the background for waterfalls, as tributary streams drop into the creeks.

The limited accessibility of these streams has resulted in clean, unlittered waterways and an abundance of wildlife and birds. The surrounding woods have many flowering plants indigenous to this area such as dogwood, wild azalea, hairy laurel, and oak-leaf hydrangea.

The North Fork flows more southerly than the other two, has a milder gradient, and is more influenced by the backup waters from the reservoir. Access to this stream is also very limited; and while it is canoeable, it is not a recommended stream.

South Fork of Cowikee Creek

The 5-mile section from Comer to Barbour C.R. 79 (Poplar Springs Road) (access A–access B) is moderately difficult paddling. From Eufaula, travel west on U.S. 82 for about 16 miles to the community of Comer. At Comer, turn left (south) on C.R. 49, cross the railroad tracks, and turn left again onto a graded road. Follow this road for less than one half mile to a bridge across the South Fork of Cowikee Creek. Access is on the southwest side of this bridge through a faint trail through the woods. An alternate access can be reached by crossing the bridge and following the graded road to the left. Just before reaching the bridge across Johnson Creek, there is a cleared access area on the left. This leads to Johnson Creek, which flows into Cowikee Creek about 100 yards downstream.

At this point, the creek is 30 feet wide and flowing very fast. The banks are 6 to 8 feet high and heavily wooded. The forest is primarily second growth hardwoods, and in the spring there are clouds of pink azalea and hairy laurel.

In this 5-mile section, the creek drops a total of 40 feet with an overall gradient of 9 feet per mile. As a result, this is a very fast run with numerous rock ledges, lots of cascading water, and several minor drops. Below the confluence of Bronson Creek, about 3 miles downstream, the creek pools for a half mile, then begins a rapid descent to the take-out. In this 1.5-mile section, beginning just above the abandoned Central of Georgia trestle under U.S. 82 and to C.R. 79, the stream drops 20 feet for a gradient of 15 feet per mile.

Despite the impressive gradient, the creek is broad, and the rocky ledges are worn smooth, posing no real danger to the canoeist. Although some degree of paddling skills would be desirable, the stream should not be hazardous except in high water or flooded conditions!

After making an easterly turn, the creek has very high rock walls in the short distance between U.S. 82 and C.R. 79. There is a very pretty waterfall on the right just above the bridge.

The next 5 miles, from C.R. 79 to C.R. 89 (access B–access C) is an easy paddle with even better scenery than the first section. From Eufaula, travel west on U.S. 82 for about 11 miles to the junction with C.R. 79, also called Poplar Springs Road. Turn right (north) on C.R. 79, and continue for less than one half mile to the bridge. Access is on the southeast side of the bridge and is extremely poor. It is very steep with poor footing.

The very high rock walls that begin below U.S. 82 continue through this section, resulting in some beautiful waterfalls on the right bank. As you paddle downstream, listen carefully for the sound of waterfalls that are not directly on the creek, but can be reached by paddling or wading upstream on some of the tributary streams that flow into it. The vegetation is very thick and characterized by upland hardwoods, some pine, and flowering trees in the spring. The creek continues to flow swiftly for the first 2 to 3 miles, but there are no further rock ledges or drops. The current on this section is highly dependent on the water level in Lake Eufaula; and, under normal circumstances, the last 2 miles can be very slow.

To reach the take-out, from Eufaula, travel west on U.S. 82 for about 5 miles to the junction with C.R. 89. Turn right (north) on C.R. 89, and continue for about 3.5 miles to a bridge across the South Fork of Cowikee Creek. Access is on the northwest side of the bridge down a trail. It is a poor access, steep and strenuous, but is clearly defined.

Middle Fork of Cowikee Creek

From C.R. 49 to David Jones Road (access A–access B) is an easy to moderate 7 miles. From Eufaula, travel west on U.S. 82 for about 16 miles to the junction with C.R. 49. Turn right (north) on C.R. 49, and continue for 6 miles to the bridge across the Middle Fork of Cowikee Creek. Access is on the southeast side of the bridge, down a faint path in the woods that leads to a small sandbar. It is a poor access, steep and poorly defined.

At this access, the Middle Fork is 30 to 40 feet wide with high, wooded banks and a good current. The gradient is 30 feet for this 7-mile trip; and, as a result, the stream is a succession of sections of cascading water and small, rocky ledges. Frequently, there are sheer rock walls up to 10 feet high on either or both sides with beautiful fern falls and green lichen on them. The woods are primarily upland hardwoods with dogwood, wild azalea, and hairy laurel blooming in the spring. In some spots, the banks are up to 50 feet high. Overall, this is a very pretty stream, easy to paddle and of a pleasant duration. It is swift, but should not be hazardous except in high water or flooded conditions!

It is possible to continue canoeing downstream on the Middle Fork to an access on C.R. 97 (3.5 miles) and even on to Lakepoint State Park on U.S. 431 (11 miles). The creek becomes a part of the Lake Eufaula system, however, and is broad, slow, and tends to be windy and populated with motorboats.

To reach the take-out from Eufaula, travel west on U.S. 82 for about 5 miles to the junction with C.R. 89. Turn right (north) on C.R. 89, and continue across the bridge over the South Fork of Cowikee Creek and for another 2 miles to the junction of a graded road on the right. Turn right on this road, David Jones Road, and continue for less than 1 mile to the bridge across the Middle Fork of Cowikee Creek. Access is on the northwest side of the bridge. This is a poor access since it is very steep, but it is well defined, and cars can be parked within a few feet of the stream bank.

North Fork of Cowikee Creek

Although the North Fork of Cowikee Creek appears to be an attractive paddling stream from Russell C.R. 12 West, it is very quickly affected by the backflow from Lake Eufaula, and access to the stream is limited between Russell C.R. 12 West and Barbour C.R. 97. This is a distance of about 9 miles, 5 or 6 of which are part of the Lake Eufaula system.

South Fork of Cowikee Creek

Section: Comer to C.R. 89
Counties: Barbour (AL)
USGS Quads: Comer, Batesville, Howe
Suitable for: Cruising
Appropriate for: Beginners, intermediates
Months Runnable: February, March, April (after heavy rainfall)
Interest Highlights: Scenery, wildlife
Scenery: Beautiful to very pretty
Difficulty: Class I, II
Average Width: 30–40 ft.
Velocity: Moderate
Hazards: Deadfalls, rocky ledges, flash flooding
Rescue Index: Accessible
Source of Additional Information: Tri-State Paddler's Association, P.O.Box 8142, Dothan, AL 36304.

Access Points	Access Code	River Miles	Shuttle Miles
A–B	2367	5.0	6.0
B–C	1468, 10	5.0	8.0
C	1467		

Access Key:
1	Paved road	7	Clear trail
2	Unpaved road	8	Brush and trees
3	Short carry	9	Launching fee charged
4	Long carry	10	Private property, need permission
5	Easy grade	11	No access, reference only
6	Steep incline		

Middle Fork of Cowikee Creek

Section: C.R. 49 to David Jones Road
Counties: Barbour (AL)
USGS Quads: Rutherford, Howe
Suitable for: Cruising, camping
Appropriate for: Beginner, intermediate
Months Runnable: February, March, April, and after heavy rainfall

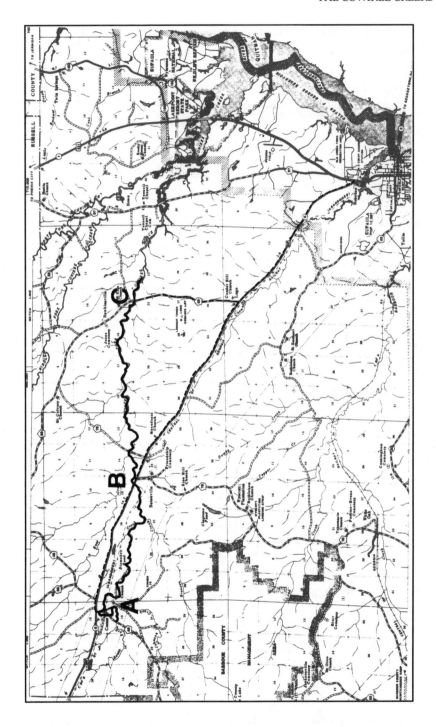

Interest Highlights: Scenery, wildlife

Scenery: Excellent

Difficulty: Class I

Average Width: 30–40 ft.

Velocity: Mild to moderate

Hazards: Deadfalls

Rescue Index: Accessible but difficult

Source of Additional Information: Tri-State Paddler's Association, P.O. Box 8142, Dothan, AL 36304.

Access Points	Access Code	River Miles	Shuttle Miles
A–B	1357	7.0	5.0
B	2367		

Access Key:

1	Paved road	7	Clear trail
2	Unpaved road	8	Brush and trees
3	Short carry	9	Launching fee charged
4	Long carry	10	Private property, need permission
5	Easy grade	11	No access, reference only
6	Steep incline		

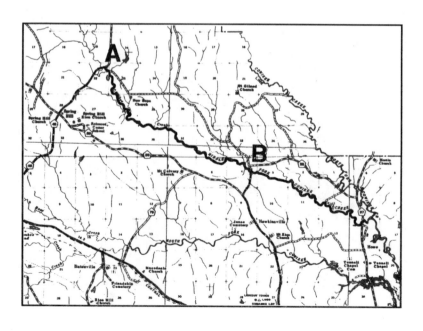

APPENDIXES

COMMERCIAL RIVER OUTFITTERS
(Canoe Liveries)

Alabama

Styx River, Perdido River

Sunshine Canoes
5460 Old Shell Rd.
Mobile, AL 36608
(205) 344-8664
Escatawpa River, Little River
Canoe rental, shuttles

Choctawhatchee River
Adventures Unlimited
160 River Annex Rd.
Cantonment, FL 32537
(904) 968-5529

Judy Creek, Pea River

The Canoe Livery
Waterford Rd.
Newton, AL
(205) 299-3888
Choctawhatchee River
Canoe rental, shuttles

Louisiana

Baton Rouge area

Backpacker
7656 Jefferson Hwy.
Baton Rouge, LA 70809
(504) 925-2667
Canoe rental

Canoe and Trail Adventures
129 North Hennessy
New Orleans, LA 70119
(504) 486-2355
Canoe and camping equipment
rental, instruction, organized
outings

Whiskey Chitto River

Pack and Paddle
301 Pinhook Rd. East
Lafayette, LA 70501
(318) 232-5854
Canoe rental

Pearl River Basin

Dreamchasers
118 Lafayette St.
Gretna, LA 70053
(504) 362-9552
Canoe rental, rental
transportation

Mississippi

Okatoma Creek

Okatoma Outpost
Route 2, Box 226C
Sanford, MS 39479
(601) 722-4297
Canoe and kayak rental,
shuttles

Lonnie's Canoe Rental
Route 1, Box 294
Seminary, MS 39479
(601) 722-4301
Canoe rental, shuttles

River Expeditions
4150 Cedar Street
Jackson, MS 39206
(601) 362-6049
Canoe rental, instruction

Black Creek

Black Creek Canoe Rentals
P.O. Box 213
Brooklyn, MS 39425
(601) 582-8817
Canoe rental, shuttles

Red Creek

Red Creek Market
Route 3, Box 72A
Perkinston, MS 39573
(601) 928-5365
Canoe rental, shuttles

Chunky and Chickasawhay Rivers,
Okatibbee Creek

Buckley Canoe Rental
Route 2, Box 147-A
Enterprise, MS 39330
(601) 659-9185
Canoe rental, shuttles

Out-N-Under
U.S. 45 South
Meridian, MS
or mail to:
    1200 Roebuck Drive
    Meridian, MS 39301
    (601) 693-5827
Canoe and kayak rental,
shuttles, instruction,
organized outings

Gappy's Fish Camp
Route 2, Box 175
Shubuta, MS 39360
(601) 776-5710
Canoe rental, shuttles

Bear Creek

Tishomingo State Park
P.O. Box 880
Tishomingo, MS 38873
(601) 438-6914
Canoe rental, shuttle only
with canoe rental
April through October only

Wolf River

Adventure Canoes
10072 Lo Buoy Road
Pass Christian, MS 39571
(601) 255-9783
Canoe rental, shuttles

Wolf River Canoe Rentals
21652 Tucker Road
Long Beach, MS 39560
(601) 452-7666
Canoe rental, shuttles

Bogue Chitto River, MaGees Creek

Sweetwater Canoe Rentals
Rt. 6, Box 82A
Tylertown, MS 39667
(601) 876-5474
Canoe rental, shuttles

Canoe and Trail Outpost
Route 6, Box 118
Tylertown, MS 39667
(601) 876-6964
Canoe rental, shuttles,
wilderness camping

Strong River

D'Lo Water Park
P.O. Box 278
D'Lo, MS
(601) 847-4310
Canoe rental, shuttles

Bogue Chitto River

Ryals Canoe Rental
Rt. 2, Box 223A
McComb, MS 39648
(601) 684-4948
Canoe and tube rental, shuttles

Riverview Grocery
Rt. 2, Box 222D
McComb, MS 39648
(601) 249-3670
Canoe rental, shuttles

Bogue Chitto Choo-Choo
Rt. 2
McComb,MS 39648
Canoe rental

Batte's River Resort
Rt. 2, Box 51
McComb, MS 39648
(601) 684-5356
Canoe and tube rental,
shuttles, camping

Appendix B

LOCAL CANOEING ORGANIZATIONS

Alabama

Birmingham Canoe Club
P.O. Box 951
Birmingham, AL 35201

Tri-State Paddler's Association
P.O. Box 8142
Dothan, LA 36304

Louisiana

Bayou Haystackers
4616 Ithaca St.
Metairie, LA 70006

Neighboring States

Apalachee Canoe Club
P.O. Box 4027
Tallahassee, FL 32315

Arkansas Canoe Association
P.O. Box 1843
Little Rock, AR 72203

Bluff City Canoe Club
P.O. Box 4523
Memphis, TN 38104

Chota Canoe Club
P.O. Box 8270, University Station
Knoxville, TN 37996

East Tennessee Whitewater Club
P.O. Box 5774
Oak Ridge, TN 37831-5774

Florida Canoeing & Kayaking Assoc.
P.O. Box 20892
West Palm Beach, FL 33416

Georgia Canoeing Association
P.O. Box 7023
Atlanta, GA 30357

Sewanee Canoe and Outing Club
The University of the South
Sewanee, TN 37375

West Florida Canoe Club
P.O. Box 17203
Pensacola, FL 32522

Tennessee Scenic Rivers
Association
P.O. Box 159041
Nashville, TN 37215-9041

Tennessee Valley Canoe Club
P.O. Box 11125
Chattanooga, TN 37401

OTHER RELATED ORGANIZATIONS

Mississippi Chapter Sierra Club
and Central Miss. Group
P.O. Box 4335
Jackson, MS 39296-4335
(601) 352-1026

Delta Chapter Sierra Club
P.O. Box 19469
Bienville St.
New Orleans, LA 70119
(505) 891-0386

Alabama Chapter Sierra Club
P.O. Box 55591
Birmingham, AL 35255
(205) 339-4692

NATIONAL CANOEING ORGANIZATIONS

American Canoe Association
P.O. Box 1190
Newington, VA 22122

American Whitewater Affiliation
146 North Brockway
Palatine, IL 60067

U. S. Canoe Association
c/o Chuck Weis
2509 Kickapoo Drive
Lafayette, IN 47905

Appendix C

WHERE TO BUY MAPS

As indicated in the introductory material, maps included in this book are intended to supplement, rather than replace U.S. Geological Survey topographic quadrangles and county road maps. Maps can be purchased from the following locations:

United States Geological Survey (USGS)
Topographic Quadrangles

Distribution Branch
U.S. Geological Survey Map Sales
P.O. Box 25286
Denver, CO 80225
(303) 236-7477
To order maps, indexes, brochures, and catalogs.

Earth Science Information
U.S. Geological Survey
12201 Sunrise Valley Drive
Reston, VA 22092
(703) 648-6045
To order state indexes and aerial photos only.

Alabama

U. S. Army Corps of Engineers
Mobile District, Attn: LO-SR
P.O. Box 2288
Mobile, AL 36628-0001
(205) 690-2631

Louisiana

U.S. Army Corps of Engineers
New Orleans District, Attn: 205
P.O. Box 60267
New Orleans, LA 70160
(504) 862-1775

New Orleans Map Company
3130 Paris Ave.
New Orleans, LA 70119
(504) 943-0878

Mississippi

Bureau of Geology
P.O. Box 5348
Jackson, MS 39296-5348
(601) 354-6228

U.S. Army Corps of Engineers

Vicksburg District, Map Sales
P.O. Box 60
Vicksburg, MS 39181-0060
(601) 631-5042

County/Parish Road Maps

Alabama

State of Alabama
Highway Dept.
1409 Coliseum Blvd.
Room 109
Montgomery, AL 36130
(205) 242-6071

Louisiana

Louisiana Department of
Transportation
General Files
P.O. Box 84245
Baton Rouge, LA 70804-9245
(504) 379-1107

Mississippi

Mississippi State Highway
Dept., Map Sales
P.O. Box 1850
Jackson, MS 39215-1850
(601) 354-6391